Guns and Violence

Guns and Violence

Other books in the Current Controversies series:

Guns and Violence

Laura K. Egendorf, *Book Editor*

Bruce Glassman, *Vice President*
Bonnie Szumski, *Publisher*
Helen Cothran, *Managing Editor*

GREENHAVEN PRESS
An imprint of Thomson Gale, a part of The Thomson Corporation

Detroit • New York • San Francisco • San Diego • New Haven, Conn.
Waterville, Maine • London • Munich

THOMSON
GALE

For more information, contact
Greenhaven Press
27500 Drake Rd.
Farmington Hills, MI 48331-3535
Or you can visit our Internet site at http://www.gale.com

LIBRARY OF CONGRESS CATALOGING-IN-PUBLICATION DATA

Guns and violence / Laura K. Egendorf, book editor.
    p. cm. — (Current controversies)
Includes bibliographical references and index.
ISBN 0-7377-2206-1 (lib. bdg. : alk. paper) —
ISBN 0-7377-2207-X (pbk. : alk. paper)
    1. Gun control—United States. 2. Violence—United States. 3. Firearms—Law and legislations—United States. 4. Firearms ownership—United States.
I. Egendorf, Laura K., 1973– . II. Series.
HV7436.G8777 2005
363.33'0973—dc22
                                                              2004052287

Printed in the United States of America

Contents

Chapter 2: Can Government Measures Reduce Gun Violence?

Yes: Government Measures Can Reduce Gun Violence

No: Government Measures Cannot Reduce Gun Violence

Chapter 3: Is Gun Control Constitutional?

Foreword

By definition, controversies are "discussions of questions in which opposing opinions clash" (Webster's Twentieth Century Dictionary Unabridged). Few would deny that controversies are a pervasive part of the human condition and exist on virtually every level of human enterprise. Controversies transpire between individuals and among groups, within nations and between nations. Controversies supply the grist necessary for progress by providing challenges and challengers to the status quo. They also create atmospheres where strife and warfare can flourish. A world without controversies would be a peaceful world; but it also would be, by and large, static and prosaic.

The Series' Purpose

The purpose of the Current Controversies series is to explore many of the social, political, and economic controversies dominating the national and international scenes today. Titles selected for inclusion in the series are highly focused and specific. For example, from the larger category of criminal justice, Current Controversies deals with specific topics such as police brutality, gun control, white collar crime, and others. The debates in Current Controversies also are presented in a useful, timeless fashion. Articles and book excerpts included in each title are selected if they contribute valuable, long-range ideas to the overall debate. And wherever possible, current information is enhanced with historical documents and other relevant materials. Thus, while individual titles are current in focus, every effort is made to ensure that they will not become quickly outdated. Books in the Current Controversies series will remain important resources for librarians, teachers, and students for many years.

In addition to keeping the titles focused and specific, great care is taken in the editorial format of each book in the series. Book introductions and chapter prefaces are offered to provide background material for readers. Chapters are organized around several key questions that are answered with diverse opinions representing all points on the political spectrum. Materials in each chapter include opinions in which authors clearly disagree as well as alternative opinions in which authors may agree on a broader issue but disagree on the possible solutions. In this way, the content of each volume in Current Controversies mirrors the mosaic of opinions encountered in society. Readers will quickly realize that there are many viable answers to these complex issues. By questioning each author's conclusions, students and casual readers can begin to develop the critical thinking skills so important to evaluating opinionated material.

Current Controversies is also ideal for controlled research. Each anthology in the series is composed of primary sources taken from a wide gamut of informational categories including periodicals, newspapers, books, United States and foreign government documents, and the publications of private and public organizations. Readers will find factual support for reports, debates, and research papers covering all areas of important issues. In addition, an annotated table of contents, an index, a book and periodical bibliography, and a list of organizations to contact are included in each book to expedite further research.

Perhaps more than ever before in history, people are confronted with diverse and contradictory information. During the Persian Gulf War, for example, the public was not only treated to minute-to-minute coverage of the war, it was also inundated with critiques of the coverage and countless analyses of the factors motivating U.S. involvement. Being able to sort through the plethora of opinions accompanying today's major issues, and to draw one's own conclusions, can be a complicated and frustrating struggle. It is the editors' hope that Current Controversies will help readers with this struggle.

Greenhaven Press anthologies primarily consist of previously published material taken from a variety of sources, including periodicals, books, scholarly journals, newspapers, government documents, and position papers from private and public organizations. These original sources are often edited for length and to ensure their accessibility for a young adult audience. The anthology editors also change the original titles of these works in order to clearly present the main thesis of each viewpoint and to explicitly indicate the opinion presented in the viewpoint. These alterations are made in consideration of both the reading and comprehension levels of a young adult audience. Every effort is made to ensure that Greenhaven Press accurately reflects the original intent of the authors included in this anthology.

"Finding answers to America's gun violence problem may require the nation's policy makers to look beyond U.S. borders."

Introduction

Gun violence is not a uniquely American problem. Indeed, many nations have grappled with the dangers that guns pose and debated ways to reduce firearms violence. One such nation is Great Britain, which has a long history of gun control. Among the gun control laws passed by Great Britain in the twentieth century were the Firearms Act of 1920—which required anyone who wanted to buy, own, use, or carry a gun or ammunition to get a special certificate—and the Firearms Amendment of 1937, which banned sawed-off shotguns and prohibited both the manufacture and sale of machine guns. The call for increased gun control became stronger in 1996, when Thomas Hamilton fatally shot sixteen children and one teacher in Dunblane, Scotland. His crime led the British government to ban all handguns in 1997. Seven years after the passage of the handgun ban, debate still rages as to its effectiveness. Gun rights advocates assert that the rising crime rate in the United Kingdom since the ban is proof that gun control makes citizens less safe. On the other hand, supporters of gun control dispute some of those crime statistics and contend that if firearms-related violence is increasing, then even stricter gun control legislation is needed.

Gun rights advocates have written extensively on the spike in violent crime in Great Britain since 1997. In an article for *Reason* magazine, Joyce Malcolm, a professor of history at Bentley College and the author of the book *Guns and Violence: The English Experience*, writes: "In the two years following the 1997 handgun ban, the use of handguns in crime rose by 40 percent, and the upward trend has continued. . . . Your chances of being mugged in London are now six times greater than in New York. England's rates of assault, robbery, and burglary are far higher than America's." Her findings are echoed by Gary A. Mauser, a professor of business administration at Simon Fraser University in Vancouver, British Columbia, Canada. In a paper published in 2002, Mauser contends:

> Despite banning and confiscating all handguns, violent crime, and firearm crime, continues to grow. The number of violent crimes involving handguns has increased from 2,600 in 1997/98 to 3,600 in 1999/00. And firearm crime has increased 200% in the past decade. The British Home Office admits that only one firearm in 10 used in homicide was legally held (British Home Office, 2001). But, the politicians continue their policy of disarming responsible citizens.

These statistics may appear irrefutable, but supporters of Britain's handgun ban maintain that gun violence has in fact declined in the United Kingdom. The weekly financial magazine *Economist* is among the stauncher advocates of the ban, lauding the policy in several editorials. According to one of those editorials, published in 2000, crimes involving guns dropped from 5,209 in 1996 to 3,143 in 1999, while the average number of gun-related homicides fell from sixty-two per year before the ban to fifty-four per year after. By contrast, the magazine writes, "There were 32,436 deaths due to gun violence in America in 1997, of which 13,252 were murders." While the *Economist* acknowledges in an April 2003 editorial that Britain's homicide rate is on the rise, the magazine notes that the majority of murders in recent years have been the result of stabbing, hitting, or kicking rather than shooting. The Gun Control Network, a pro–gun control organization based in London, has pointed to government statistics indicating that fewer than one hundred people became gun-related homicide victims between April 2001 and April 2002.

Even still, those who support the ban on handguns have had to acknowledge that the prohibition has had a surprising consequence: More crimes are being committed by people using replica guns or air guns, which utilize compressed air or a spring to shoot ammunition. While they do not inflict the same level of damage as do real guns, the pellets released by air guns (also known as BB guns) can cause injuries such as serious lacerations or permanent eye damage. Replica guns, like real guns, can be used to intimidate and threaten, and are increasingly used to do so. According to the Gun Control Network, "In England and Wales in 2002/03 . . . [there] were a total of 24,070 firearm offences of which 57% (13,822) involved air weapons, the highest number of offences ever. The largest increase in offences was seen with imitation firearms for which there was an annual increase of 46% to 1815 offences." The growing use of replica guns and knives suggests that when real guns become legally unavailable, criminals will find other ways to intimidate and harm their victims. The threat has become so great that some Britons are now calling for bans on air and replica weapons. Peter Squires of the Gun Control Network, in a report by the British Broadcasting Corporation, contends, "Replicas are responsible for a record rise in firearms in the national crime statistics. If something is not done, there is a massive coat because it is an important public safety issue." Banning air guns may be inevitable because some air guns can be converted into weapons that fire live rounds, thereby giving criminals yet another way to get around the handgun ban.

The debate over whether Britain's handgun ban has increased or decreased crime inevitably leads to an argument on how to best to reduce gun violence elsewhere in the world. Advocates of the ban contend that if gun violence is increasing, then the appropriate response is tougher laws. Suggestions include increasing funds to fight firearm trafficking and taking more steps to keep guns away from minors. Gun rights supporters maintain that more guns, not more laws, are the answer. Backers of concealed-carry laws assert that giving citizens the right to carry weapons reduces crime by causing potential criminals to think twice before threatening others, who may very well be armed. They point to the decline in violent crime in the United States, where more than thirty states have concealed-carry laws, as proof that such policies are successful.

While Great Britain is not a perfect parallel to the United States—it is smaller both in size and population, with different demographics—the success or failure of its gun control laws can provide U.S. policy makers with more information to consider when weighing new gun control legislation. Indeed, finding answers to America's gun violence problem may require the nation's policy makers to look beyond U.S. borders. As long as there are guns, there will be people who will use them for unlawful proposes, but fair and effective policies may lessen the scope of the problem.

Chapter 1

Is Gun Violence a Serious Problem?

Overview: The Extent of Gun Violence

by Linda Schmittroth

About the author: *Linda Schmittroth is the author and editor of several reference works.*

Firearm-related incidents are a leading cause of preventable injury and death, particularly among young people. Doctors Against Handgun Injury, a coalition of 12 clinical and professional medical societies, calls handgun injuries a public health problem, a political issue, and a criminal justice concern. The group contends: "While we have enough data in the area of firearm injuries to know there is a problem, we do not have enough detailed information to fully understand its dimensions or properly evaluate efforts to ameliorate it."

The public health establishment, represented at the national level by the Centers for Disease Control and Prevention (CDC), believes that collecting comprehensive data on firearms injuries and deaths—such as who was shot, under what circumstances, and with what kind of weapon—is the first step in reducing those injuries and deaths. The next step might be a campaign like those that eradicated polio and reduced traffic fatalities. The HELP Network, an international coalition of medical, public health, and allied organizations, described the form such a campaign might take ("The Public Health Approach to Firearm Injury Prevention," [online] http://www.helpnetwork.org/frames/resources_factsheets_pubhealth.pdf). "Most firearm deaths in the U.S. are caused by handguns, yet handguns account for a minority of all firearms owned. The handgun can be recognized as a high-risk weapon, and perhaps even as the primary agent of the modern epidemic of gun death. One strategy to reduce these risks may be to restrict civilian access to certain kinds of handguns."

A National Tracking System

The CDC, in collaboration with the U.S. Product Safety Commission, administers the only national system that tracks firearm-related injuries—the National

Electronic Injury Surveillance System (NEISS). Established in 1992, as of 2003, NEISS collected data from 91 participating hospital emergency departments. Expansion of the surveillance system beyond the 91 hospitals is a CDC goal.

State and local health departments report that they lack the funding to conduct a thorough surveillance of firearms injuries. To see how many health agencies do surveillance, a survey of all 50 state health departments and the city and county health departments of the 50 largest urban areas was done by Roger Hayes et al. for the report *Missing in Action: Health Agencies Lack Critical Data Needed for Firearm Injury Prevention* (HELP Network, Chicago, IL, 1999). . . . Thirty-one states (62 percent) maintain some type of firearm injury surveillance, but 19 (38 percent) do

> *"More than 50 percent of victims of nonfatal gunshot wounds from crime were younger than 25."*

not. More than one-half of the states (56 percent) track mortality data, 30 percent track hospital data, and 38 percent track the type of firearm. Twenty-six percent of the states track circumstances. Only 18 percent issue a report. According to the HELP report, the main obstacles to adequate surveillance were funding and staffing. . . .

About one-half of the city and county health departments collected data on firearm injuries and deaths. Less than one-quarter collected information on firearm types involved in injuries or on the circumstances, and 35 percent issued a report. The health departments without surveillance identified funding and staffing as the reasons they did not collect data.

Concerned about the lack of firearms injury data, in September 2002 the CDC awarded $7.5 million to six states (New Jersey, Maryland, Massachusetts, Oregon, South Carolina, and Virginia) to develop the nation's first comprehensive system for collecting data about violent deaths, the National Violent Death Reporting System. When data are released (perhaps as soon as 2004), more will be known about factors such as the involvement of alcohol or drugs in violent deaths, the type and source of the weapons used, and whether social service agencies or the police had prior warning of domestic violence or child abuse.

Firearm Injury Statistics

Data on gunshot injuries and firearm-related deaths for the period 1993 to 1997 were collected from victim surveys, hospital emergency room surveillance, and government entities such as the National Center for Health Statistics (death certificates), the Federal Bureau of Investigation (FBI) (reported homicides), and the CDC (firearms injury studies) for the report *Firearm Injury and Death from Crime, 1993–97* (U.S. Department of Justice, Bureau of Justice Statistics, Selected Findings, October 2000). The authors note that efforts to count injuries were complicated by limitations such as the failure of some sources to provide data on victims who later died, or the inability of other sources to make estimates because of too few cases reported. The authors estimate that there were 19.2 million incidents of nonfatal violent crime committed from 1993 through 1997, excluding simple assault. . . . The following are highlights:

- Of serious nonfatal violent victimizations, 28 percent were committed with a firearm, 4 percent resulted in serious injury, and 1 percent resulted in gunshot wounds.
- Assault accounted for 62 percent of the 411,800 nonfatal firearm-related injuries treated in emergency departments. . . . Of 180,533 firearm-related fatalities, 44 percent were homicides and 51 percent were suicides.
- Gunshot wounds from assaults treated in emergency departments fell by 39 percent, from 64,100 in 1993 to 39,400 in 1997. . . . Homicides committed with a firearm declined by 27 percent, from 18,253 in 1993 to 13,252 in 1997.
- Four of five victims of both fatal and nonfatal gunshot wounds from crime were male. About half were black males, and about half of those were between the ages of 15 and 24. About one in five victims of nonfatal gunshot wounds from crime was Hispanic.
- More than 50 percent of victims of nonfatal gunshot wounds from crime were younger than 25, while older victims were more common in gun-related homicides.

Of all victims of nonfatal firearm injury who were treated in emergency departments, more than half were hospitalized overnight.

Most of the nonfatal incidents occurred during the commission of a crime (assault or homicide, or legal intervention, which means injuries inflicted by the police in the course of arresting or attempting to arrest lawbreakers). . . .

An estimated average of 115,000 firearm-related injuries (including about 35,200 fatal and 79,400 nonfatal injuries) occurred each year from 1993 through 1998, with actual numbers decreasing over most of the period. Far more men than women were treated for gunshot wounds or died of them, with black men aged 15 to 34 being the most vulnerable. . . .

> *"In some states the number of firearm deaths is greater than the number of deaths from car crashes."*

Firearm Fatalities

The overall death rate has generally dropped steadily from the highs of the 1970s. Firearm injuries were the second leading cause of injury deaths in the United States in 1995, surpassed only by motor vehicle-related injuries, a circumstance that had not changed in 2001. In some states the number of firearm deaths is greater than the number of deaths from car crashes. As of 1996 firearm death rates were higher than motor vehicle death rates in Alaska, California, Louisiana, Maryland, Nevada, and Virginia. . . .

Age

People aged 15 to 24 years [are] the age group most conspicuously afffected by firearms deaths. The rate of 15.5 firearms-related deaths per 100,000 in 1970 in this age group rose to a high of 27.2 in 1995 before declining to 17.1 in 2000. [There are also] very high rates of firearms deaths among elderly males. The *Los Angeles Times* (December 15, 2000), citing a study by the Los Angeles–based Women Against Gun Violence, reported that although gun deaths were down overall in Los Angeles County in 1999 from the previous year, firearm deaths for senior citizens, including suicides, rose 14.6 percent. Dr. David Trader, medical director of geriatric psychiatry services at Cedars-Sinai Medical Center in Los Angeles, pointed out that loss is a characteristic of old age, including the loss of health, family, occupation, income, and friends. Trader believes the elderly may see guns as a finality, or a sure end. . . .

Race

Black males, [are] the racial group most conspicuously affected by firearms deaths. Black men aged 25–34 experienced a death rate of 145.6 in 1970, which declined to 77.9 by 2000. For black men aged 15–24, the rate fell from 97.3 in 1970 to 89.3 in 2000. . . .

International Comparisons

[For] a National Center for Health Statistics comparison of injury mortality among 11 of the countries participating in the International Collaborative Effort on Injury Statistics, a group of researchers sponsored by the CDC [worked] together to identify and develop issues for research on injury statistics. In 1994 the motor vehicle–related death rate among males 15–24 years of age was 41 per 100,000 in the United States. Compared with the selected countries, only New Zealand had a higher motor vehicle death rate than the United States, at 63 per 100,000 in 1992–93. France had a motor vehicle death rate similar to that of the United States.

The firearm death rate among males 15–24 years old was 54 per 100,000 in the United States. This was far higher than the rate in 10 other countries. The United states had a firearm death rate 4.5 times the rates of Norway, Israel, and Canada, which averaged 11 to 12 per 100,000. Death rates in Scotland, the Netherlands, and England and Wales were the lowest, at about 1 per 100,000.

The firearm death rate among males 15–24 in the United States was 32 percent higher than the motor vehicle death rate. In no other comparison country did the firearm death rate exceed the motor vehicle death rate.

In the United States, 63 percent of the firearm deaths among males in this age group were homicides, and 30 percent were suicides. In no other country, except the Netherlands, were more than 25 percent of the firearm deaths homicides. Firearm suicide accounted for at least 70 percent of firearm deaths in Norway, Sweden, France, Canada, New Zealand, and Australia.

Gun Violence Is a Serious Economic and Public Health Problem

by the Firearm Injury Center at Penn

About the author: *The Firearm Injury Center at the University of Pennsylvania is a collaboration of communities, researchers, and health care professionals that addresses the issues of firearm violence and injury.*

Firearm injury in the United States has averaged 32,703 deaths annually between 1970 and 2000. . . . It is the second leading cause of death from injury after motor vehicle crashes and, in several states, is the leading cause of injury death. An estimated two nonfatal injuries occur for every firearm death. Firearms are involved in approximately 70% of homicides, 60% of suicides, 40% of robberies, and 20% of aggravated assaults. The fatality rate of firearm violence is similar to HIV, which is recognized as an epidemic by the Centers for Disease Control and Prevention (CDC), and is more than twice as high as the U.S. Department of Health and Human Services' "Healthy People" goals for the year 2010.

Several additional facts compel the interdisciplinary study of firearm injury and development of interventions to reduce its impact.

- Firearm injury and its subsequent repercussions are preventable. Research on firearm injury provides evidence that specific changes can be made that will reduce the deaths, disability, and costs to society.
- Firearm injury disproportionately affects young people, resulting in lives cut short or forever affected by violence. . . .
- Compared to other causes of death, the number of firearm injury and death in the United States demonstrates its impact on American society. Firearms, especially handguns, are effective lethal weapons with the capability to escalate often-impulsive acts of interpersonal violence or suicidal thoughts into death.

Compared to other industrialized countries, violence and firearm death rates in the United States are disproportionately high. Of the approximately 50 upper- and middle-income countries with available data an estimated 115,000 firearm deaths occur annually and the U.S. contributes about 30,000. Among industrialized nations, the U.S. firearm-related death rate is more than twice that of the next highest country. The firearm death rate in the U.S. (14.24 per 100,000) is eight times the average rate of its economic counterparts (1.76).

- Compared to high-income Asian countries (Taiwan, Singapore, Hong Kong, and Japan), the firearm mortality rate in the U.S. is over 70 times higher (14.24 per 100,000 in the U.S. compared to 0.1925 per 100,000 in Asia).
- The correlation between firearm availability and rates of homicide is consistent across high-income industrialized nations: where there are more firearms, there are higher rates of homicide overall. The U.S. has the highest rates of both firearm homicide and private firearm ownership. In 1998 an estimated 38% of U.S. households had a firearm.
- Rates of youth violence and death are high worldwide. In the U.S., the youth firearm death rate is high relative to other countries. The death rate for all causes of firearm mortality (homicide, suicide, and unintentional) is higher for people less than 25 years old in the U.S. than in other high-income nations.

> *"The fatality rate of firearm violence is similar to HIV."*

- In 1995, the overall firearm-related death rate among American children younger than 16 years was nearly 12 times higher than for children in 25 other industrialized countries combined.
- Excluding firearm suicides, the rate of child suicide in the U.S. would be similar to that of other countries.
- Among all industrialized countries, more men are killed by firearms than women. However, women in the U.S. die from firearm injuries in a higher proportion than in most other high-income countries.

The Use of Handguns

Compared to other weapons commonly used in interpersonal violence, firearms have the highest lethality. The fraction of firearm injuries resulting in death (the case fatality rate) is reported in some studies to be as much as five times higher than for knives. The likelihood and severity of injury depends on the type of weapon used and the intent of the person using the weapon.

Case fatality rates (CFR) vary across intent. It is estimated that nearly one-third of all gunshot injuries are fatal. The fatality rate depends on the intent of the firearm event and the body part injured in a shooting. . . .

- Intentional self-directed firearm injuries resulted in death in 76.6% of cases.
- Intentional interpersonal firearm injuries resulted in death in 21.6% of cases.
- Unintentional firearm injuries resulted in death in 7.3% of cases.
- The CFR for firearm injuries to the head (61.0%) was more than triple the CFR for injuries to other parts of the body (18.7%).

Types of Guns

Firearms refer to all guns, with two major subsets being long guns (i.e., rifles and shotguns) and handguns (i.e., revolvers and pistols). Handguns are lightweight, concealable, easy to fire, and powerful, relative to their size. This makes them the weapon of choice for self and home protection. For many of the same reasons, handguns are more likely to be used in interpersonal violence and crime, as well as self-directed injury.

- Handguns comprise about one-third of all firearms owned in the U.S. (65 million of 192 million total), but they are used in half of all homicides, approximately 80% of all firearm homicides, and 70% of all firearm suicides.
- Of the 38% of American households that had a firearm in 1998, 23% had a handgun.
- Handguns account for 77% of all traced guns used in crime.
- Semi-automatic and automatic pistols are capable of inflicting greater injury, as more bullets can be fired in a shorter period of time. The increased use of semi-automatic weapons has resulted in changed wounding patterns with an increased number of bullet wounds per incident per body and a subsequent higher mortality.
- Of the two major types of handguns, revolvers and pistols, pistols currently are more popular. Revolvers typically hold 5–6 cartridges in a rotating cylinder and must be manually reloaded when the cylinder is empty. A revolver fires one bullet with each trigger pull. Pistols are typically semi-automatic, hold 7 or more cartridges, and have an internal magazine where ammunition is stored. The chamber of a semi-automatic weapon is reloaded automatically after each round is fired, but the trigger must be pulled for each firing (a fully-automatic weapon would fire multiple rounds with a single pull of the trigger).
- In 1999 semi-automatic pistols were the most frequently traced handguns by law enforcement for all age groups (52%). Among juveniles less than 17 years old arrested in 1999, handguns were the most common type of firearm recovered by law enforcement (87%). Semi-automatic pistols were the weapon of choice for juveniles, with 58% traced among youth under age 18 and 60% for those ages 18–24, compared to 47% among persons age 25 or older.

The Widespread Effects of Firearm Injuries

The impact of firearm injury extends beyond the fatal statistics, with widespread repercussions throughout society. Though many of these effects are difficult to quantify, they are gaining recognition and interdisciplinary research has begun. Areas of study include nonfatal firearm injury, health care, economics, psychology, and sociology.

For every person who dies from a gunshot wound, at least two others are shot and survive. However, these numbers vary widely based on intent, with self-inflicted injuries much more likely to be fatal. There were more than 100,000 firearm injuries in the five-year period between 1993 and 1998.

Nonfatal firearm-related injuries in all intent categories from 1993–1998 had the following characteristics:

- 20% occurred in the home
- 35% involved a handgun
- Approximately 60% were transported to the [emergency room] by ambulance or other emergency services.
- Approximately 2% were job-related

Injury patterns by intent:

- More than half of the intentionally self-inflicted nonfatal injuries involve gunshot wounds to the head or neck and are highly fatal.
- In contrast, approximately 15% of firearm-related assaults and those of undetermined intent were head or neck injuries, and more than 30% were gunshot wounds to the leg or foot.
- More than 70% of unintentional nonfatal injuries were gunshot wounds to the legs or arms, resulting in lower fatality.

The Role of Trauma Centers

Trauma centers, primarily located in metropolitan areas, disproportionately treat gunshot wounds and serve a critical role in managing these injuries, thereby improving outcomes for firearm injury survivors and decreasing fatalities. New approaches to diagnosis and management of wounds, including damage control and temporary shunts, have decreased mortality, but less is known about the long-term emotional and sociological sequalae.

- Each year approximately 100,000 people survive a gunshot injury long enough to be taken to emergency departments. Of these, nearly 60% are injured seriously enough to require hospitalization. The average length of hospital stay for mild to moderate firearm injuries is 10–13 days.
- The establishment and growth of trauma centers and trauma response systems may partially account for the decline in the nation's homicide rate in the late 1990s. There is some evidence that a part of the downward trend seen in firearm homicide is due to expert clinical care provided in trauma systems.
- The most serious disabilities for firearm injury survivors result from amputation, and brain and spinal cord injuries. Nationally, 16.5% of spinal cord injuries are caused by gunshot injuries.

Beyond the Physical Effects

Firearm injury is cosily to individuals and society. A small percentage of the total estimated cost of firearm injury comes from medical expenses and lost productivity. Change in quality of life and deterioration in community living and society have far greater economic tolls. Public and private efforts to reduce the risks of gun violence carry much of the burden.

- In a study of U.S. firearm injuries from 1994, cost was estimated at $2.3 billion in lifetime medical costs, an average of $17,000 per injury. Of these costs, 74% are accounted for by assaults. Most of the costs of firearm injuries are due to long-term consequences, not acute care.
- U.S. taxpayers pay about half ($1.1 billion) of the total lifetime costs of treating gunshot injuries, with private insurance, victims, and other sources covering the rest.
- Survivors of firearm injuries incur losses in productivity, ongoing medical costs, long-term disability, as well as physical and psychological problems. Some research shows that when these factors are considered in the context of a willingness to pay methodology and quality of life cost estimates, the price tag reaches $100 billion annually.

Firearm injury is the fifth leading cause of years of potential life lost (YPLL) for all injury and the second leading cause of YPLL for injury-related deaths in those under the age of sixty-five, a ranking surpassed only by motor-vehicle crash injuries.

Studies have shown an increase in depression and stress as the result of violence, but few studies have discussed the consequences of firearm violence in particular. People living with the threat of violence change their social behavior as they adapt to the increased risk of violence.

Given the unexpected nature of physical trauma, a violent event can become a defining moment in the injured person's life. In response to the injury, the survivor separates his/her life into "before injury" and "after injury." Survivors of traumatic injury experience increased levels of posttraumatic psychological distress and depression and are forever changed by their injury.

> *"U.S. taxpayers pay about half ($1.1 billion) of the total lifetime costs of treating gunshot injuries."*

Children are exposed to community violence at disturbingly high rates, particularly in the inner city. It is estimated that one quarter of low income urban youth have witnessed a murder. Frequent exposure to violence can result in posttraumatic stress symptoms, depression, dissociation, aggression and distress.

In addition to the impact highlighted above, firearm injury has longer term psychosocial repercussions. For example, children exposed to violence experience substance abuse, school failure, anxiety, and behavioral problems at higher levels. The pervasive threat to society's sense of safety is not easily quantified. Whether a person's experience of firearm violence is firsthand, shots heard outside a window, or a story in the morning newspaper, his/her safety is called into question. As a result, many youth feel they must carry a weapon for a sense of protection, as well as to establish status and social identity. In one study of youth, fear seems to contagiously drive violence as it feeds into the development of an "ecology of danger."

The Public Health Framework

Scholars from many disciplines including criminology, law, nursing, medicine, public health, sociology, psychology, and economics study firearm injury. Interdisciplinary teams continue to seek explanations for the complex causes and effects of violence and firearm injury. The root causes include poverty, illicit drug markets, lack of educational or employment opportunities, fear, stress, racial and income inequalities, substance abuse, and mental health. Explanations for the dramatic rise of firearm violence in the 1980s that peaked in 1993 generally focus on changes among youth violence, including involvement in illicit drug sales, especially crack cocaine, and increased availability of firearms.

Public health provides a useful framework to address firearm injury because it seeks to prevent harm to both individuals and the community. This approach is informed by epi-

> *"Public health provides a useful framework to address firearm injury."*

demiology [defined by *A Dictionary of Epidemiology* as] "the study of the distribution and determinants of health-related states or events in specified populations and the application of this study to control of health problems." In the 1970's, William Haddon applied this approach to injury prevention, specifically motor vehicle crashes, bringing about significant changes to motor vehicle design and operation. The recently released World Health Organization report on violence and health recommends a public health approach to understand the complex social, psychological, economic and community underpinnings of violence, as a complement to the law and order approach.

A similar approach can be taken for firearm injury. Before interventions can be designed, it is important to understand what factors contribute to the injury event. Firearm data should include factors related to the weapon used (design, sale, and storage), the people who misuse weapons, people who could be injured by the misuse of weapons (behavior, attitudes, and intent), and factors in the environment (such as social, physical, political, and economic circumstances).

A visual representation of the pathway of a firearm injury event depicts three critical factors that must converge in order for the event to occur: 1) the agents must be available (firearm and ammunition), 2) a person must acquire and use the weapon (host: carrier), and 3) there must be a person at risk of being shot (host: at-risk). Note that the carrier and at-risk host are the same person in the case of a self-inflicted injury (whether intentional or not). The timeline of a firearm event involves factors from long before the event (pre-incident) to those immediately around the event (peri-incident), to after the event (post-incident). The social and physical environments may influence whether and how the factors intersect. For example, rural areas are disproportionately affected by firearm suicide while urban areas experience greater rates of firearm homicide.

Physical environments enhance or inhibit the chances of firearm involvement in an interaction. Social environments, such as a concentration of poverty, may support community norms that increase levels of violence. The trajectories for firearm injury do not end with a firearm injury. A given event can result in different outcomes for the injured person, ranging from immediate death, a lifetime of disability, or other life changes. The shooter's trajectory could continue with involvement in other firearm events, move through the criminal justice system or also end in a subsequent death from firearm violence. The discharged firearm may be found and traced, destroyed, or continue to be used in other events. Communities and individuals must deal with the fallout of a traumatic firearm event or events, which can, in turn, affect the community environment as a whole. Each factor identified along the pathway represents a potential point of intervention to reduce firearm injuries. . . .

Violence is a problem worldwide, but measures are being taken to reduce its toll and burden. In the United States, there is a significant problem with firearm violence and injury, one that affects all aspects of American life and disproportionately affects youth. While there are many other mechanisms of violence, a firearm adds an element of lethality to any situation, intentional or unintentional. The resulting death and injury is extremely costly, economically, psychologically, and socially. Over time, it changes and destroys millions of lives and communities. Given the magnitude of the problem, addressing firearm injury can seem an insurmountable task, but the public health precedent for making motor vehicles safer can lead to sensible and effective policies. Surveillance and data analysis can inform communities of their specific problem with firearm injury and focus their decisions for intervention. While firearm policy has been the subject of long and heated debate in the United States, the fact remains that people have continued to die and be injured by firearms, mostly handguns. This [viewpoint] is an attempt to present the problem of firearm injury and appeal to a wide range of disciplines working in the areas of medicine, law, social services, and public health to expand their knowledge and redirect new energies to address the urgent problem of firearm injury and death in America.

Youth Gun Violence Is a Serious Problem

by Kathleen Reich, Patti L. Culross, and Richard E. Behrman

About the authors: *Kathleen Reich is a policy analyst and editor at the David and Lucile Packard Foundation; Patti L. Culross is a program officer in the Children, Families, and Communities program at the foundation; and Richard E. Behrman is the editor in chief of* The Future of Children.

Guns are exceptionally lethal weapons, and they are easily available to young people. In the late 1980s and early 1990s, the lethality and availability of guns, particularly handguns, fueled a youth gun violence epidemic that peaked in 1994, when nearly 6,000 young people under age 20 died from firearm injuries. That crisis has abated, but the number and rate of youth gun homicides, suicides, and unintentional shooting deaths remain unacceptably high in this country. Nearly 4,000 children and youth under age 20 were killed with firearms in 1998, and more than 18,000 others were injured.

Unfortunately, data regarding the extent of and circumstances surrounding youth gun violence are limited, and the need for better data remains a major concern. This [viewpoint] summarizes what is known about youth gun deaths and injuries, and makes recommendations for obtaining better information.

The Lethality and Easy Availability of Guns

Youth violence is a complex problem, influenced by psychological, economic, and social factors. But the problem is worsened substantially because of the lethality and accessibility of firearms. Guns cause deaths and severe injuries more frequently than knives, clubs, or fists, and with guns, even transitory violent impulses can have lethal consequences. Guns also are easily available to young people, even though federal law, with a few exceptions, prohibits those under 21 from purchasing handguns and those under 18 from purchasing rifles and shotguns or possessing handguns. Exceptional lethality, combined with

Kathleen Reich, Patti L. Culross, and Richard E. Behrman, "Children, Youth, and Gun Violence: Analysis and Recommendations," *The Future of Children*, vol. 12, Summer/Fall 2002, p. 5. Copyright © 2002 by The David and Lucile Packard Foundation. Reproduced by permission.

easy access, accounts at least in part for the fact that firearm-related injuries remain the second leading cause of death among children and youth ages 10 to 19. Only motor vehicle accidents claim more young lives.

Guns are more lethal than other weapons. For example, robberies committed with guns are 3 times more likely to result in a fatality than are robberies with knives, and 10 times more likely than are robberies with other weapons. Between 1996 and 1998, there was 1 death for every 4.4 visits to emergency departments by young people under age 20 for treatment of a firearm injury. In comparison, the ratio of deaths to emergency department visits for nonfirearm-related injuries for the same age group was 1:760.

Guns have become more lethal over the past few decades. . . . The increase in youth gun violence in the late 1980s coincided with the diffusion of high-powered semiautomatic pistols into the legal and illegal gun markets. These pistols had higher calibers (the higher a gun's caliber, the higher its destructive potential) and held more ammunition than their predecessors. Semiautomatic pistols, particularly inexpensive ones, quickly became weapons of choice for criminals, including young people; by 1999, these pistols accounted for one-half of all guns traced by the U.S. Bureau of Alcohol, Tobacco and Firearms (ATF) after being recovered by law enforcement following a crime. With the increasing use of these guns came increases in rates of firearm violence, the average number of bullet wounds per person injured, and the proportion of victims who died before reaching the hospital.

The increased lethality of guns, particularly handguns, coincided with their increasing availability to and use by young people. . . . The carrying of guns by youth began to rise in the late 1980s in tandem with the explosive growth of markets for crack cocaine. As young drug dealers in urban communities began using guns to protect the cash and narcotics they carried, other young people in the community also began carrying guns, often for self-protection. This process was exacerbated by the growth of youth gangs, which tightened social networks among teenagers and served as conduits for the diffusion of guns.

A Violence Epidemic

Overall homicide rates in the United States rose to nearly unprecedented levels between 1985 and 1993, and the entire increase was attributable to homicides committed by young people with guns. Guns were not the only reason for this increase; the rise of crack cocaine, an increase in child poverty, and expanded gang activity also were important factors. But the increasing lethality and availability of guns undoubtedly played a key role in the explosive growth of youth gun homicide. As the Surgeon General reported in 2001:

> The epidemic of violence from 1983 to 1993 does not seem to have resulted from a basic change in the offending rates and viciousness of young offenders. Rather, it resulted primarily from a relatively sudden change in the social environment—the introduction of guns into violent exchanges among youth. The

violence epidemic was, in essence, the result of a change in the presence and type of weapon, used, which increased the lethality of violent incidents.

Since the early 1990s, both youth gun carrying and youth gun violence have declined dramatically. Several articles in [the summer/fall 2002 issue of *Future of Children*] offer theories to explain the decrease; these include a drop in illegal drug market activity (particularly surrounding crack cocaine), stronger law enforcement against youth gun carrying, and increased public education efforts promoting safe storage of guns and violence prevention. Still, many young people apparently have little difficulty obtaining guns, either from home, from friends, through illegal purchase from gun dealers or "on the street," or through theft.

"Firearm-related injuries remain the second leading cause of death among children and youth ages 10 to 19."

For example, an estimated 34% of children in the United States live in homes with firearms. In addition, in a national study of male high school sophomores and juniors conducted in 1998, 50% of respondents reported that obtaining a gun would be "little" or "no" trouble. A 1999 national survey estimated that 833,000 American youth between the ages of 12 and 17 had carried a handgun at least once in the previous year. Many teens who carry guns cite the need for self-protection as their primary reason for doing so. With so many children and youth reporting easy access to guns, high rates of youth gun death and injury should not be surprising.

In 1994, the number of gun deaths among children and youth under age 20 reached a historic high of 5,833; by 1998, annual deaths had fallen to 3,792. Still, gun death rates among children and youth due to homicide, suicide, and unintentional shooting are far higher in the United States than in other industrialized nations. The risk of gun death is not spread evenly throughout the youth population, however. Certain groups of young people are at greatest risk. Moreover, a February 2002 study found that children ages 5 to 14 were more likely to die from gunshot wounds if they lived in states where firearm ownership was more common. This finding held true even after the researchers controlled for state-level poverty rates, education, and urbanization.

Youths and Homicide

An estimated 58% of firearm deaths among children and youth under age 20 in 1998 were homicides. . . . Older teens, males, minority youth, and young people residing in urban areas are more likely than other children and youth to die in gun homicides. Adolescent African American males are at highest risk for youth gun homicide; in 1998, some 63 out of every 100,000 African American males ages 15 to 19 died in a firearm homicide, compared with a rate of 29 per 100,000 for their Hispanic counterparts and 3 per 100,000 for white male teenagers.

Children and youth are perpetrators as well as victims of gun violence. In 1998, juveniles and youth under age 25 committed 54% of gun homicides in which the offender was known; juveniles under age 18 alone accounted for 12% of gun homicides in which the offender was known. African American teenage males are more likely to commit gun homicides than are white or Hispanic youth. Thus, African American youth are overrepresented both as victims and perpetrators of youth gun deaths.

Even without firearms, American children are more likely to die in homicides than their counterparts in other industrialized nations. However, guns worsen the violence. The firearm-related homicide rate among children under age 15 in the United States is nearly 16 times higher than in 25 other industrialized nations combined. If the United States could reduce youth gun homicide to levels more comparable to those of other nations, youth homicide rates in general would decline significantly, giving more children and youth—particularly adolescent males, minority youth, and young people living in inner cities—a better chance of reaching adulthood. An important first step in this process is to forge a national commitment to reduce youth gun homicide. The effort should be led by the federal government and include active involvement by a wide range of stakeholders such as public health experts, law enforcement personnel, religious leaders, community leaders, educators, and parents.

Youth Gun Suicides

Suicide is the second leading cause of firearm-related deaths among children and youth, accounting for 33% of these deaths in 1998. Although youth gun suicides declined somewhat in the late 1990s, firearms remain the most common method of suicide among youth. . . . Youth are more likely to use guns to commit suicide than are older, nonelderly adults; in 1994, about 67% of 15- to 24-year-olds used firearms to commit suicide, compared with 56% of 25- to 64-year-olds. White adolescents, males, and youth living in rural areas are more likely than other youth to die in gun suicides, although the gun suicide rate among African American adolescent males has risen sharply in the past 20 years, and is approaching the rate for white adolescent males.

Numerous studies have documented a clear association between the presence of firearms in the home and suicides, particularly suicides by adolescents and young adults. One study found that guns were twice as likely to be present in the homes of teen suicide victims as in the homes of suicide attempters or a comparison group of teen psychiatric patients who were not suicidal. Household firearm ownership is positively associated with the firearm suicide rate for 15- to 24-year-olds, even after controlling for education, unemployment, and urban residence.

> *"Firearms remain the most common method of suicide among youth."*

The rate of nonfirearm suicides among 5- to 14-year-olds in the United States is roughly equal to the rate in other industrialized countries combined. However, the firearm suicide rate among children in this age group is nearly 11 times higher. As a result, children in the United Stares commit suicide at twice the rate of children in 25 other industrialized nations combined.

Despite the prevalence of youth gun suicide, it has been something of a silent killer, not attracting nearly as much attention from policymakers, researchers, and the media as youth gun homicide or even unintentional shootings. One unresolved issue in academic literature is whether youth who commit suicide with a gun would simply have found another way to kill themselves if guns were nor available to them. Given the extreme lethality of firearms, it seems plausible that at least some young people might not have succeeded in their suicide attempts if they had not had access to a gun. Therefore, convincing young people, parents, and the public to keep guns away from youth at risk of suicide should be a high priority.

Unintentional Shooting Deaths and Firearm Injuries

Unintentional shootings among young people most frequently happen when children or youth obtain a gun and play with it, not realizing that it is real, or loaded, or pointed at themselves or a friend. In 1998, more than 7% of children and youth under age 20 killed by firearms died in unintentional shootings, and these shootings accounted for 27% of firearm deaths among children under age 12. . . . Boys, African American children, and Hispanic children are more likely to die in accidental shootings than are other groups of children. The death rate from unintentional shootings among children is nine times higher in the United States than in 25 other industrialized nations combined.

Although accidental shootings of children have declined significantly in recent decades, they still attract a great deal of public attention, perhaps because the victims, and sometimes even the perpetrators, are seen as blameless and the deaths preventable. If guns were not present in the home, if they were designed with safety features making them difficult for children to fire, or if they were stored safely—unloaded and locked, with ammunition stored separately from the guns—the risk to young children could be virtually eliminated.

For every gun death among young people under age 20, there are more than four injuries. Although the data about nonfatal firearm-related injuries to children and youth are incomplete, the article by [Lois A.] Fingerhut and [Katherine Kaufer] Chrisroffel summarizes what is known: From 1996–1998, an estimated 18,400 children and youth visited emergency departments for gun injuries each year, with nearly one-half of these visits requiring hospitalization. About 85% of these firearm injuries were among older teens, ages 15 to 19. Males were 7 times more likely than females to be injured. African American youth were 10 times more likely and Hispanic youth 2 times more likely to be injured than were white youth. . . .

The Economic Costs of Gun Violence

In addition to the human toll, gun violence among young people imposes significant financial and psychological costs on society. For children and youth, these costs can be especially high; those exposed to gun violence are at risk for significant and lasting psychological effects. Moreover, children do not have to be injured themselves to experience these negative effects. Exposure to gun violence at home, at school, in the community, or through the media all can cause harm.

The most obvious economic costs associated with gun violence in the general population are health-related, in the form of increased medical costs due to injury and death. Other economic costs include those associated with strengthening law enforcement to combat gun crime, and prosecuting and incarcerating gun offenders.

> *"Gun violence among young people imposes significant financial and psychological costs on society."*

Together, these costs total an estimated $4 billion to $5 billion annually. However, [an] article by [Philip J.] Cook and [Jens] Ludwig . . . notes that these costs account for only a small share of the total costs of gun violence to society. Other, less tangible costs related to gun violence—such as higher taxes to ensure public safety, higher housing costs as families move to areas that are perceived as safe from gun violence, and the psychological costs associated with fear—make up most of the costs of gun violence.

Such costs affect not only the families of gun violence victims, but all Americans, through increased taxes, decreased property values, limits on choices about where to live and work, and concerns about safety, particularly children's safety. These intangible costs can be difficult to quantify, but Cook and Ludwig argue that the costs of gun violence can be considered equivalent to the value that people place on safety from gun violence. Therefore, they estimate the costs of gun violence by assessing how much Americans would be willing to pay to reduce or eliminate gun violence from their lives.

A 1998 national survey that asked people about their willingness to pay for policy interventions to reduce gun violence found that the average American household was willing to pay $239 a year to reduce the threat of gun violence in its state by 30%. Based on these answers, Cook and Ludwig estimate that the total annual cost of gun violence in the United States is $100 billion, of which $15 billion is attributable to costs associated with gun violence against children and youth.

Gun Violence Has Psychological Costs

Just as the economic costs of gun violence are substantial, so are the psychological costs. Children exposed to gun violence, whether they are victims, perpetrators, or witnesses, can experience negative psychological effects over the short and long terms. Psychological trauma also is common among children who are exposed to high levels of violence in their communities or through the media. [An] article by [James] Garbarino, [Catherine P.] Bradshaw, and [Joseph A.] Vorrasi . . . details common effects associated with exposure to gun violence, including sleep disturbance, anger, withdrawal, posttraumatic stress, poor school performance, lower career aspirations, increased delinquency, risky sexual behaviors, substance abuse, and desensitization to violence. All of these effects can make children and youth more prone to violence themselves, feeding a continuing cycle of violence within some families, peer groups, and communities.

Arguably, every child in the United States is exposed to gun violence through media coverage of shootings, films and television shows, and violent video games that allow young people to shoot lifelike targets on the screen. More than 1,000 studies have documented a link between violent media and aggressive behavior. Children exposed to media violence have been shown in experimental studies to become more aggressive, to view more favorably the use of aggression to resolve conflicts, to become desensitized to violence, and to develop a belief that the world around them is a frightening place.

However, the children and youth at highest risk for psychological trauma from gun violence are those exposed to it directly: children who are injured, who witness gun violence at close proximity, or who are exposed to high levels of gun violence in their homes, schools, or communities. School and community violence are particularly worrisome because they can affect large numbers of children at one time.

A December 2001 study of 119 African American 7-year-olds living in inner-city Philadelphia, for example, found that three-quarters had heard gunfire, one-third had seen someone shot, and one-tenth had someone in their own family or household who had been shot or stabbed. Among children in the study, exposure to higher levels of violence was correlated with more anxiety, greater likelihood of depression, lower self-esteem, lower grade point average, and more absences from school. More than 60% of the chil-

> *"There is no broad-based commitment to a wide range of strategies that will reduce unsupervised youth access to and use of guns."*

dren worried that they might be killed or die, and 19% sometimes wished they were dead.

Despite widespread recognition of the psychological costs to children and youth associated with gun violence, physicians and mental health professionals have been slow to develop treatments that help young people cope with gun-related trauma. Even children and youth who are injured often go without psychological help. One group of doctors has observed, "When patients present with suicide attempts, evaluation for future risk and follow-up treatment are considered standard practice. However, individuals treated for violent injuries generally receive no further evaluation." Government, schools, and health care practitioners should work together to ensure that children and youth who are exposed to gun violence get the psychological help they need. Two examples of innovative programs . . . include a pioneering project developed at the University of California, Los Angeles, that provides school-based group therapy for adolescents who have sustained or witnessed violent injury, and a collaboration between the New Haven Police Department and Yale University School of Medicine to train police officers in how to deal with children who are victimized by or witnesses to violence. Additional programs are needed to help youth overcome gun-related psychological trauma, especially because treating traumatized young people may make them less prone to violent acts in the future.

Addressing the Problem

No single policy solution will end youth gun violence in the United States; a wide repertoire of approaches is needed to address different aspects of the problem. Key strategies that may reduce youth gun violence include: reducing unsupervised exposure to guns among children and youth; strengthening social norms against violence in communities; enforcing laws against youth gun carrying; altering the design of guns to make them less likely to be used by children and youth; and, perhaps most importantly, implementing new legal and regulatory interventions that make it more difficult for youth to obtain guns. Parents, community leaders, policymakers, and researchers all have vital roles to play in implementing these strategies. . . .

Guns are unique weapons, highly lethal, and easily available. Their use by and against children and youth has exacted an enormous toll on American society. The economic costs associated with youth gun violence have been estimated in the billions of dollars. But the most significant costs—lost lives or diminished futures for children and youth affected by gun violence—are probably incalculable. The federal government and state governments, working in partnership with local communities and parents, should adopt a unified, comprehensive strategy for reducing youth gun violence in the United States.

Precedent exists for such a broad injury prevention strategy. Over the past 40 years, Congress, federal agencies, public health practitioners, and law enforcement professionals have worked together in a systematic effort to reduce motor vehicle deaths and injuries. The approaches they have adopted include: national data systems that track all motor vehicle fatalities; federal safety standards for motor vehicles and equipment; federal and state requirements for driver training and licensing; strict enforcement of motor vehicle laws, especially against drunk driving; federal, state, and private-sector investment into research to improve motor vehicle safety and treatment of injuries; and extensive public awareness activities. As a result, the federal government estimates that 243,400 lives were saved between 1966 and 1990.

Obviously, the task of reducing gun injury and death poses different and perhaps more difficult challenges than reducing motor vehicle injury and deaths, most of which are unintentional. Still, the motor vehicle example points to what is lacking in youth gun violence prevention efforts. As yet, no broad national consensus exists on how to approach the problem. There is no broad-based commitment to a wide range of strategies that will reduce unsupervised youth access to and use of guns.

There needs to be. Without more concerted efforts to reduce youth gun violence, children and youth will continue to die, unnecessarily and senselessly, from gunshot wounds. A national campaign against youth gun violence should be strongly grounded in research, and encompass [a] broad range of strategies. . . . Such strategies should include promoting parental monitoring and safe gun storage; strengthening community norms against gun violence; implementing creative collaborations between law enforcement and communities; regulating guns as consumer products; and tightening federal and state laws regarding gun sales.

Common ground often proves elusive on an issue as polarizing as gun violence. Both gun control and gun rights advocates surely can agree, however, that it is unacceptable for the United States to have a higher rate of gun-related deaths and injuries to children and youth than all other industrialized nations combined. Hopefully, that point of agreement can serve as the foundation for aggressive efforts to reduce youth gun violence in the United States.

Gun Violence Is a Global Problem

by Philip Alpers

About the author: *Philip Alpers is a senior fellow at the Harvard Injury Control Research Center.*

This journal [*Injury Prevention*] often publishes papers on gun injury, almost all of them American. Readers on other shores could be forgiven for asking if the topic concerns them, given the sharp disparities in firearm related mortality. For example in the United States, 4% of the world population possesses 50% of the planet's privately owned firearms; America's gun death rate stands head and shoulders above those of 35 similar high and upper middle income nations. Of the 35, 29 suffer less than half the firearm related death rate in the United States.

Despite a recent spike in drug related shootings in a handful of cities, including London, a resident of England or Wales remains 26 times less likely to die by gunshot than an American. In Japan, the risk of gun death is at least 100 times lower than in the United States.

Gun Violence Outside America

Yet America is far from alone in suffering high rates of firearm related mortality. Close competitors include Mexico, South Africa, Colombia, Estonia, and Brazil—nations with whom Americans rarely see themselves in the same league.

As the World Health Organization, the Small Arms Survey and others push out the fringes of research into gun death, it seems clear that worse is to come. In scores of less wealthy countries the toll has barely been measured—entire societies which lack the resources to accurately count injury deaths, let alone centralise data on method or intent.

In South Africa, where firearm mortality overshadows all other external causes of death, and whose data collection is among the most effective in the Global South, only one third of unnatural death records are available for analy-

Philip Alpers, "Yes, Americans Are Often Shot—and So Are Many Others: The Public Health Community Is Crucial to Any Solution," *Injury Prevention*, vol. 8, December 2002, p. 262. Copyright © 2002 by the British Medical Association. Reproduced by permission from the BMJ Publishing Group.

sis. Even that fraction is perforce an estimate. The current discussion of inadequacies in United States firearm related health data highlights the comparative transparency (and excellence by world standards) of American gun death and injury statistics.

That said, best estimates show that gunshots cost us 500,000 lives each year, worldwide. Of these, 300,000 people die in regional conflict and 200,000 in interpersonal violence and suicide. The majority of victims are non-combatants, many of them women and children. Where estimates are available, non-fatal firearm related injuries are said to number three for every gun death.

Gun injury has been labelled a "disease" (American Medical Association, International Red Cross), a "public health emergency" (Centers for Disease Control), an "epidemic" (US Surgeon General), and a "scourge" (UN Secretary General, the Vatican).

Political and Social Effects

The global proliferation of small arms increases both the lethality of violent encounters and the number of victims. With 639 million firearms in circulation worldwide, guns increasingly transform minor disputes into shootings and make it easier for children to become killers. In Papua New Guinea, intertribal disputes once settled with bows, arrows, and machetes are now fought out with firearms. Across great swathes of Africa and South Asia, child soldiers are enabled with AK-47s, exploited by adult combatants, their lives ended or distorted, their weapons still available for banditry and domestic violence even if peace does arrive.

No community seems immune from this pandemic of gun violence. It overwhelms health services and undermines personal security, economic development, good governance, and human rights. And the involvement of the public health community will be crucial to any solution.

The emergency room is no place for geopolitics or for blame. To a trauma surgeon delving into gunshot wounds in Pretoria, London or Islamabad, it matters little if the weapon was fired by a terrorist/freedom fighter, by a mobster, a soldier, or an angry husband. Nor does it matter if the gun was military in appearance or had previously been used only to shoot pigeons. Whether the gunshot is by accident, suicide, crime or conflict, the damage done to the victim, the family, and wider society is remarkably similar.

> *"Gunshots cost us 500,000 lives each year."*

Public health professionals are ideally placed to act as lynchpins for firearm related policy swings in their own countries. When guns are discussed and regulated matter-of-factly as vectors of injury, ideological barriers can be moved aside, much as they were in the prevention of HIV/AIDS.

Then the healing—and even more importantly, the prevention—can proceed.

Gun Violence Is Not a Public Health Crisis

by Miguel A. Faria Jr.

About the author: *Miguel A. Faria Jr., MD, is an author and editor emeritus of the* Medical Sentinel, *the journal of the Association of American Physicians and Surgeons.*

I have related previously (*Medical Sentinel*, Spring and Summer 1997) how the 1991 American Medical Association's (AMA) campaign against domestic violence launched for public relation consumption went hand in hand with the public health establishment's 1979 stated objective of eradication of handguns in America, beginning with a 25 percent reduction by the year 2000. Toward that objective, in the 1980s, hundreds of articles describing politicized, biased, result-oriented research funded at taxpayers' expense were published in the medical journals. One of the principle investigators was Dr. Arthur Kellermann, who now heads the Emory University School of Public Health.

A significant portion of the gun control agenda, not only of the public health but the entire health advocacy establishment, in fact, comes from Dr. Kellermann's landmark articles, particularly "Gun Ownership as a Risk Factor for Homicide in the Home," published in *The New England Journal of Medicine (NEJM)* in 1993. And yet, much of the methodology, not to mention conclusions in the article, have been questioned by numerous investigators.

Error-Laden Research

Since at least the mid-1980s, Dr. Kellermann (and associates), whose work had been heavily-funded by the CDC [Centers for Disease Control and Prevention], published a series of studies purporting to show that persons who keep guns in the home are more likely to be victims of homicide than those who don't. In a 1986 *NEJM* paper, Dr. Kellermann and associates, for example, claimed their "scientific research" proved that defending oneself or one's family with a firearm in the home is dangerous and counter productive, claiming "a gun owner is 43 times more likely to kill a family member than an intruder."

In a critical review and now classic article published in the March 1994 issue of the *Journal of the Medical Association of Georgia (JMAG)*, Dr. Edgar Suter, Chairman of Doctors for Integrity in Policy Research (DIPR), found evidence of "methodologic and conceptual errors," such as prejudicially truncated data and the listing of "the correct methodology which was described but never used by the authors." Moreover, the gun control researchers failed to consider and underestimated the protective benefits of guns. Dr. Suter writes: "The true measure of the protective benefits of guns are the lives and medical costs saved, the injuries prevented, and the property protected—not the burglar or rapist body count. Since only 0.1–0.2 percent of defensive uses of guns involve the death of the criminal, any study, such as this, that counts criminal deaths as the only measure of the protective benefits of guns will expectedly underestimate the benefits of firearms by a factor of 500 to 1,000."

In 1993, in his landmark and much cited *NEJM* article (and the research, again, heavily funded by the CDC), Dr. Kellermann attempted to show again that guns in the home are a greater risk to the victims than to the assailants. Despite valid criticisms by reputable scholars of his previous works (including the 1986 study), Dr. Kellermann ignored the criticisms and again used the same methodology. He also used study populations with disproportionately high rates of serious psychosocial dysfunction from three selected state counties, known to be unrepresentative of the general U.S. population. For example, 53 percent of the case subjects had a history of a household member being arrested, 31 percent had a household history of illicit drug use, 32 percent had a household member hit or hurt in a family fight, and 17 percent had a family member hurt so seriously in a domestic altercation that prompt medical attention was required. Moreover, both the case studies and control groups in this analysis had a very high incidence of financial instability. In fact, in this study, gun ownership, the supposedly high risk factor for homicide was not one of the most strongly associated factors for being murdered. Drinking, illicit drugs, living alone, history of family violence, living in a rented home were *all* greater individual risk factors for being murdered than a gun in the home. One must conclude there is no basis to apply the conclusions of this study to the general population.

All of these are factors that, as Dr. Suter pointed out, "would expectedly be associated with higher rates of violence and homicide." It goes without saying, the results of such a study on gun homicides, selecting this sort of unrepresentative population sample, nullify the authors' generalizations, and their preordained conclusions can not be extrapolated to the general population.

Sampling Bias in One Study

Moreover, although the 1993 *New England Journal of Medicine* study purported to show that the homicide victims were killed with a gun ordinarily kept in the home, the fact is that as Kates and associates point out 71.1 percent of the victims were killed by assailants who did not live in the victim's household using guns presumably not kept in that home.

While Kellermann and associates began with 444 cases of homicides in the home, cases were dropped from the study for a variety of reasons, and in the end, only 316 matched pairs were used in the final analysis, representing only 71.2 percent of the original 444 homicide cases.

This reduction increased tremendously the chance for sampling bias. Analysis of why 28.8 percent of the cases were dropped would have helped ascertain if the study was compromised by the existence of such biases, but Dr. Kellermann, in an unprecedented move, refused to release his data and make it available for other researchers to analyze.

Likewise, [Professor] Gary Kleck of Florida State University has written me that knowledge about what guns were kept in the home is essential, but this data in his study was never released by Dr. Kellermann: "The most likely bit of data that he would want to withhold is information as to whether the gun used in the gun homicides was kept in the home of the victim."

As Kates and associates point out, "The validity of the *NEJM* 1993 study's conclusions depend on the control group matching the homicide cases in every way (except, of course, for the occurrence of the homicide)."

> *"The health care costs incurred by gun shootings have been greatly exaggerated."*

However, in this study, the controls collected did not match the cases in many ways (i.e., for example, in the amount of substance abuse, single parent versus two parent homes, etc.) contributing to further untoward effects, and decreasing the inference that can legitimately be drawn from the data of this study. Be that as it may, "The conclusion that gun ownership is a risk factor for homicide derives from the finding of a gun in 45.4 percent of the homicide case households, but in only 35.8 percent of the control household. Whether that finding is accurate, however, depends on the truthfulness of control group interviewees in admitting the presence of a gun or guns in the home."

The Problem with Scientific Surveys

Professor Gary Kleck has written extensively that false denial of gun ownership is a major problem in these survey studies, and yet Kellermann and associates do not admit or mention this fact. And this is critical. It would take only 35 of the 388 controls *falsely* denying gun ownership to make the control gun ownership percentage equal that of the homicide case households. As Kates and associates write, "If indeed, the controls actually had gun ownership equal to that of the homicide case households (45.4 percent), then a false denial rate of only 20.1 percent among the gun owning controls would produce the thirty-five false denials and thereby equalize ownership."

Consider the fact that Kellermann and associates' pilot study had a higher percent false denial rate than the 20.1 percent required to invalidate their own study, and yet, he and his associates concluded that there was no "underreporting of gun ownership by their control respondents," and their estimates, they claim were, therefore, considered not biased.

In the *Medical Sentinel*, we have considered this type of bias in response to a *JAMA* 1996 gun ownership survey. We reported on question #20 of that survey: "If asked by a pollster whether I owned firearms, I would be truthful? 29.6 percent disagreed/strongly disagreed." So according to this survey, 29.6 percent would falsely deny owning a firearm. We know that nearly one-third of respondents intentionally conceal their gun ownership because they fear further confiscation by the police as has happened in cities such as Washington, D.C., Detroit, and New York.

One must conclude on the basis of these errors that the findings of the 1993 Kellermann study are invalidated, just as those of 1986 are tainted. Nevertheless, these errors have crept into and now permeate the lay press, the electronic media, and particularly, the public health literature and the medical journals, where they remain uncorrected and are repeated time and again and perpetuated. And, because the publication of the data (and their purported conclusions) supposedly come from "reliable" sources and objective medical researchers, it's given a lot of weight and credibility by practicing physicians, social scientists and law enforcement. These errors need to be corrected to regain the loss of credibility of public health in this area of gun and violence research.

Guns Save Lives

What we do know, thanks to the meticulous scholarship of Prof. Gary Kleck and Doctors for Integrity in Policy Research (DIPR), is that the benefits of gun ownership by law-abiding citizens have been greatly underestimated. In *Point Blank: Guns and Violence in America* (1991), myriads of scientific publications, and his latest book, *Targeting Guns* (1997), Prof. Kleck found that the defensive uses of firearms by citizens amount to 2.5 million uses per year and dwarf the offensive gun uses by criminals. Between 25–75 lives are saved by a gun for every life lost to a gun. Medical costs saved by guns in the hands of law-abiding citizens are 15 times greater than costs incurred by criminal uses of firearms. Guns also prevent injuries to good people and protect billions of dollars of property every year.

Incidentally, the health care costs incurred by gun shootings have been greatly exaggerated. DIPR, in an article published in the June 1995 issue of the *JMAG*, estimated that the actual U.S. health care costs of treating gunshot wounds is approximately $1.5 billion which amounts to 0.2 percent of annual health care expenditures. The $20–$40 billion figure, so frequently cited by the mass media, and even medical journals, is an exaggerated estimate of *lifetime productivity lost* where criminals are given inflated, unrealistic life productivity estimates, as if their careers were suddenly expected to blossom into that of pillars of the community with projected salaries equaling those of managed care CEOs. Yet, despite these major detractions, the health advocacy establishment clings to the erroneous figures and extrapolations of Dr. Kellermann and other public health researchers, and use these erroneous figures in propounding health and gun control policies, to the detriment of public policy.

To catch up with the lost ground on the gun and violence research that has been accumulating in the criminologic and sociologic body of literature in the last couple of years, we have to look not only to the data collected by Prof. Gary Kleck and Dr. Edgar Suter, but also other prominent investigators.

The Positive Effects of Concealed Carry Laws

Recent data by Prof. John R. Lott, Jr., formerly with the University of Chicago and now at Yale University, in his book *More Guns, Less Crime—Understanding Crime and Gun Control Laws* (1998) has also been suppressed from dissemination in the medical journals and public health literature, except for the *Medical Sentinel*. In his book, Prof. Lott studied the FBI's massive yearly crime statistics for all 3,054 U.S. counties over 18 years (1977–1994), the largest national survey on gun ownership and state police documentation in illegal gun use, and he comes to some startling conclusions:

1. While neither state waiting periods nor the federal Brady Law is associated with a reduction in crime rates, *adopting concealed carry gun laws cut death rates from public, multiple shootings* (e.g., as those which took place in Jonesboro, Arkansas, and Springfield, Oregon, in 1998; the Columbine High School shooting in Littleton, Colorado, in 1999; or the 1993 shooting on the Long Island subway)—*by a whopping 69 percent.*

2. Allowing people to carry concealed weapons deters violent crime—without any apparent increase in accidental death. *If states without right to carry laws had adopted them in 1992*, about 1,570 murders, 4,177 rapes, and 60,000 aggravated assaults would have been avoided annually.

3. Children 14 to 15 years of age are 14.5 times more likely to die from automobile injuries, 5 times more likely to die from drowning or fire and burns, and 3 times more likely to die from bicycle accidents than they are to die from gun accidents.

> *"Allowing people to carry concealed weapons deters violent crime."*

4. Prof. Lott found that *when concealed carry laws went into effect in a given county*, murders fell by 8 percent, rapes by 5 percent, and aggravated assaults by 7 percent.

5. For each additional year concealed carry gun laws have been in effect, the murder rate declines by 3 percent, robberies by over 2 percent, and rape by 1 percent.

Let me now say a word about suicide and gun availability. Both Drs. Arthur

Kellermann and John H. Sloan have written about suicides and have attempted to link these fatalities to the availability of guns in articles published in *The New England Journal of Medicine.*

In reality, the overwhelming available evidence compiled from the psychiatric literature is that untreated or poorly managed depression is the real culprit behind the high rates of suicide. The evidence is authoritative on this point as classified in the *Diagnostic and Statistical Manual of Mental Disorders* of the American Psychiatric Association and any standard psychiatric text. From the social science of criminology, in fact, we solve the seeming paradox that countries such as Japan, Hungary, and in Scandinavia which boast draconian gun control laws and low rates of firearm availability have much higher rates of suicide (2 or 3 times higher) than the U.S. In these countries where guns are not readily available, citizens simply substitute for guns other cultural or universally available methods for killing oneself, such as Hara-kiri in Japan, drowning in the Blue Danube as in Hungary, suffocation (with poisonous gases such as carbon monoxide from automobile exhausts), or simply hanging like in Denmark and Germany, or even drinking agricultural pesticides as is commonly done in Sri Lanka. And in these countries, citizens commit suicide quite effectively by these methods at higher rates than in the U.S. I believe the health advocacy establishment must consider the fact that guns and bullets are inanimate objects that do not follow Koch's Postulates of Pathogenicity (which prove definitely and scientifically a micro-organism is responsible for a particular disease), and recognize the fact that behind every shooting there is a person pulling the trigger—and who should be held accountable. The problem is more complex than just easy availability of firearms and guns and bullets as animated, virulent pathogens, needing to be stamped out by limiting gun availability, and ultimately, eradicating guns from law-abiding citizens.

And, within the context of gun availability, much has been said about the "crimes of passion" that supposedly take place impulsively, in the heat of the night or the furor of a domestic squabble. Criminologists have

> *"Why [is there] faulty research and concealment of . . . valuable, potentially life-saving information by the medical establishment?"*

pointed out that homicides in this setting are the culmination of a long simmering cycle of violence. In one study of the police records in Detroit and Kansas City it was revealed, for example, that in "90 percent of domestic homicides, the police had responded at least once before during the prior two years to a disturbance," and in over 50 percent of the cases, the police had been called five or more times to that dysfunctional domicile. Surely, these are not crimes of passion consummated impulsively in the heat of the night by ordinary citizens, but the result of violence in highly dysfunctional families in the setting of repeated alcohol or illicit drug use; it is also the setting of abusive husbands who after a long history of spousal abuse finally commit murder, and increasingly, wives defending themselves against those abusive husbands, representing acts of genuine self-defense.

Another favorite view of the gun control, public health establishment is the myth propounded by Dr. Mark Rosenberg, former head of the NCIPC [National Center for Injury Prevention and Control] of the CDC who has written: "Most of the perpetrators of violence are not criminals by trade or profession. Indeed, in the area of domestic violence, most of the perpetrators are never accused of any crime. The victims and perpetrators are ourselves—ordinary citizens, students, professionals, and even public health workers."

That statement is contradicted by available data, government data.

Faulty Research

The fact is that the typical murderer has had a prior criminal history of at least six years with four felony arrests in his record before he finally commits murder. The FBI statistics reveal that 75 percent of all violent crimes for any locality are committed by 6 percent of hardened criminals and repeat offenders. Less than 0.2 percent of crimes committed with firearms are carried out by licensed (e.g., concealed carry permit holders) law-abiding citizens. Violent crimes continue to be a problem in the inner cities with gangs involved in the drug trade. Crimes in rural areas for both blacks and whites, despite the preponderance of guns in this setting, remain low. Gun availability does not cause crime. Prohibitionist government policies and gun control (rather than crime control) exacerbates the problem by making it more difficult for law-abiding citizens to defend themselves, their families, and their property. In fact, there was a modest increase in both homicide and suicide after prohibition and passage of the Gun Control Act of 1968.

As to how one can protect oneself from assailants when the police, as more often than not, are not around, National Victims Data suggests that "while victims resisting with knives, clubs, or bare hands are about twice as likely to be injured as those who submit, victims who resist with a gun are only half as likely to be injured as those who put up no defense." Of particular interest to women and self-defense, "among those victims using handguns in self-defense, 66 percent of them were successful in warding off the attack and keeping their property. Among those victims using non-gun weapons, only 40 percent were successful. The gun is the great equalizer for women when they are accosted in the street or when they, particularly single mothers, are defending themselves and their children at home.

But let us return to public health and gun research. Why this faulty research and concealment of this valuable, potentially life-saving information by the medical establishment? In a comprehensive and widely discussed Tennessee Law Review article, constitutional scholar and criminologist Don B. Kates and associates declare: "Based on studies, and propelled by leadership from the Centers for Disease Control and Prevention, the objective [of public health] has broadened so that it now includes banning and confiscation of all handguns, restrictive licensing of owners of other firearms and eventual elimination of all firearms from American life, excepting (perhaps) only a small elite of extremely wealthy collectors, hunters or target shooters. This is the case in many European countries."

In the chapter "Bad Medicine—Doctors and Guns," Kates and associates describe a particularly egregious example of editorial bias and censorship by the *New England Journal of Medicine*. In 1989, two studies were

> *"The subject of guns and violence is reported by the media with bias and sensationalism."*

independently submitted for publication to *NEJM*. Both authors were affiliated with the University of Washington School of Public Health. One study by Dr. John H. Sloan was a selective two-city comparison of homicide rates in Vancouver, British Columbia, and Seattle, Washington. The other paper was a comprehensive comparison study between the U.S. and Canada by Dr. Brandon Centerwall. Predictably, the editors of the *NEJM* chose to publish Sloan et al.'s article with inferior but orthodox data claiming erroneously that severe gun control policies had reduced Canadian homicides and rejected Centerwall's superior study showing that such policies had not affected the rate of homicides in Canada.

In fact, the homicide rates were lower in Vancouver before the restrictive gun control laws had been passed in Canada and in fact, rose after the laws were passed. The Vancouver homicide rate increased 25 percent after the institution of the 1977 Canadian law. Sloan and associates glossed over the disparet ethnic compositions of Seattle and Vancouver. When the rates of homicides for whites are compared in both of the cities it turns out that the rate of homicide in Seattle is actually lower than in Vancouver, while the fact that blacks and hispanics have higher rates of homicides in Seattle was not mentioned by these investigators. Dr. Centerwall's paper on the comparitive rates of homicides in the U.S. and Canada was finally published in the *American Journal of Epidemiology*, but his valuable research was not really made widely available to the public. In contradistinction to his valuable gun research data, Centerwall's other research pointing to the effects of TV violence affecting homicide rates have been made widely available, but his data exculpating gun availability and homicide rates has not.

More Examples of Bad Research

Another example of faulty research was displayed by the AMA's [American Medical Association] Council of Scientific Affairs when it endorsed, on the basis of "scientific research," the ban on assault weapons. Obviously, the Council had a public relations axe to grind rather than expert knowledge of the sciences of criminology and ballistics. Instead of doing its own scholarly work or at least relying on the expert work of Dr. Martin Fackler, the foremost wound ballistic expert in the United States, it unfortunately relied, for political purposes, on unscientific data and even sensationalized newspaper articles, one of which claimed that watermelons fired upon and blasted with "assault weapons" are appropriate human tissue simulants to demonstrate wound ballistics!

It has been pointed out, correctly, I may add, that if that were the case, an 18" drop of a watermelon would also be appropriate for the study of head injuries.

As a physician and medical historian, I have always been a staunch supporter of public health in its traditional role of fighting pestilential diseases and promoting health by educating the public as to hygiene, sanitation, and preventable diseases, as alluded to in my books, *Vandals at the Gates of Medicine* and *Medical Warrior: Fighting Corporate Socialized Medicine;* but I deeply resent the workings of those in public health with the proclivity toward the promulgation of preordained research such as the gun and violence research conducted by many investigators with a gun control agenda and disseminated in the medical journals over the past two decades. Much of this information, unfortunately, is tainted, result-oriented and based on what can only be characterized as poor science.

Mass Shootings and Media Bias

In his celebrated book, *The Samurai, the Mountie, and the Cowboy*, David Kopel makes the point that such disparate countries as Japan and Switzerland have low crime rates regardless of gun control laws, because of close ties engendered in the traditional family in which parents spend time with their children, children who are then imbued with a sense of civility as well as civic duty. And yes, in my opinion, law-abiding citizens should be allowed to own guns and be candidates for "shall issue" concealed carry permits.

Felons (and mentally unstable people) forfeit this right by virtue of the fact they are a threat (or a potential threat) to their fellow citizens. And anyway, not everyone would want to carry a firearm, for regardless of what you have been led to believe, criminologists have pointed out that criminals do make quick risk versus benefit assessments. Empirical evidence and criminologic studies consistently reveal that just the knowledge that one in 5 or 6 citizens in a public place could very well be armed can deter crimes and could very well avert massacres, as has been the case in Israel (repeatedly), Switzerland, and the U.S. In Switzerland, for example, where guns are notoriously liberalized, there was not a single report of armed robbery in Geneva in 1993!

Another problem with public health and gun control is the way the subject of guns and violence is reported by the media with bias and sensationalism. Let us, for example, take a look at how the media reports mass shootings in America. Three illustrative cases will help us draw inferences as to the nature of these incidents and their reporting by the media.

In Pearl [Mississippi,] in 1997, 16-year-old Luke Woodham used a hunting rifle to kill his ex-girlfriend and her close friend and wound seven other students. It was Assistant Principal Joel Myrick who retrieved his handgun from his automobile and halted Woodham's shooting spree. Myrick held the young delinquent at bay until the police arrived. Later it was discovered that Woodham had also used a knife to stab his mother to death earlier that morning. While the shooting was widely reported, the fact that Mr. Myrick, an armed citizen, prevented a larger massacre with his gun was ignored by the media.

In Edinboro [Pennsylvania,] in 1998, a deadly scenario took place when 14-year-old Andrew Wurst killed one teacher and wounded another as well as two other classmates. The shooting rampage here was halted by merchant James Strand who used his shotgun to force the young criminal to halt his firing, drop his gun, and surrender to police.

But yet, in another unreported incident in Santa Clara, California, Richard Gable Stevens, rented a rifle for target practice at the National Shooting Club on July 5, 1999 and then began a shooting rampage, herding three store employees into a nearby alley, and stating he intended to kill them. When Stevens became momentarily distracted, a shooting club employee, who had a .45-caliber handgun concealed under his shirt, drew his weapon and fired. Stevens was hit in the chest and critically wounded. He was then held at bay until the police arrived.

A massacre in the making was prevented. The unknown employee was an unsung hero ignored by the major media. Why are these and other similar incidents, where the tables are turned and citizens use guns to protect themselves and others, not reported by the mainstream media?

By and large, to read about acts of citizens using guns for self or family protection, one has to read Robert A. Waters' excellent book, *The Best Defense*, for rarely do these acts get publicized in the mass media, nor do these cases get compiled, studied and published in the medical journals, as public health investigators do with their "gun and violence" research.

Moreover, rarely, if ever, are constitutional or historical issues covering the Second Amendment aired in the most widely utilized medium—television. Mass murders and street violence on the other hand, get the lion's share of coverage—particularly, when committed with firearms. And as anyone who takes even a cursory look and flips the pages of medical journals knows, these criminal shootings are studied and reported extensively in the medical journals, such as the *NEJM*, *JAMA*, *Western Journal of Medicine*, and even the state medical journals.

> *"In the last decade, constitutional scholars 'from across the political spectrum' have concluded that the Second Amendment protects an individual right."*

Let me tell you about one more atrocious incident where innocent victims were killed or injured, and yet, this episode was not given the attention others are given simply because it was not committed with firearms. In May 1999, a deranged individual wreaked deadly havoc at a Costa Mesa, California, daycare center playground, killing two toddlers and injuring 5 people. Steven Abrams, the 39-year-old assailant told police, "I was going to execute these children because they were innocent." After this barbaric act, Abrams calmly and unhurt sat and waited for police.

Needless to say, there was a big difference in how this incident was reported as compared to the saturation coverage of the Pearl, Miss.; Edinboro, Pa.; or the Littleton, Colo., shooting,[1] which had occurred only a few days earlier. The difference: In this 1999 incident, the assailant used an automobile, a Cadillac to be exact, not a firearm.

Guns and the Constitution

The Bill of Rights was added to the Constitution to limit the power of leviathan government, and individual rights were enumerated in this document, so that they would provide extra protection from the monopolistic tendency of government to wrest power away from and usurp the liberties of the individual citizen. [Political philosopher] John Locke (1632–1704), admired by our Founding Fathers, once wrote, "I have no reason to suppose, that he, who would take away my Liberty would not when he had me in his Power, take away everything else."

And for his part, Thomas Jefferson added, "the natural progress of things is for liberty to yield and for government to gain ground." The solution to this dilemma—namely, government as a necessary evil, according to Joseph Story (1779–1845), foremost American jurist and intellectual alter ego of Chief Justice John Marshall—was found in the Second Amendment. Supreme Court Justice Story thus wrote (1833): "The right of the citizens to keep and bear arms has justly been considered the palladium of the liberties of a republic; since it offers a strong moral check against usurpation and arbitrary power of rulers; and will generally, even if these are successful in the first instance, enable the people to resist and triumph over them."

These are strong words but better said by our forefathers in explaining the reason for the Second Amendment than to be left unsaid to a posterity that may have forgotten why the right was written into the Constitution.

In more recent times, Dr. Edgar Suter, Chairman of Doctors for Integrity in Policy Research, and 37 other Second Amendment supporters including legal scholars, correctly pointed out in the June 1995 issue of the *Journal of the Medical Association of Georgia* that Supreme Court decisions have been thoroughly reviewed in the legal literature. Since 1980, of 39 law review articles, 35 note the Supreme Court's acknowledgment of the individual right to keep and bear arms and only four claim the right is only a collective right of the states (three of these four were authored or co-authored by employees of the gun control lobby).

---

1. This was a shooting at a high school that left thirteen people dead, after which the two assailants committed suicide.

And so in the last decade, constitutional scholars "from across the political spectrum" have concluded that the Second Amendment protects an individual right, a view that is referred to as the "Standard Model" by University of Tennessee Professor Glenn Harlan Reynolds. The nation's leading legal and constitutional scholars—including Laurence Tribe of Harvard, Akil Reed Amar of Yale, William Van Alstyne of Duke University, Sanford Levinson of University of Texas Law School, Don B. Kates of the Pacific Institute for Public Policy Research, attorney David Kopel of the Independence Institute, and noted Fairfax, Virginia, attorneys Jeffrey Snyder and Stephen P. Halbrook—all subscribe to this "Standard Model" or individual right view.

Though the gun control debate has focused on the Second Amendment, legal scholarship also finds support for the Right to Keep and Bear Arms in Ninth Amendment "unenumerated" rights, Fourteenth Amendment "due process" and "equal protection" rights, and natural rights theory. Also, in the absence of explicit delegated powers, the Tenth Amendment guarantees that the powers are reserved to the States and the people.

This latter fact was spelled out in two major Supreme Court cases. In *U.S. v. Lopez* (1995), in striking down the Gun Free Schools Zones Act, U.S. Chief Justice William Rehnquist wrote that the law was unconstitutional because it would otherwise convert the Commerce Clause of the Constitution to a general police power it does not possess. And in *Printz et al. v. U.S.* (1997), the Court went a step further and, to the chagrin of the gun control lobby, struck down a major section of the federal Brady Law. Associate Justice Antonin Scalia quoted a passage from James Madison (*The Federalist No. 51*): "Just as the separation and independence of the coordinate branches of the federal Government serve to prevent the accumulation of excessive power in any one branch, a healthy balance of power between the States and the Federal Government will reduce the risk of tyranny and abuse from either front." Attorney Elizabeth Swasey, Director of NRA/ILA Crime Strike, noted this was the same passage Chief Justice Rehnquist cited in the *Lopez* case.

It was also in 1999 that we had the momentous court ruling of the Northern District of Texas, *U.S. v. Emerson*, in which U.S. District Court Judge Sam Cummings overturned a federal gun law on Second Amendment grounds stating, "The right of the Second Amendment should be as zealously guarded as the other individual liberties enshrined in the Bill of Rights."

Children and Guns

Recall professor John Lott's finding that children 14 to 15 years of age are 14.5 times more likely to die from automobile injuries, 5 times more likely to die from drowning or fire and burns, and 3 times more likely to die from bicycle accidents than they are to die from gun accidents. A child's death from any cause is a tragedy. In 1991, for example, a typical year, 145 children between the ages of 1 and 14 years died of accidental gunshot wounds, 310 children died from suffocation (choking), 1,075 children died from burns, 1,104 died of drowning, and 3,271 died in motor vehicle accidents. These are all tragedies, but do we want to ban food, matches, swimming pools, and automobiles?

The fact is that the firearm accident rates in the United States (including those for children) have been declining steadily since the turn of the [twenty-first] century, particularly after 1975, because of the emphasis that has been placed on gun safety education courses, including the NRA's [National Rifle Association] Eddie Eagle program, which has now touched providentially in excess of 9 million youngsters in the U.S. As far as teen-age violence is concerned, more than 20,000 laws are already on the books, including a sizable number pertaining to the proscription of handgun possession by minors and banning guns on school grounds. These laws need to be enforced. Despite all the media hype regarding guns and violence, the naked truth is that this year's latest available FBI statistics show that, like the not-so-well known drop in gun accident rates, there has also been a steady decline in homicide rates for every segment of American society. In fact, murder and violent crimes have reached 30 and 25-year low rates, respectively. And, mass shootings, despite what you have been led to believe and contrary, sensationalized reporting, notwithstanding, are not more frequent today, only more publicized. For example, Northeastern University criminal justice professor James Fox reports that the highest casualty rate for mass murders in the past three decades occurred in 1977! In that year, 38 criminals killed 141 victims. Compare this to 1994, which had the lowest number of mass murders—31 criminals murdered 74 people.

> *"The fact is that the firearm accident rates in the United States (including those for children) have been declining steadily since the turn of the [twenty-first] century."*

Again, despite perception, violence in school is down. Of the more than 2,000 unfortunate children who die in acts of violence each year, only 34 died in school-related violence during the 1997–1998 school year, according to the Department of Education's *Annual Report on School Safety*. The difference between perception and reality is more reporting, saturation coverage, more gun control hype and sensationalism, which may, in fact, result in more copy cat killings by deranged predators craving media attention. Sensationalized violence and the debate regarding the Gun Free Schools Act of 1994, may have been, in fact, behind the school shootings of 1997–1999, which culminated with the Littleton, Colo., Columbine High School shooting of April 20, 1999.

Israeli anti-terrorist expert and editor of the European magazine *Visier*, David [Thomas] Schiller, commenting on the U.S. school shootings, wrote: "Schools/kindergartens make for very attractive targets for the deranged gunman as well as for the profit-oriented hostage gangsters or terrorist groups. If you crave media attention, as for instance the PLO did [in Israel] in the '70s, nothing will catch the headlines better than an attack on a school full of kids."

Mr. Schiller concludes: "We in the terrorism research field have argued for decades that it was exactly the media coverage that spurred more and each time more violent and extreme terrorist incidents. Could we stop the media from advertising the terrorist message? Certainly not." Given what we know now about the psychology of these shootings and Hollywood's excesses with movie violence, perhaps, the question should be rephrased: Is it time to regulate Hollywood and the media? Obviously, the answer now requires more excogitation.

A Permissive Culture

Moral declivity. And yes, the death of any child by any cause is a tragedy. Yet, we must be honest and lay the blame where it belongs: A culture that for three decades has been mired in permissiveness: increasingly devoid of intellectual guidance for our youth and lacking a moral compass for our children. Consider some of its characteristics:

Moral relativism. Schools no longer teach traditional morality, the discernment between right and wrong and moral absolutes, leading to situational ethics and a value free society. Building the self-esteem of children is placed ahead of personal morality and doing what is right.

Lack of discipline. Consider the fact parents and teachers in today's environment are afraid of reprimanding the young for fear of being charged with child abuse and prosecuted. Often, parents are not at home (both working, one of them to pay taxes to Uncle Sam) so children, lacking parental guidance and discipline, do as they please.

Lack of accountability. There is a persistent crisis of conscience in our society. There is a trend to absolve the individual of personal responsibility and a penchant for blaming inanimate objects such as guns for the level of violence in our society. This lack of personal responsibility and accountability trickles down to young impressionable minds, which then fail to take responsibility for their actions as they grow up.

More gun control (i.e., law-abiding citizen disarmament, whereas criminals, who by definition do not obey the laws, keep their guns) rather than crime control. Data from the *FBI Uniform Crime Report* show that states with permissive gun laws have lower homicide rates than states with restrictive gun control laws. Draconian gun control surely is not the answer. As stated previously, there are already 20,000 gun laws on the books including illegal possession of firearms by minors. These laws should be applied and enforced. And when inner city teenagers or juvenile delinquents from suburbia act as criminals, they should be tried as adults.

Parents Are Important

In a study that was not given the attention it deserved, the U.S. Department of Justices Office of Juvenile Justice and Delinquency Prevention tracked 4,000 juveniles aged 6–15 in Denver, Pittsburgh and Rochester, N.Y., from 1993–1995, and contrary to what was expected by conventional wisdom, the investigators reached these unexpected conclusions: Children who get firearms from their parents are less likely to commit acts of violence and street crimes (14 percent) than children who have no guns in their homes (24 percent), whereas children who obtain guns illegally do so at the whopping rate of 74 percent.

The study also found that "boys who own legal firearms have much lower rates of delinquency and drug use (than boys who own illegal guns) and are even slightly less delinquent than non-owners of guns."

This study also provides more evidence that in close nuclear families, where children learn from their parents, youngsters can be taught to use guns responsibly. These youngsters, in fact, become more responsible in their conduct and more civil in their behavior.

Children should be taught moral absolutes and universal truths so that, as they journey through life, they will exercise their free will to distinguish right from wrong and choose the former, as to fulfill their destinies in a spirit of goodness.

Do Not Subordinate Science and Medicine

We can be compassionate and still be honest, but we must have the moral courage to pursue the truth and find viable solutions through the use of sound, scholarly research. We have an obligation to reach our conclusions based on objective data and scientific information rather than on ideology, emotionalism, political expediency, or budgetary consideration.

Public health should not be subverted and medical science should not be perverted. The lessons of history sagaciously reveal that whenever and wherever science and medicine have been subordinated to the state and individual will has been crushed by tyranny, the results have been as perverse as they have been disastrous, as the examples of Nazi Germany and the former Soviet Union so aptly testify in the 20th Century. We must preserve the free flow and exchange of information that is essential for academic freedom and the preservation of a free society. The individual should never, ever, be subordinated to the collective.

The Media Exaggerate the Problem of Youth Gun Violence

by Mike Males

About the author: *Mike Males is a sociologist and the author of several books on adolescents.*

Monitoring the Future, an annual survey of 12,500 high school seniors by the University of Michigan's Institute for Social Research, is one of America's most widely quoted surveys on youth behavior. Its release every December provokes a media and official frenzy over student drug use. Curiously, one of the survey's most interesting findings relevant to one of this era's biggest fears is never quoted: its findings regarding school violence trends.

Despite their worshipful citation in press and official forums, self-reporting surveys are weak, highly suspect research tools. However, *Monitoring* is the only long-term consistently-administered survey of school violence available, and its trends follow the crime cycles in larger society. Its finding that both white and black students report less weapons-related victimization in school today than in the 1970s is consistent with other self-reported violence (students also report fewer instances of being deliberately injured by persons without weapons, being threatened with weapons, or being threatened with any kind of violence at school). The stable, generally declining pattern of violence among white students and the higher, cyclical pattern among black students is consistent with FBI crime reports.

School Violence Is Declining

In 2000, 3% of black high school seniors report being injured by someone with a weapon at school, on the way to or from school, or at a school event sometime in the year—down from 4% in 1999 and the lowest percentage in the survey's 24-year history. If that makes schools seem pretty dangerous, reflect on these even more unsettling perspectives: school safety and crime reports show only one-sixth of 1% of the nation's murders occur in schools, and hospital emergency department records analyzed by the U.S. Bureau of Justice Statistics found homes, workplaces, and streets account for eight, five, and 2.5 times more violence-related injuries, respectively, than do schools.

School and police agencies report the rate of injury with weapons in senior high schools is 46 per 100,000 students, and while they don't learn about most assaults, serious injuries would not escape notice. American schools are the site of a good deal of violence, but apparently not as much as other institutions, led by the family. Thus, statements that students are safer from murder and serious injury at school than at home, in the streets, or at work are factual but not necessarily comforting. The only comforting aspect is that most school violence is apparently low-level.

The *Monitoring* findings also directly contradict anecdotal quotes in the press from school personnel, experts, and teen-book authors that today's students are far more violent than those of past generations. These anecdotal quotes also appear at odds with what most teachers report. A 1997 *Los Angeles Times* survey of 545 students, 1,100 teachers, and 2,600 parents and other adults that found that 91% of students and 92% of teachers in Los Angeles (supposedly America's arch-drug/gang/gunplay capital) rated their schools as "safe." Only 14% of students had ever been in a fight at school, and only 1% had been in a fight involving a weapon.

However, adults not involved with public schools as teachers or parents—that is, ones whose impressions derive from media images and quotable authorities—were six to 10 times more likely to rate schools as imperiled by gangs, violence, and drugs than were the teachers and students inhabiting those schools. *Times* editors (the same ones who editorially lament lack of public support for school funding) apparently thought the public was insufficiently terrified of public schools. . . .

That there is some violence in public schools—led by the school shootings of 1997–2001 that received gargantuan media attention—properly draws concern, outrage, even (in cases such as the Columbine High School slaughter) horror. But there is no excuse for Americans being surprised that schools are not violence-free. The lack of perspective was pointed out by Justice Policy Institute president Vincent Schiraldi in a November 22, 1999, commentary in the *Los Angeles Times:*

> Nowadays, it is impossible to talk about juvenile crime and not discuss school shootings. Yet school shootings are extremely rare and not on the increase. In a population of about 50 million schoolchildren, there were approximately 55 school-associated violent deaths in the 1992–93 school year and fewer than half that in the 1998–99 school year. By comparison, in 1997, 88 people were killed by lightening—what might be considered the gold standard for idiosyncratic events. Children who are killed in the United States are almost never

55

killed inside a school. Yes, 12 kids were killed at Columbine. But by comparison, every two days in the U.S., 11 children die at the hands of their parents or
guardians.

Prejudice Toward Youth

The term "youth violence," a media and official staple, is inherently prejudicial. To understand this, consider how we treat other demographic groups. Example: About one million Orthodox Jews live in the United States. Crime statistics aren't kept by creed, but assume a half-dozen commit murder every year.

This would give Orthodox Jews one of the lowest homicide rates of any
group—probably the case. That means that every two months, on average, an Orthodox Jew is arrested for murder. Let's further assume that powerful political
demagogues want to depict Jews as the font of violence, and the major media and
institutions, as always, go along. Every couple of months, then, the press erupts,
headlining "another Jew violence" tragedy, with sensational pictures and overwrought speculation as to "why Jews are so violent." The press and politicians
resolutely ignore thousands of intervening murders by non-Jews, including murders of Jews by Gentiles, while connecting every Jewish homicide, no matter how
occasional, into a "spate of Jew killings." Conservatives angrily demand tougher
policing of Jews. Liberals blame violent Jewish cultural messages. Politicians and
private institutions form a National Campaign to Prevent Jew Violence.

We need not add the seig-heils to realize that equating Jews and violence isn't
an expression of science or genuine concern, but rank anti-Semitism. Linking
an entire population class with a negative behavior practiced by only a few of
its members is bigotry, regardless of
which group is singled out. The
politician-media-institution campaign
on "youth violence" is bigoted and devoid of genuine concern for youths.
Real concern would involve lamenting
the major causes of violence against youths, yet politicians and institutions de-
ploring "school violence" and pushing the National Campaign to Prevent Youth
Violence concern themselves only with the tiny fraction of murdered children and
youth that is politically advantageous to highlight while downplaying larger dangers to the young.

> *"School shootings are
> extremely rare and not
> on the increase."*

The target of aging America's rage is all youths, not just the 13 kids who
committed the recently publicized shootings taking 31 lives in 12 schools in
four years (in Pearl, Mississippi; West Paducah, Kentucky; Jonesboro,
Arkansas; Edinboro, Pennsylvania; Springfield, Oregon; Littleton, Colorado;
Conyers, Georgia; Fort Gibson, Oklahoma; Mount Morris, Michigan; West
Palm Beach, Florida; Santee, California). These aren't all the school shooters;
only the young ones with white victims we choose to care about. Compare: 25
million teenagers, 18 million of them white, attend 20,000 American secondary

schools every day. Another 25 million pre-teens attend elementary schools.

"Columbine" (it seems a grievous injustice on top of tragedy to equate a school's name with mass murder) revealed the individual pathologies of two high school boys; "post-Columbine" revealed the mass pathology of America's institutions. In [2002], I still can't pick up a copy of *Youth Today* without seeing program ads blaring, "The Lessons of Columbine," crack a newspaper without seeing some Ph.D. declaiming "the new face of youth violence," glance at a magazine rack or turn a TV knob without confronting, "the secret life of suburban teens." The only blessing is that *Rolling Stone* fear-monger Randall Sullivan hasn't (yet) unburdened another of his fact-free histrionics anointing [Columbine shooters] Eric Harris and Dylan Klebold the new Everyteens.

Media Manipulation

The lesson of reporting on Columbine is pretty simple: America sports an ugly new face of adult hostility, and it doesn't care about kids. It's the "quality," not the quantity, of school violence victims that sets off panic, with the paradoxical result that school murders actually are underreported. The late-1990s tactic by the media and officials to focus on demonizing suburban and small-town youth as the fright-provoking face of American savagery means that murders of poorer students and murders by adults in schools are systematically ignored. In a bizarre twist that reveals reams about official America's true concern for young people, whether kids are more likely to get hurt or killed in schools today than in the past, or more in danger in schools than elsewhere in society, is of little importance. The alarmism surrounds the supposedly new development that victims now are white—and thus politically useful.

The National School Safety Center's excellent tabulation of "School Associated Violent Deaths" (http://www.nssc1.org), covering the period from August 1992 through May 2003 (the latest as of this writing),[1] reveals how the press and politicians have relentlessly manipulated school violence. In truth, there were 39 additional school murders during 1999–2001 which received practically no publicity, resulting from 35 incidents involving 37 killers in cities from Hoboken, New Jersey, to Pomona, California. What made these 35 school murders worthy of silence? They fell into two categories. Thirty involved student victims who were black, Hispanic, Asian, or of unknown race (the eight whose races were not reported attended mostly-minority schools), killed by other students or by adults. Nine involved white victims: six were adults murdered by adults, two were students murdered by adults, and one student died from a previously undiscovered aneurysm after a fistfight. And if the NSSC's tabulation included preschools, the deliberate mowdown of two toddlers by an enraged middle-aged driver in Costa Mesa, California, would add to the school murder toll the media ignored.

---

1. Males made some revisions to this viewpoint in 2004.

In the super-charged 1999 school year when the media feverishly awaited any new school shooting, three were shrugged off. An Elgin, Illinois, 14-year-old was shot to death in his classroom in February. Not news: he was Latino and in special ed. On June 8, two girls were gunned down in front of their high school in Lynwood, California, south of Los Angeles. Not news (even to the *Los Angeles Times*, which ran a modest 440-word story on an inside page); they were Latinas. On November 19, a 13-year-old boy shot a 13-year-old girl to death in a Deming, New Mexico, middle school. Also Latinos, not the news editors' kind and therefore not news.

Similarly, the Santana High School shooting in Santee, California, on March 5, 2001, involving a white 15 year-old shooting to death two other white students alleged to have bullied him, received massive press attention. Reporters absurdly depicted Santee, site of considerable racial and domestic violence, as a pristine suburb menaced only by drug-taking teens. The school superintendent suspended friends of the student shooter, who were also badgered by the press for not reporting their vague suspicions; popular students suspected of bullying unpopular kids were not similarly taken to task. In addition, gun murders of two black and one Latino student in the two months surrounding Santee's killings were ignored. And, in a major irony that escaped much attention, a law enforcement officer training to respond to school shootings at a Texas high school accidentally shot a fellow officer to death on June 7, indicating that gunners who create danger at school are not all students.

> *"If even one in 100,000 high schoolers harbored [a] murderous mentality, we'd have several Columbines and Jonesboros every week."*

In fact, several of the unheralded school murders (the multiple killings of white adults in Hoboken and Fort Lauderdale, Fla., in lover-triangle shootings, or of Latino students in Pomona and in Lynwood) had death tolls equaling or exceeding nationally headlined killings (Pearl and Springfield involved two killings, Edinboro and West Palm Beach one, Conyers and Fort Gibson none). Why, then, did the media, politicians, and quotable experts deem white-suburban-student murders an apocalypse and white-adult, minority-student, and inner-city killings of no importance?

To ask the question is to answer it: in the crass logic of reporters and editors, things like that are "supposed to happen" to darker skinned youth. The press's new mission was to demonstrate that school shootings proved white, suburban youth were out of control. If reporters had to ignore school killings that didn't confirm their narrow agenda, ignore them they did. . . .

No Lesson to Be Learned

The problem with deriving any "lessons" from Littleton is that the rare psychopath, by definition, does things for reasons the mass of non-psychopaths never consider. Nevertheless, books, documentaries, and "youth violence" treatises for years to come will feature highly credentialed authors selectively choosing whatever over-generalized "explanation" for the "why why why" suits their preconceived ideologies. I suggest we should pay more attention to Harris's quiet video aside: "I can make you believe anything." For this is all we really know about Klebold and Harris: along with Kip (Springfield) Kinkel, Michael (West Paducah) Carneal, and the handful of other school shooters, their kind is vanishingly rare among teenagers. Here is the irrefutable fact the school gunners proved: any youth can obtain hefty firepower within scant hours or days of wanting it, so if even one in 100,000 high schoolers harbored their murderous mentality, we'd have several Columbines and Jonesboros every week, not two or three a year. The most accurate conclusion is also the least satisfying to those bent on divining larger cultural "messages" from Columbine: Klebold and Harris represented Klebold and Harris, not a generation, not even alienated boys.

Now, what is preventing *Rolling Stone's* Randall Sullivan and other "experts" from pronouncing such an inescapable conclusion based on the evidence—the job of an expert, after all? In all the mass media freakout, I saw only one bit of sanity: CDC violence prevention epidemiologist Jim Mercy, who told *New York Times* reporter Sheryl Stolberg that school shootings are "the statistical equivalent of a needle in a haystack. The reality is that schools are very safe environments for kids."

Middle-Aged Predators

Wait a minute, some might argue, when adults kill en masse, they get lots of bad press, too. Oklahoma City bomber Timothy McVeigh was deplored by the president and media for months. Daytrader Mark Barton, who gunned down 13 and wounded 25 at an Atlanta brokerage firm in August 1999, got on the covers of national magazines.

Are youthful killers being treated unfairly, then? No—youthful killers are not being mistreated, except in the sense that their evil deeds are more likely to be featured in the press and deplored by luminaries than similar murders by adults. (Dylan Klebold, Eric Harris, and Kip Kinkel remain far bigger names than Mark Barton, Buford Furrow, and Larry Gene Ashbrook, middle-agers who committed similar, more recent public massacres.) The unfairness involves the fact that middle-aged killers are treated by the press and experts as crazed individuals committing isolated acts while youthful killers are treated as part of a connected pattern demonstrating today's younger generation is uniquely barbaric. Consider recent murders in Ventura County, California, among the nation's richest suburban havens. Its three cities of over 100,000 people are regularly cited as among the safest in the United States from violent crime. Yet in . . . 36 months, three affluent, suburban Ventura grownups in their 40s blew away 10 people in multiple-victim rage shootings—six children and four adults.

That's more than the combined toll of headlined shootings by high schoolers in Pearl, Mississippi; West Paducah, Kentucky; and Jonesboro, Arkansas—all in just one county.

Horror? The Ventura grownup shootings had that: 44-year-old man guns down screaming wife and three children on pastoral lane, 43-year-old man rakes two neighbors with bullets as one's three-year-old shrieks in terror; 42-year-old mom blasts three boys in their beds in ritzy rural enclave. All the usual big story ingredients were there: well-off perpetrators coldly mowing down innocent children in communities where "murder just doesn't happen," carnages so bloody law enforcement veterans required counseling, etc. Yet none made national headlines. No CNN continuous coverage, no Ph.D.s shaking heads at society's degeneration, no tearful presidential condolences. The only ingredient missing: the murderers were not youths.

The "post-Columbine" events proved the school shootings were not a youth, but a "dissed suburban male" phenomenon. The crucial point being missed is that Klebold, Harris, Kinkel, and other middle-class student gunmen had practically nothing in common with other kids (their isolation, in fact, was a big part of their rage), but they had a lot in common with adult middle-class mass killers. . . .

Not Representative of All Youth

"They're not drunk or high on drugs. They're not racists or Satanists or addicted to violent video games, movies, or music," began an April 9–10, 2000, *New York Times* series on school shooters and other "rampage killers," entitled, "They threaten, seethe, and unhinge, then kill in quantity." Reporters led by Ford Fessenden catalogued hundreds of rampage killings in the U.S. since 1950. They profiled 102 teenage and adult rampage murderers whose 100 multiple, public killings left 425 dead and 510 injured. As is nearly always the case when an issue is studied rather than butchered by experts' and pundits' anecdotal pontifications, the *Times* analysis uncovered major challenges to popular myths. Politicians' and programs' favorite culprits turned out to be trivial. Very few of the rampagers patronized violent media; practically none harbored occult or satanic interests. "Cultural *influences* seemed small," the *Times* concluded. However, there was "an extremely high association between violence and mental illness." Half had been formally diagnosed with serious maladies, led by schizophrenia and depression. When it came to ignoring warning signs of catastrophe, psychiatrists, family members, and peers were equally blind. Rampage killers overwhelmingly were male (96 of 102) and white (79). They tended to be older (high proportion in 30s and 40s) than

> *"Youthful killers are treated as part of a connected pattern demonstrating today's younger generation is uniquely barbaric."*

single-victim murderers. A large majority were suburban, small-town, or rural.

Their mass killings were not new—not even school massacres. Two examples in the *Times* sample: in 1974, Olean, New York, honor student Anthony Barbaro, 17, opened fire at his school, killing three and wounding nine. In 1979, Brenda Spencer, 16, gunned two to death and injured nine at a San Diego elementary school. (Those two mass killings by white students in the 1970s merited only inside stories in *Time* and *Newsweek*, which is why experts don't remember them.) But rampage killers of all ages, though rare, appear somewhat more plentiful today—23 per year in the 1970s and 1980s, 34 per year in the 1990s.

As noted, the FBI reports that youths under age 18 accounted for about 6% of the 50,000 murders in the U.S. in the last four years. The famous school shootings comprised one-twentieth of 1% of the murders in the United States, and half of these were at Littleton. By contrast, in a few months, over-30 men slaughtered three times more in multiple-victim shootings than all school students in four years. This raises a blunt question: do the authorities, from President Clinton to institutional and media commentators, view Cyrano Marks as a symbol of general murderousness among black men? Andrew Cunahan as a harbinger of gay male rage? Mark Barton as symbolic of suburban businessman savagery? Cora Caro as the image of the new killer soccer-mom? None I'm aware of has so labeled. In fact, most would consider those who define racial or other groups by their most brutal individuals as bigots of a particularly ugly and hostile mindset—especially if followed with proposals to inflict mass controls on the disfavored groups. It is exactly this kind of prejudicial thinking that grownups lecture teenagers to avoid.

Certainly there is no National Campaign to Prevent Middle-Aged Violence (which is a far more prevalent problem, statistically than "youth violence"). But if adults would not elevate our most murderous few as symbols of the moral disintegration of the groups we occupy, by what right do we hold up Klebold, Harris, or Kinkel as symbols of suburban youth, or of all youth?

The Media Ignore Incidences Where Firearms Are Used to Save Lives

by Bernard Goldberg

About the author: *Bernard Goldberg is an award-winning television journalist.*

A student at the Appalachian School of Law in Grundy, Virginia, who has just been told he will be suspended for failing grades, storms through the campus, clutching a handgun.

As terrorized students run for their lives, they hear him say, "Come get me, come get me." But before anyone can get him, the student, a forty-two-year old immigrant from Nigeria, goes on a shooting spree, killing the dean, a professor, and a fellow student.

He also shoots and wounds three other students—one in the abdomen, one in the throat, and another in the chest.

Finally, as the *Washington Post* reports, "Three students pounced on the gunman and held him until help arrived." Later in the story, the *Post* says, "The students then tackled the gunman."

John Roberts at CBS News reported the story the very same way: "Three people were killed . . . before students tackled the suspect."

At NBC News, Kevin Tibbles said the students "overpowered the gunman and held him until police could arrive."

An Important Fact Ignored

The bloody incident happened on January 16, 2002, and was picked up by news organizations all over the country, almost all of which covered the story the way the *Washington Post* and the networks did. Which means virtually all of them left out one tiny, little fact.

Two of the three students who "pounced on" and "tackled" and "overpowered" the gunman, also had guns.

They had them in their cars, and when they heard the gunshots and learned what was happening, they got their guns and used them to subdue the killer who had just shot up the campus.

One might think this was an important element that should have been reported in the *Washington Post* story, especially since the man who had already killed three people and wounded three others would probably have tried to kill a lot more if he had not been stopped by the other students *who themselves had guns.*

Doing the Research

An honest mistake? You decide. Soon after the law school rampage, criminologist and scholar John Lott ran a LexisNexis search on the story and came up with this: Only 4 of 208 news reports that he found mentioned that the rescuers had guns. James Eaves-Johnson did his own Nexis search for the *Daily Iowan* (at the University of Iowa) and found that just two of eighty-eight stories reported that guns were used to subdue the killer. A third search conducted by Eaves-Johnson, this time using a database called Westnews, which specializes in news about the law, turned up 112 stories on the subject—and

> *"To a lot of [people in the mainstream media], guns are destructive and evil. Period."*

again only two mentioned that the gunman was subdued by students using guns themselves.

None of this sounded like it made any sense. Yes, I'm a critic of how big news organizations slant the news, but even I couldn't believe these numbers. All of them struck me as so incredible that I finally decided to run my own Nexis search. I sampled one hundred news sources, which included the major TV outlets and most every big city daily in the country. And what I found stunned me. Sure enough, only a few papers in the whole country reported that the rescuers had guns. I counted a grand total of six out of a hundred. Six! (Giving credit where it's due, the papers were the *New York Times*, the *Richmond Times-Dispatch*, the *Lexington Herald-Leader*, the *Charlotte Observer*, the *Asheville Citizen-Times*, and the *Roanoke Times and World News*.)

Ah, but it gets worse. Many of those newspapers that failed to report the whole story then seized upon the horror at the Appalachian School of Law to editorialize once again against handguns.

No matter whose count you use, the fact could not be more clear: Only a tiny handful of reporters in the entire country were willing to report an essential part of the story: that it wasn't just the killer who used a gun on campus that day, but the rescuers, too.

Pro-Gun and Antigun

In America, there are pro-gun people and antigun people. The pro-gun people love everything about guns. They love to touch guns and fondle guns and smell guns, and mostly they love to have guns close by. Guns give them peace of mind.

To tell you the truth, I'm not one of those people. I don't like to touch guns or smell them or feel them. I grew up in the Bronx. I played basketball and baseball. Those were my sports. Not hunting. In fact, the only animals I ever got close to were at the Bronx Zoo, and they don't let you hunt any of them. So, unlike kids who grew up with guns in rural America, I never got close to a gun early on—and it carried over to my adult life. But I'll tell you this: It would be just fine with me if everyone on my block now had a gun or two at home, just to discourage criminals from even thinking about preying on the neighborhood. I wouldn't even care if they sat out on their lawns brandishing their guns alongside homemade signs reading, "Attention bad guys: If you're thinking that someone's gonna get hurt around here, you're right—and it's gonna be you!"

But here's an important point: While I'm not exactly comfortable around guns myself, I am not *anti*gun.

The antigun people don't like anything about guns. Guns do not give them peace of mind. Just the opposite. And the vast majority of mainstream media people—certainly those who work in the biggest, most important newsrooms in the country—fall into this antigun category. To a lot of them, guns are destructive and evil. Period. In fact, they think there *are* no credible arguments on the other side, just the irrational rants of all those crazy "gun nuts."

Media Attitudes Toward Guns

A poll in the *Los Angeles Times* once showed that while 50 percent of Americans are for tougher gun controls, 78 percent of journalists favor stricter gun laws. Bob Herbert of the *New York Times* spoke for a bunch of those antigun journalists when he wrote that "Gun violence in America is as common as the sunrise. The truth is, we are addicted to gun violence. We celebrate it, romanticize it, eroticize it."

Okay, maybe for some losers, having a big gun at home is a substitute for having a small something else, but that doesn't give the media elite some kind of 007 license to kill certain inconvenient facts that don't mesh with their particular biases. After all those years on the inside, I am more than a little familiar with how the big-time media operate; I know how biased they can be when it comes to certain issues. Still, even I found the coverage of the shootout at the Appalachian School

> *"There have been many studies that indicate the use of guns to prevent violence may be quite common."*

of Law absolutely astounding. I mean, only a handful of news stories pick up on such an important fact—that the students who stopped the killing spree used their own handguns to do it!

Not long ago I was talking to a pro-gun person, a very bright guy, who said he often asks people a simple question: "When was the last time you watched the national evening news and heard a story about someone using a gun to save a life?" "Most people," he went on, "can't think of a single case."

Actually, I told him, I did just such a story myself, not for the evening news, but for *48 Hours* at CBS. It was about a young woman who lived in rural North Carolina, whose father had just given her a gun for self-protection. Late one night, she went to a deserted post office to pick up her mail from her lock box and was ambushed by a man with a gun, who forced her into her car and demanded that she drive away with him. At this point, fearing she would not be alive when the sun came up, the young woman pulled out her own brand-new gun and stuck it in the gunman's face, which not only took him by surprise but also apparently scared the hell out of him, because he jumped out of the car and fled.

The producer I worked with . . . was practically in a state of depression. "We should never have done the story," he told me some time later in full mea culpa mode.

"Why not?" I asked him, naively not having a clue where he was going.

"Because it gave the impression that this [defensive use of guns] was far more common that it really is."

I remember saying something like, "How do we know how common or uncommon it is?" I knew he had no idea, no facts to marshal, just knee-jerk antigun biases. Living as he does in a well-to-do community in Westchester County outside New York City, where most people have never shot a gun and almost everyone is as liberal on guns as they are on everything else, my pal the liberal producer *knew* because . . . well, because *he just knew.*

The Michael Bellesiles Controversy

In fact, there have been many studies that indicate the use of guns *to prevent violence* may be quite common. In 1995, for example, Dr. Gary Kleck, a criminologist at Florida State University, found that Americans use guns defensively 2.5 million times a year. They almost never actually fire the gun; its presence alone is enough to scare off a criminal. But this isn't the sort of data you're likely to see mentioned in the mainstream press. And its absence stands in marked contrast to the attention generated in 2000 by the publication of *Arming America: The Origins of a National Gun Culture*, a fiercely antigun book by Michael Bellesiles of Emory University. Bellesiles claimed that a review of probate records dating back to the Colonial era proved that gun ownership in early America was far less common than believed—suggesting, therefore, that the Second Amendment was intended to protect not individual rights but only organized militias.

The book was widely hailed in the press for its important ground-breaking research. A front-page review in the *New York Times Book Review*, for instance, gushed that *Arming America* "has dispelled the darkness" in the debate on guns in America. "Furiously researched," is how the *Rocky Mountain News* put it, right there in the heart of gun country, adding that "Bellesiles has performed heroically in plumbing the depths of our history."

"Thinking people who deplore Americans' addiction to gun violence have been waiting a long time for this information," said Stewart Udall, the Democratic former secretary of the interior. "Michael A. Bellesiles," he went on, "has uncovered dramatic historical truths that shatter the 'Ten Commandments' promulgated by the National Rifle Association."

In no time at all the book received the Bancroft Award, the most prestigious prize given for historical research in the United States.

There was only one problem—some of *Arming America's* most provocative claims were completely unsupported.

Conservatives and Second Amendment activists quickly discovered that the probate records Bellesiles cited had been grossly misrepresented—or didn't exist at all. For an inexcusably long time, liberals in thee media and elsewhere resisted these findings, but the evidence against Bellesiles was overwhelming, and in the end he was discredited. In October 2002, after an Emory University panel of independent scholars accused him of "unprofessional and misleading work" that "does move into the realm of falsification," he resigned in disgrace from Emory, calling the university's findings against him "just plain unfair." Two months later, the Bancroft Prize was rescinded.

> *"There are millions of Americans out there who never hear anything but arguments against gun ownership."*

The real question is, why was he so readily believed in the first place? His claim that few early Americans owned guns should have seemed ludicrous on the face of it. There were all those letters and diaries of the era that had so many gun references; there was the art and literature of the time; there was work by other scholars about guns in colonial America. But none of that sounded the alarm. Because, as in all the other issues involving core liberal beliefs, the eagerness to believe overcame all skepticism and reason—with journalists leading the way.

Liberal Groupthink

All of which brings us back to the way the media handled the story about the shootout at the Appalachian School of Law in Grundy, Virginia, and what seems to be the only plausible reason so much of the media left out the salient fact that the students who finally subdued the gunman also had guns. If they had reported that, it would lend support to an argument liberal media elites detest, namely, that having guns around sometimes actually does some good. That maybe, to put it bluntly, in some instances more guns really do mean less crime.

I have always argued that there is no formal media conspiracy—*because there is no need for one.* The real problem, I have said, is liberal groupthink—the idea that if everyone at all the right Manhattan cocktail parties thinks guns should be banned, there's nothing more to be said on the subject. Being against guns becomes the noncontroversial, reasonable, civilized position. End of discussion.

But the Appalachian Law School shootout raised groupthink to a whole new category of duplicity. This *was group lying.* Because there's no way the media's failure to tell the whole story can be written off as an honest mistake.

On February 7, 2003, I spoke to one of the students who used his gun that day to end the violence. Tracy Bridges told me he spoke to about a hundred reporters about what happened at the law school, and told every one of them that he and another student had gone to their cars to get their guns to try to stop the killer.

"It was kind of shocking [to learn that they didn't use the gun angle]. At first I thought maybe they didn't hear the whole story, but then after you read about it time after time it becomes obvious why they left it out."

And why was that? I asked him.

"I believe they didn't want to put out an image that a gun was actually used in defense to help someone out. They definitely did not want to put a story out that a handgun was used for some good. I've collected handguns for a number of years, and the short time I've been on this earth [he's twenty-seven] I've never read a story where they've put a favorable light on someone using a handgun. I only read the negatives. And I just *know* there have to be good stories out there, but I haven't read one."

A Lack of Responsibility

This time the bias was as bad as it looked, and then some. On this one, as much as on any story I've encountered, the media gave their critics all the ammo (pardon the expression) necessary to make the case that Big Journalism was more interested in promoting an agenda than in promoting the truth.

So much for the responsibility to present as many sides of the debate as possible. So much for the responsibility of seeking to fully inform the American people on this vital issue. There are millions of Americans out there who never hear anything but arguments against gun ownership. Do you think the gun debate in America would be different today if even some of these stories got news coverage?

Yet in failing the public, once again reporters also fail themselves. Because there are great stories on this subject just waiting to be told—if only they would tell them. And not only small, riveting stories like the one about the rescuers at the Appalachian School of Law, but larger stories of potentially great significance to society at large.

Chapter 2

Can Government Measures Reduce Gun Violence?

Chapter Preface

Many criminals have been able to buy firearms at gun shows because background checks, which are intended to make sure that potential buyers do not have criminal records, mental illness, or other conditions that bar them from legal purchases, are not always required at these events. Concerned that gun show purchases lead to violent shooting sprees, Congress passed the Lautenberg Amendment in 1999. Named for its writer, New Jersey senator Frank Lautenberg, the law requires licensed dealers or law enforcement personnel to perform background checks at gun shows where at least fifty firearms are offered for sale. However, many organizations and politicians believe the Lautenberg Amendment is not a sufficiently strong law and have proposed adding further checks to gun shows. None of those proposed laws made it to a vote as of spring 2004.

Many gun control advocates contend that strengthening background checks at gun shows is necessary in order to reduce violence. In its paper "The Gun Show Loophole and Crime," the organization Americans for Gun Safety (AGS) states, "Gun shows, particularly where the loophole is open, are a major source of crime guns." According to the organization, more than twenty-five thousand firearms that had been purchased at gun shows were recovered in 1998 and 1999 as a result of Bureau of Alcohol, Tobacco, and Firearm trafficking investigations. In addition to those investigations, AGS details a number of crimes that can be tied to gun show purchases. For example, three men bought 239 guns at Ohio shows and resold them to criminals in Buffalo; one of the guns was later linked to a homicide.

Those opposed to increased background checks maintain that these laws are unnecessary and make gun buying unfairly time-consuming. Gun rights supporter Dave Kopel argues that only 2 percent of guns used in crimes were bought at gun shows. Furthermore, Kopel argues, the purportedly instant background check frequently takes days to complete. He maintains, "If [Americans] learn the facts about gun shows, they will discover that there is no gun show loophole, no gun show crime problem and no reason to adopt federal legislation whose main effect would be to infringe on First and Second Amendment rights."

Supporters of gun control believe that gun show background checks and other types of government-mandated measures will help reduce firearms violence. Gun rights advocates, on the other hand, argue that these measures are part of a wider attempt to eliminate the right of Americans to own guns. The authors in this chapter evaluate the effectiveness of several gun control measures. Finding ways to keep guns out of the hands of criminals may improve the safety of law-abiding Americans.

Gun Control Reduces Violent Crime

by Bill Clinton

About the author: *Bill Clinton was the forty-second president of the United States.*

Editor's Note: The following viewpoint was originally given as remarks at a Democratic National Committee dinner in Baltimore, Maryland, on March 15, 2000.

The most important thing that we're doing right now, of course, is we're embroiled in this fight over gun safety. And I always—I suppose I should be glad because they're kind of unmasked, but it's always kind of sad to me when one of these fights turns real mean and personal. I have a pretty thick hide after all these years, and it's not really very effective when they say things like they've been saying [in March 2000,] the gun lobby. But it obscures the reality.

Sometimes people just don't like you, and you don't know why. Have you ever had that happen to you? One of my favorite stories is this story about this guy that's walking along the edge of the Grand Canyon, and he slips off, and he's careening to his certain demise. And all of a sudden he sees this little twig sticking out of the canyon, and he grabs onto it, and it breaks his fall. And then all of the sudden the roots start coming out of the twig. And he looks up in the sky and he says, "God, why me? I'm a good man. I've taken good care of my family. I've worked hard, and I've paid my taxes all my life. Why me?" And this thunderous voice comes out of the sky and says, "Son, there's just something about you I don't like."

Bill Clinton Versus the NRA

Now, everybody has been in that situation. I know why the NRA [National Rifle Association], however, doesn't like me. They don't like me because I was shooting cans off a fencepost in the country with a .22 when I was 12 years old.

Bill Clinton, remarks at a Democratic National Committee dinner, Baltimore, MD, March 15, 2000.

They don't like me because I governed for 12 years in the state where half the people had a hunting license. And therefore, I know how to talk to people they try to scare up against us, those of us that want to have a safer world.

But the real issue is not the spokesman for the NRA saying that I want more deaths in America or that somehow we're responsible for the death of that wonderful, former basketball coach from Northwestern [Ricky Byrdsong] and all these absurd claims, which they will doubtless use to raise money on. The real issue is, we have the lowest crime rate in 25 years and the lowest gun death rate in 30 years, but no one in their right mind believes America is as safe as it ought to be or could be. And no one believes we should stop

> *"[Because of the Brady bill] 500,000 people have been kept from getting handguns because they were felons, fugitives, and stalkers."*

until we make America the safest big country in the world. Now, that's what I believe.

You know, when people start batting around responsibility for people's lives—one of the jobs that I was not prepared for as president—I never dreamed about, and I confess, I never thought about it—was the responsibility to comfort the grieving when their loved ones had died. I never thought when I was running for president I'd be meeting a plane carrying the body of my friend and brother, Ron Brown, and all those people who died in Croatia, trying to give those people a better life. I never thought I'd have to go down to one room after another at a military base and greet 19 families of 19 airmen that were killed by terrorists because they were serving us in Saudi Arabia. I never thought I'd have to go to a place like Oklahoma City, where nearly 170 people were killed by a man consumed by his hatred for our Government.

I never thought I'd have to have parents like the grieving mother and stepfather of young Kayla Rolland sit in the Oval Office. And what can you tell them, that you've got a little girl and their little girl is gone? So I don't really think we should be talking about this debate in these terms.

Gun Control Saves Lives

When they fought me on the Brady bill, because they said it would be so burdensome to hunters and sports people, and I said it wouldn't, and we won. We had evidence now: 500,000 people have been kept from getting handguns because they were felons, fugitives, and stalkers. Unfortunately, the man [white supremacist Benjamin Smith] who killed Ricky Byrdsong in Chicago, and a young Korean Christian walking out of his church and several other people, was able to get a gun illegally in another way.

Well, one of the ways people get guns, as the NRA said way back in '93, when they were against the Brady bill, they said, "Oh, well, people don't buy these guns at gun stores. They get them at these gun shows and these urban flea markets." So I said, "Well, let's just do a background check there." That's what this is about: child safety locks, money for smart gun technology, banning the importation of large ammunition clips—assault weapons are illegal in this country; then we let people import the ammunition clips that can convert legal weapons into assault weapons—and closing the gun show loophole.

And oh, there's been the awfulest outcry about how terrible this is and how burdensome this will be. And one of the reasons they don't like me is I've actually been to these country gun shows. You're the Governor of Arkansas, you've got to get out there and hustle around and go where the people are. And I've got a lot of friends that have bought hunting rifles at these country gun shows. And it's true, if you're out in the country and somebody has to go someplace else, it's a little bit of an inconvenience if you have to wait a day to get your gun. But every one of these places has a nearby police office or a sheriff's office where those guns could be deposited while a background check is done.

Most people I know of good conscience, that love to go into the deer woods, would do anything to keep another child alive. This is not what this is about. And 95 percent of these people could be checked in a day, and the other 5 percent that I want to wait 3 days to make sure we can check—their denial rate, because of their background problems, is 20 times the denial rate for the 95 percent to clear in a day.

We're going to hold up the whole United States Congress, go 8 months after the Columbine slaughter? I didn't even talk about that, going to Columbine High School, going out to

> *"The death rate from accidental gun shootings is 15 times higher in this country than it is in the next 25 biggest countries combined, for kids."*

Springfield, Oregon, calling those people in Jonesboro, Arkansas, where I knew the people in the school.[1] You know, I'm sorry, but I think it's worth a little inconvenience to save a lot of lives, and I think you do, too.

Efforts in Congress

[Maryland congressman] Ben Cardin was with me today when they won a great legislative victory over a tiny thing, because the NRA was trying to beat a resolution by Representative Zoe Lofgren from California, that simply said: Look, the Senate passed a good gun safety bill [in July 1999] and the House passed one that wasn't so good, but at least they passed a bill—and what Congress does when the Senate and House pass different bills, they get together, just like you do in Maryland, and you have a conference committee, and you work out a compromise, and you send it to the chief executive, and he signs or vetoes it. They haven't met in 8 months. And the reason is, they know that our

---

1. A gun massacre occurred at Columbine High School in which two students killed thirteen people and then committed suicide. School shootings also occurred in Springfield and Jonesboro.

friends in the media back there cannot run a headline story every day for 8 months saying they haven't met. I mean, they can't. They've got a lot of work to do. Tomorrow there will be something else on the news. So they thought this thing will just go away if we just don't meet. But if we meet and we have to say what our position is, we'll get hurt, or something might happen. So they just never met.

So Zoe Lofgren introduced a resolution in the House [on March 15, 2000] that simply said one thing: Meet. You draw a paycheck every 2 weeks, earn it. Meet. Do something on this bill. Even if it's wrong, do something. That's all it said. Well, the NRA acted like we were going to go confiscate guns. And they were up there pressuring people, handing out these awful pamphlets, running all these ads and everything.

So a bunch of them came down to the White House [on March 15, 2000] a bunch of the members of the House, including about three Republicans, including Connie Morella from Maryland, who spoke, and Carolyn McCarthy spoke, whose husband was killed and whose son was nearly killed by the man who was using an automatic weapon on the Long Island subway 7 years ago. She was a lifelong, Irish Catholic Republican. She switched parties, ran for Congress, became one of our members. And I can tell you, we're really proud of her. She got up and talked about how callous it was for people who disagree with us on the issue to act like we don't care whether people die or not.

And the point I made was that—I was trying to get a little levity in the situation because it's so profoundly sad, but I also wanted people to think. I said— but these people at the NRA, what their position is, is that guns are different from every other single safety threat. Every other threat, we do as much prevention as possible. And then if somebody does something wrong and we catch them we punish them. But we try to prevent.

A Serious Issue

I mean, every one of us was raised with that old "ounce of prevention is worth a pound of cure," right? But they say, "No, no, no, no prevention. Just throw the book at them if they do something wrong.". . .

What if somebody said to you, "You know, most people who drive cars are really good people. They're responsible drivers. They're never drunk when they drive. They're just as good as they can be. And I'm just tired of them being burdened with having to get a license and having to observe the speed limit. And by the way, we're going to rip all the seatbelts out of all the cars, because most people do the right thing anyway." I mean, it's absurd, right? You know it's absurd. That is the argument: no prevention, only punishment.

So this is a huge deal, much bigger than just the issue at hand. Look, I know what the Constitution says and, quite apart from the Constitution, the American people believe they ought to have the right to hunt; they ought to have the right to sports shooting. But the death rate from accidental gun shootings is 15 times higher in this country than it is in the next 25 biggest countries combined, for kids.

I had a fellow call me yesterday when he saw all the press about this, an old friend of mine, just to remind me that once in his garage many years ago his little boy and his little boy's best friend were playing with a gun that they got somewhere else. The gun went off and killed his little boy's best friend. I've known this guy forever. He said, "I just want to remind you of that; don't forget that." He said, "It took my son years to get over that. He had no wounds, no burdens, himself, but he had to live with seeing his friend die, and in front of him as a kid, in a game they were playing together with something they had no business [holding] in their hands."

Lawsuits Against the Gun Industry Will Help Reduce Violence

by David C. Anderson

About the author: *David C. Anderson is an author and a contributor to* American Prospect *magazine.*

The street guy told the dealer he needed some guns to replace one he had lost the previous Saturday. The dealer was sympathetic. Were you caught with the gun? he wanted to know. No, the man said. He had run and hadn't been caught, but along the way he ditched the gun and the cops got it. Now he wanted new guns because he had figured out who had "ratted me out" to the police, he said, and he had to "settle up." They agreed on replacement guns and the dealer said to come back in a few days to pick them up.

This was a disturbing episode of retailing, certainly—and all the more disturbing because it did not take place on an inner-city street corner or a booth in a bikers' bar, but over the counter of a store in a Chicago suburb. The customer was an undercover officer, part of a sting operation mounted by Chicago police to support the city's lawsuit against firearms manufacturers and distributors. The Chicago suit, part of a fast-growing legal trend, suggests the potential for litigation to open a new front in the decades-old war of attrition between promoters of gun control and the gun lobby. Some experts still dismiss the suits as grandstanding. Others, citing a . . . New York case, see them as in line with emerging legal trends.

How the Gun Industry Sells Its Wares

America remains one of the world's leading gun markets. Private citizens are believed to own 200 million firearms, a third of them handguns, and the industry, with revenues estimated between $1.4 billion and $2.5 billion annually, distributes several million new guns each year. Even so, gun makers fret over flagging sales. Guns are durable, and most of the people interested in buying one for legitimate reasons have already done so. Recent surveys now find guns present in about 35 to 40 percent of American households, a decline from earlier estimates of 50 percent.

As Tom Diaz documents in [the 1999] book, *Making a Killing*, the need to sustain sales has taken the industry in troubling directions: appeals to macho fantasy and efforts to exploit a criminal market that developed rapidly in the 1980s and 1990s as a by-product of the boom in crack cocaine. More precisely, the industry attracts potential customers by pitching a new gun's ability to kill better than an old one. "Lethality is the nicotine of the gun industry," Diaz writes. "Time and time again, the gun industry has injected into the civilian market new guns that are specifically designed to be better at killing—guns with greater ammunition capacity, higher firepower in the form of bigger caliber or power, increased concealibility, or all three."

Apparently calculating that gun buyers who begin early remain buyers for life, gun marketers appeal shamelessly to kids. Diaz quotes appalling copy from the voyeuristic "gun press"—magazines that promote the industry. It "is one mean looking dude," says a *Guns & Ammo* review of an assault weapon, "considered cool and Ramboish by the teenage crowd; to a man they love the AP9 at first sight. Stuffed to the brim with Nyclad hollow points, the pistol is about as wicked a piece as you can keep by your pillow. . . . Take a look at one. And let your teenage son tag along. Ask him what he thinks."

Most recently, the industry has bet on "pocket rockets"—guns that combine higher caliber with smaller size. "The concealibility and firepower of these guns make them among the most lethal weapons America's streets have ever seen," Diaz writes. They also coincide with a national movement to reduce authorities' discretion in denying permits to carry concealed weapons. Diaz quotes *Shooting Industry* magazine: "Two bright rays of sunshine gleam through the dark clouds of the slump in the firearms market. One is the landslide of 'shall issue' concealed carry reform legislation around the country. The other is the emergence of a new generation of compact handguns."

The Costs of Gun Violence

Such marketing imposes huge social costs. Guns killed about 34,000 people in the United States in 1996 and were second only to automobiles as a non-natural cause of death. (The Centers for Disease Control and Prevention estimates that by 2003, guns will surpass cars.) The shooting deaths included 14,300 homicides, or 68 percent of all homicides committed that year. The other fatal shootings included 18,100 suicides and 1,100 accidents. (Circumstances of the rest weren't clear.) A study based on 1992 data found that about 99,000 people were treated in hospitals each year for nonfatal gun wounds, about 20,000 the result of accidents. Recent studies of the surge in crime that accompanied aggressive marketing of crack in the late 1980s and early 1990s blame most of the violence on guns in the hands of young people. The number of homicides committed by juveniles with guns nearly tripled between 1986 and 1993, while the number of killings with other weapons remained unchanged.

The burden for an innocent public is financial as well as emotional. Medical treatment of a single serious gunshot wound may easily exceed $100,000; a medical journal article in 1995 estimated the cost for treating gun injuries nationwide that year at $4 billion. Taxpayers pay most of these bills. A 1996 California study, for example, found that 81 percent of hospitalized gunshot victims did not have medical insurance.

> *"Private [American] citizens are believed to own 200 million firearms, a third of them handguns."*

Costs of emergency medical, law enforcement, and other public services mount quickly: Philadelphia estimates that nonmedical expenses of gun violence cost the city $72.2 million per year. Chicago estimates $78.1 million in 1997 for gun-related police and emergency medical service and for prosecution of gun violations. A 1997 study calculated $2.8 million in direct and indirect costs (lost productivity, pain and suffering, quality of life) for a single gun fatality. For nonfatal wounds, the figures were $249,000 for those admitted to hospitals and $73,000 for those who required only emergency treatment. Overall, the study estimated total costs of U.S. gun violence at $126 billion per year. The idea that an industry reliant on perverse appeals to immature judgment should impose that level of grief and fiscal burden makes the case for serious regulation seem obvious, yet it has eluded legislatures for years.

Gun Control Has Been Limited

The modern era of federal gun control began in the 1960s with laws passed after the assassinations of the Kennedy brothers and Martin Luther King, Jr. These laws banned mail-order gun sales and required buyers to attest to their sobriety, sanity, and lack of a felony record. They also restricted purchases to the buyer's state of residence.

Subsequent laws banned importation of cheap handguns ("Saturday night specials") and sales of assault weapons and imposed a waiting period between purchase and delivery of a gun so that police could scrutinize the buyer. (Congress [has] allowed that requirement to expire, substituting a procedure that requires dealers to check a buyer's identity against databases of criminal records.) While leaders of the National Rifle Association denounce all such regulation in apoplectic terms, it is remarkable for its laxity. In addition to fending off more serious gun control, the gun lobby over the years has carved out remarkable exemptions for its constituents.

For example:

• A law specifically prohibits the Consumer Product Safety Commission—whose role it is to judge the fitness for market of everything from lawnmowers to baby cribs—from testing or ruling on guns.

• Congress bars the Bureau of Alcohol, Tobacco and Firearms [ATP] from assembling gun data in a centralized electronic database. Tracing ownership of a gun recovered at a crime scene requires a call to the manufacturer, who may or may not be able to say what wholesaler sold it to which retail shop, then a call to the retail shop where clerks may or may not have records of the gun's last sale on file.

• In many states, virtually nothing regulates sales of guns between private individuals. Nearly every weekend in America, tens of thousands of people interested in buying and selling guns gather at "gun shows," where many are able to carry on private transactions beyond any official scrutiny.

Real gun control would impose the level of sensible regulation long accepted for automobiles: universal registration of firearms and licensing of gun owners based on gun handling skills and knowledge of gun safety and gun law. It might also impose a liability insurance requirement and limit gun purchases to one per month. These measures, financed by licensing and registration fees, could do much to inhibit flows of guns to criminals and kids, limit panic buying of guns in the wake of riots or media-inflamed "crime waves," and elevate the general level of gun safety.

It is a measure of the gun lobby's effectiveness that such an idea seems radical even in the wake of national soul-searching over [spring 1999's] school shootings in Colorado and Georgia. All the White House could push through the Senate, with a vote from Vice President [Al] Gore required to break a tie, were relatively modest

> *"Real gun control would impose the level of sensible regulation long accepted for automobiles."*

measures, like requiring background checks of buyers at gun shows and including child safety devices with sales of new guns. When an interviewer challenged President [Bill] Clinton, saying he should have pressed for more, he responded in anger.

"Let's join the real world here," he said, pointing out that he was the first president ever to stand up to the gun lobby. "Should we do more? Should people ought to have to register guns like they register their cars? Do I think that? Of course I do. . . . But I tell you, the American people may have one opinion, but they elected the Congress, and the Congress doesn't have that opinion." As he spoke, a version of the mild Senate bill was being weakened in the House. Could lawsuits circumvent the legislative stalemate? Skepticism abounds. Authorities like Franklin Zimring, the Berkeley law professor who has written extensively on gun policy, reflect the view of many who assert that the legal issues remain hopelessly complicated by the fact that in most cases an "intervening agent"— the criminal—shares responsibility for harm to the plaintiff. And low barriers to entry the gun business may limit the effectiveness of any legal victories. As suits force some producers to settle or fold, others can easily replace them.

Chapter 2

The Promise of Lawsuits

Even so, the results of litigation so far are intriguing. Until recently, tort claims against gun producers and dealers based on gun injuries were considered unlikely so long as guns remain legal to buy and sell. Whatever the suffering of gunshot victims, they couldn't very well argue the product that injured them was defective. And judges shrugged off assertions that people selling guns should be held responsible for how customers use them. This began to change in the 1990s when lawsuits against the tobacco industry demonstrated that persistent, muscular lawyering could force an industry to account for negligent product design and marketing. In addition, juries were finding drug companies and other defendants liable based on proof of general negligent business conduct rather than specific harm to a specific person.

A group of lawyers who had helped with the tobacco effort worked with the city of New Orleans to file one of the first gun suits. Mayor Daley of Chicago ordered his police department to develop an elaborate sting, "Operation Gunsmoke," that produced startling evidence of suburban gun shops helping to supply inner-city street criminals and gangs. In New York, meanwhile, a lone legal practitioner named Elisa Barnes produced a surprising early win, persuading a jury to find several gun makers collectively liable for "negligent marketing."

[By September 1999] 21 cities and counties have filed suits against scores of gun manufacturers, wholesalers, retailers, and their trade organizations [the number reached 24 by early 2004]. The suits raise different issues, depending on the laws in states where they are filed. The New Orleans, Miami, Atlanta, and Cleveland suits focus on "negligent design," asserting that guns are inherently dangerous and that the industry should be held liable for neglecting to make them safer. They argue, for example, that the industry failed to develop guns that can be fired only by their owners, when technology exists to make this possible. Suits filed by Bridgeport, Detroit, Cincinnati, and St. Louis raise issues of "negligent distribution." "Defendant dealers have sold and continue to sell handguns even when they know or should know that the handguns will be used illegally in the City of Bridgeport. . . ." A similar claim by Los Angeles and San Francisco engages a California business practices law. Courts have ruled that it may be violated by otherwise legal conduct that undercuts established public policy and inflicts economic damage or physical harm on society. Lawyers for the cities point to a California Supreme Court decision holding it an unfair business practice for tobacco companies to advertise and promote cigarettes to minors, even though it was otherwise legal for them to do so.

The Chicago Lawsuit

The Chicago suit elaborates on these themes with support from the undercover operation in which police officers posing as gang members and other suspicious people easily bought guns. The suit cites examples of guns purchased at suburban stores later used in gang shootings, armed robberies, and a number of murders, including one of a police officer.

The complaint points out that 57 percent of firearms recovered after illegal use in Chicago were first sold only three years before they were recovered, a percentage of new guns that exceeds figures for the rest of Illinois and the United States as a whole. Only 10.5 percent of guns recovered by Chicago police were reported stolen. The complaint also documents a more chilling development: legitimate gun dealers who cultivate business and close sales by acting as weapons consultants to criminals, bending the rules on waiting periods and record keeping when they threaten to get in the way of a customer's street business. Some excerpts:

• Officer 1 quietly asked the sales clerk to recommend a 'throw-away' 9mm or .380 caliber firearm. [A throw-away is a cheap gun likely to be ditched by a person, like a drug lookout, with a high risk of apprehension.] The sales clerk told him that one should not buy a 'throwaway' gun from a gun store. Instead, he said, one should buy one from a second party, such as a friend, so that if it is recovered and ATF questions the friend from whom you bought it, then the friend can call and let you know that you will soon be approached by the ATF.

• On August 19, Officer 2 returned . . . with Officer 3. Officer 2 told the same sales clerk with whom he had dealt on August 14 that Officer 6 owed him money and was likely on the run. Officer 2 stated that Officer 6 had to be dealt with before he left town, and said he needed to 'get a Tec for his ass.' Officer 3 agreed that they had to 'take care of business today.' The sales clerk recommended an Intratec 9mm assault weapon that could fire 100 rounds per load, telling them, 'You made a good choice. It will take care of business.' The sales clerk then added the Intratec 9mm assault weapon Officer 2 had just selected to the purchase order he had created for August 14.

The Chicago complaint argues that the industry creates a public nuisance by flooding these suburban stores with far more guns than the legal market can absorb, and by selling them to people who appear likely to use them for crime.

The complaint requests monetary damages of $433 million and a list of injunctions that would require the industry to enforce restrictive practices: limiting purchases to one gun per person per month, requiring customers who are Chicago residents to show proof of a legal place to keep a gun outside the city, requiring manufacturers and distributors to monitor dealers and terminate shipments to those who sell guns to people "whom the dealer has noticed will not use them lawfully and responsibly."

> *"The industry creates a public nuisance by flooding . . . suburban stores with far more guns than the legal market can absorb."*

How likely is the suit to succeed? The manufacturers and the dealers that were subjects of the undercover operation have not responded yet, and they could come up with ways to challenge the police officer's testimony. The suit might also be challenged on civil liberties grounds, because asking dealers to assess the possible criminal intent of customers invites racial profiling.[1]

Even so, says David Strauss, of the University of Chicago Law School, "The idea that [the sale of guns to likely criminals] is a public nuisance is actually mainstream and straightforward. One way to think about it would be to suppose that Chicago had an anti-pollution ordinance and someone set up a factory right on the outskirts of the city and operated in a way that polluted Chicago air. There would be no problem suing them to get them to stop. This is the same thing, if you accept the factual allegations." The city can already claim a small victory. In April [1999], one dealer, Bob's Sports Headquarters, Inc., signed a consent decree. In exchange for dismissal of damage claims, Bob's agreed to give testimony against the industry and either go out of business or accept strict conditions on the way it sells guns.

Success in New York

Chicago and other cities pursuing the negligent distribution/public nuisance strategy can also look for encouragement to the lawsuit Elisa Barnes brought in federal court in New York. A lawyer who specializes in product liability, Barnes sued 25 gun manufacturers to recover damages for the families of six people killed by gunfire and for a young man who survived a shooting but remains permanently disabled. She presented the shooting victims as the inevitable consequence of the industry's irresponsible distribution practices. At the trial, Barnes paraded families of victims with tales of grief along with experts on youth violence and marketing of dangerous products. She also used information forced from the manufacturers in discovery to document the idea of negligent distribution. Specifically, she alleged that the manufacturers and distributors were selling far more guns in states with weak gun-control laws than the legitimate users in those states could be expected to purchase, and that the excess guns wound up in the hands of criminals in New York.

To demonstrate this, she hired a team of economists who combined the manufacturers' data with ATF reports and other sources to document trafficking between New York and states with weaker gun laws. The defense hired its own economists to rebut the plaintiff's assertions, sometimes leading the argument into the arcana of statistical regression analysis.

After a turbulent deliberation, the jurors found 15 of the 25 defendants liable and ordered three of them to pay damages of $522,000 to the surviving gunshot victim, Stephen Fox. This was stunning: the gun used to shoot Fox was never recovered. All police found at the scene was a spent .25 caliber shell casing. The jury, acting on a theory of "collective liability," awarded damages against

---

1. The suit was initially dismissed in 2000, but the Illinois Appellate Court overturned that ruling and reinstated the action.

manufacturers with no proof that any of them had distributed the gun that caused the injury.

A few days after the verdict, the *Wall Street Journal* published an account of the deliberation based on interviews with jurors and attorneys. It depicted an irrational process—an adamant juror who favored the plaintiffs buffaloed others sympathetic to the industry into a compromise. In May (1999), however, District Judge Jack B. Weinstein, who had presided over the case, filed a 113-page memorandum that provided a different spin.

The judge dismissed the complaint against the 12 manufacturers who escaped damage payments, ruling that "finding of liability requires proof of damages." But he also cited with approval a modern legal trend to find collective liability when a plaintiff cannot identify a precise defendant for reasons beyond anyone's control. He pointed to litigation over DES, the synthetic estrogen blamed for cancer in adult daughters of women who used it during pregnancy. DES raised "unique problems of proof" because much time had

"The suits have strained relations between industry trade groups willing to consider a settlement and the National Rifle Association."

elapsed between the time mothers ingested the drug and the development of cancer in their children. Many could not identify who had actually produced the drugs their mothers took. Courts reluctant to deny the victims any remedy "eliminated the identification requirement, predicating liability instead on defendants' creation of risk through participation in the DES market."

In the gun suit, Judge Weinstein acknowledged the plaintiff's argument that "it is the underground market itself, created and stocked by the defendants' negligence—rather than any one manufacturer's product—which the plaintiffs regard as the cause of their injuries." The language he used suggested the idea of public nuisance as well: "Apt is the analogy to a stream polluted by many manufacturers at once, overwhelming the water's ability to purify itself by the huge influx of the many polluters."

A jury considering a case where the type of product is known but the manufacturer is not may assign damages according to the market share of manufacturers found to market the product negligently—the "market share" version of collective liability. That is what the jurors did in the case of Stephen Fox, awarding him damages from defendants who manufactured .25 caliber guns, prorated according to their market share.

The Benefits of Litigation

Extending such liability to the marketing of guns intensifies the heady atmosphere surrounding the other lawsuits; the industry, at least, is no longer willing to dismiss the litigation as frivolous. If nothing else, the suits have strained relations between industry trade groups willing to consider a settlement and the National Rifle Association, which puts the convenience of gun owners first.

Appeals courts might still cause all this to implode, of course. But in the meantime, the suits will have put invaluable new information on the public record. Elisa Barnes now regularly receives reporters and other interested parties who want to rummage through the boxes of trial transcripts, statistical analysis, depositions, and other documents stacked up in a room of her financial district office. In addition to the extensively argued clash of economists on the question of interstate trafficking, they will find:

• The testimony of David Stewart, a University of Southern California professor of marketing, who points out that industry-wide agreements are common to reduce the risks products create to consumers or to society. Producers of fertilizer and herbicides make sure they are sold only by people trained to instruct customers in their proper use. Producers of spray paint, concerned about graffiti, make sure retailers keep the spray cans in locked cabinets and don't sell them to minors. He offers a list of similar steps gun manufacturers might take, should they decide to reduce the risk their products create.

• The testimony of Jeffrey Fagan, a professor of public health at Columbia University who compiles interviews with young men about episodes of violence in their lives. He discusses the pervasiveness of guns on the streets and the "vicious cultural dynamic" they generate.

• The testimony of Robert Hass, former senior vice president for marketing and sales for Smith & Wesson. He asserts that "the company and the industry as a whole are fully aware of the extent of the criminal misuse of handguns. . . . In spite of their knowledge, however, the industry's position has consistently been to take no independent action to insure responsible distribution practices."

Lawyers for the cities are likely to extract more damning statements as they depose more executives and otherwise assemble information in discovery. Each new revelation generates new publicity, adding to the pressure on legislatures to act and the industry to settle. The train, in other words, is leaving the station. Once rolling, it could be hard to stop.

Requiring That Handguns Be Made to Recognize Authorized Users Can Reduce Gun Violence

by John D. Cohen

About the author: *John D. Cohen is the director of the Progressive Policy Institute's Community Crime Fighting Project.*

Just when it seemed the carnage in America's schools could not get any worse, dreadful news came from Michigan—a six-year-old boy shot and killed his classmate, Kayla Rolland, in their first-grade classroom. Once the shock over the killer's age had faded, people wanted to know the answer to a simple question: how in the world does a six-year-old get a gun?

As it happened, the boy found the gun, which had been stolen, in the flop house where his mother had left him in the supposed care of relatives. Similarly, the guns used in the Columbine slaughter[1] found their way into the killers' hands through a third party. Unfortunately, it's a recurring theme. The U.S. Treasury Department reports that 60 percent of all guns used to commit crimes are either purchased for a criminal by another person, or stolen from their legal owner.

That statistic alone should lead public policy makers to an easy conclusion: if guns were manufactured so that only their legal owners could fire them, much of the death and destruction caused by illegal gun use could be prevented.

A Political Gunfight

The technology exists to do just that—and by focusing on the development of technological solutions, Congress might actually be able to break the ideologi-

---

1. an April 1999 incident in which two high school students fatally shot twelve students and one teacher and then committed suicide

cal impasse that has repeatedly sunk even modest gun control measures (even in the face of clear public support for strong action to reduce gun violence).

The White House has asked Congress for $10 million to continue the research on "smart guns"—weapons with internal features that prevent their unintended or criminal use. The Republican-controlled Congress shot down an even smaller request for smart gun research in the [1999] budget. But Republican leadership should reconsider this time around, because the fact is gun technologies make it easier to do what the National Rifle Association (NRA) and its GOP allies have long said they favor: target only the improper or illegal use of guns without trampling on the rights of law-abiding gun-owners.[2]

> *"If guns were manufactured so that only their legal owners could fire them, much of the death and destruction caused by illegal gun use could be prevented."*

Up to this point, the contours of the gun debate have broken down largely along traditional conservative-versus-liberal lines. Conservatives demand more aggressive enforcement of existing laws, but they oppose any new provisions to keep guns out of the hands of the wrong people. Most recently, top National Rifle Association (NRA) officials have launched shrill attacks on President [Bill] Clinton for daring to propose common sense gun control measures. For their part, some liberals want to restrict access to guns or even ban handguns outright—even if that means violating what a majority of Americans regard as a basic constitutional right. Meanwhile, as the left and the right fight each other to a standstill, more children die and the cycle of violence that has become a part of our neighborhoods, our schools, and our workplaces remains unbroken.

Building Safer Guns

Smart guns make it possible to transcend the false choice between gun rights and gun control by adopting a "consumer product safety" approach. This approach does not aim to stigmatize gun owners or deny law-abiding citizens the right to own arms. It would simply assign gun manufacturers the responsibility for building safer products.

Like tobacco, motorcycles, or prescription drugs, guns are undeniably dangerous products. Most Americans not only expect but also demand that our government act to protect consumers from unsafe uses of perfectly legal products. Safety caps are required on aspirin bottles, seatbelts are required in automobiles and children's toys, and even toy guns must be safe or they are subject to recall. With current and emerging technologies, it is reasonable to require that guns be made with internal safety features that minimize accidental injury and/or criminal misuse.

---

2. As of spring 2004, Congress had not passed smart gun–related legislation.

Currently, a manufacturer sells an internal trigger lock that requires a gun user to push three buttons on the handle of a gun—in specific order—before the gun will fire. Through the use of this type of internal mechanical device, we can improve gun safety right away—and in the near future, safety-enhancing capabilities will improve even further. For example, one manufacturer has produced a gun that contains a small radio receiver. In order to fire the weapon, a person must be wearing a special ring containing a radio transmitter that communicates with the receiver. Eventually, advancements in microchip technology will enable the programming of guns to read a user's fingerprints and preclude its use by an unauthorized person. It would be a good use of federal money to help fund such research.

For the most part, the gun industry has resisted efforts to promote new product safety standards. This is not surprising. Historically, companies have improved consumer product safety only after prodding from the government or the threat of lawsuits. In an effort to force the industry to develop these new technological capabilities and include them in gun designs, some U.S. cities, including Chicago, Bridgeport, and Detroit have filed lawsuits against gun manufacturers. Meanwhile, policy makers in Maryland, New Jersey, Massachusetts, and Connecticut have introduced state legislation requiring the gun industry to adopt product safety standards.

> *"With current and emerging technologies, it is reasonable to require that guns be made with internal safety features."*

[An] agreement between Smith and Wesson and the federal government may represent an important breakthrough. Smith and Wesson has agreed to safety, design and distribution standards that include a commitment that within three years they will market primarily "smart guns"—weapons with internal features that prevent their unintended or criminal use.[3]

Making Gun Enforcement Work

It will take time to put product safety requirements into effect. Meanwhile, millions of unsafe guns are in circulation, and we must redouble our efforts to prevent them from getting into the hands of criminals and unstable people. Waiting periods on gun purchases, mandatory background checks, and the ban on assault weapons all help. However, we must also provide federal, state, and local law enforcement with the tools they need to aggressively target for arrest and prosecution illegal gun traffickers, people who illegally supply guns to children, and those who use guns to commit crimes. Among the highest priorities are integrated criminal justice information systems that facilitate proactive, data-driven enforcement efforts and information sharing between courts and

---

3. The company has continued its research, but as of spring 2004 these guns were not yet available.

law enforcement so that the felons, persons under psychiatric care, and domestic abusers are prevented from buying guns.

Effective gun enforcement efforts also require that federal, state, and local law enforcement agencies work together to arrest and prosecute criminals who use guns and those who illegally sell guns. State governments can play an active role in facilitating statewide law enforcement efforts. For example, the State of Maryland has implemented a statewide "crime gun" enforcement initiative that directs state and local law enforcement to trace seized guns when those guns have been used in the commission of a crime. The measure also expands the use of ballistic imaging, as well as funding for proactive law enforcement efforts that target violent criminals and illegal gun traffickers.

The Clinton Administration . . . proposed a $280 million enforcement initiative as part of the President's FY 2001 budget. In addition to expanding the funding for development of smart guns, it would fund the hiring of 500 new Bureau of Alcohol Tobacco and Firearms (BATF) agents and more than 1000 new prosecutors at all levels of government. It would also fund crime gun tracing and ballistics imaging, in order to catch more criminals. Further, the Administration has proposed $30 million to support computerized mapping of gun violence to help law enforcement agencies develop better strategies to protect the public.

Ironically, while Republicans and the NRA now criticize the Administration for a lackluster performance in enforcing gun laws, they have continually opposed efforts to increase resources for the BATF (the agency within the Federal government that has primary jurisdiction over gun related crime). In fact, the NRA has called for the abolition of BATF, whose agents were once described as "jack-booted government thugs" in an NRA fundraising letter.

It's time to move beyond this false and polarizing stage of the debate. Supporting the development of smart guns would be a logical and productive first step.

Gun Control Does Not Reduce Gun Violence

by Edmund F. McGarrell

About the author: *Edmund F. McGarrell is a professor and the director of the School of Criminal Justice at Michigan State University.*

Laws Have Unclear Effects

Since the brutal murders at Columbine High School in April 1999,[1] the long, contentious debate over gun control has reached fever pitch and become a forum for the president and congressional allies to demonstrate "leadership." A plethora of new proposals regularly emanates from the White House to reflexive squawks of disapproval from gun owners and manufacturers and their allied organization. Essentially, however, the debate boils down to a choice between new regulations over sale, purchase, and possession of firearms or increased enforcement of criminal laws against those who use firearms illegally. That is, do we focus on legal possession of firearms or their illegal possession and use—on controlling gun owners or controlling criminals?

One element of the debate has to do with the effectiveness of these proposals on reducing deaths from firearms. The truth is, we know very little about the likely impact of many of the new gun-control proposals. We do know that gun registration in Great Britain and Australia ultimately led to bans on firearms. We also know that confiscation in these countries was followed by increasing rates of predatory crime. Yet, we do not know whether registration would affect crime in the United States.

One popular proposal that President [Bill] Clinton and the Department of Housing and Urban Development are implementing is gun-buyback programs. Unfortunately, the available research suggests that these programs do not reduce violent crime (see Benjamin Styring, *American Outlook*, Winter 2000).

---

1. Twelve students and one teacher were murdered, and the two perpetrators committed suicide.

Experience with another proposal, laws punishing parents for failing to lock guns away from children, has generated conflicting research findings. A study conducted at the University of Washington found that states with these laws achieved reductions in accidental shootings by children. However, Yale Law School researcher John Lott Jr. and John Whitley from the University of Chicago found that states passing safe-storage laws suffered dramatic increases in rape, robbery, and burglary (see http://papers.ssrn.com/paper.taf?abstract_id= 228534). The point is that we do not know whether these laws decrease accidents, increase other types of violent crime, or have no effect. Other gun-control proposals suffer from even greater deficiencies of systematic research.

Given the evidence we now have and the number of gun-control laws in place, it seems clear that increased regulation of legal gun possession is unlikely to reduce firearms violence in the United States. This conclusion is based on two key points. More than 99 percent of U.S. firearms are never used illegally, and almost all gun violence is perpetrated by a very small group of criminals using illegal guns, people who would be utterly unaffected by any new regulations. Further, any potential reductions in gun accidents such laws might accomplish would probably be more than offset by increases in gun crime resulting from the disarming of legal gun owners. The news, however, is not all bad. Research shows that firearms crime can be affected by aggressive enforcement of existing laws aimed at gun criminals. These issues have been addressed in depth in previous issues of *American Outlook* (see "More Guns, Less Crime," Fall 1999) and need not be further discussed here.

During recent years the gun-control debate has turned on symbolism: concern for victims of accidents versus concern for constitutionality. These are valid considerations, but both research and common sense require that the next president and Congress start to think seriously about firearms legislation in terms of *effectiveness.* State and local governments have the constitutional mandate to handle these matters, and they can serve as laboratories for practical application of firearms crime policy while fulfilling that responsibility. The federal government's key role is to ensure that state laws are enforced fairly, not mandate or supersede them. Behavior that has been legal here for four centuries should certainly not be transformed into a federal crime unless the very survival of the republic is in danger. Thus, a central principle for the new president and Congress should be to refrain from enacting federal legislation criminalizing heretofore legal behavior when there is no evidence that such policies will reduce deaths by firearms.

Fundamental Conflicts

There is, however, another dimension to the debate, which has received almost no attention: what the contrasting proposals on reducing gun violence tell us about the nation and the principles guiding the nation's legal system, and what they tell us about the future of America's legal system. A close look at the gun-control debate sheds light on conflicts in American society over fundamental positions on liberty, personal responsibility and accountability, federalism, and the position of the individual vis-à-vis the state.

The Second Amendment to the Constitution of the United States reads, "A well-regulated militia being necessary to the security of a free state, the right of the people to keep and bear arms shall not be infringed." Although legal scholars debate whether the Second Amendment applies to the individual right to bear arms as opposed to a collective right to maintain an armed militia, the current gun-control debate clearly signals a fundamental disagreement over the issue of individual rights versus state control, especially as regards the federal government's role. Advocates of more gun regulations clearly see the right of the federal government to control firearms as superseding citizens' rights to individual freedom. For example, Dennis Henigan of Handgun Control Incorporated has stated that there is no "federally guaranteed constitutional right" to self-defense (*USA Today*, November 20, 1991). Rather than viewing the right to self-defense as inherent in the individual unless appropriately restricted by rule of law, many gun-control advocates clearly presume that this is a right to be granted by the state—in this case the federal government—at its own discretion.

> *"Increased regulation of legal gun possession is unlikely to reduce firearms violence in the United States."*

Those who advocate increased enforcement of laws against gun offenders and oppose further restrictions on law-abiding citizens, especially by the federal government, see the Second Amendment as a fundamental assertion of the primacy of the individual over the state. Thus, liberty, in this case the unfettered right of law-abiding adults to bear arms, trumps the state's interest in regulation.

With freedom, of course, come responsibility and accountability. Thus, advocates of intensified prosecution of those using firearms to commit crimes view such policies as not only effective but also as the appropriate state action given the social contract: maximum liberty to all who do not break the contract. Gun-control advocates, by contrast, view government restrictions on liberty as a worthwhile price to pay for enhanced safety. Given the restriction on liberty, however, it is only wise to place on advocates of gun regulations the burden of demonstrating how, in each case, the price of freedom is justified by increased safety and security.

This last point raises issues related to federalism. First, one of the features of a federalist structure is that the variations across states and localities provide a vehicle for assessing private and public policy options. Thus, we can compare the extremely high rates of firearm violence in the most restrictive gun-law jurisdiction in the country (Washington, D.C.) with jurisdictions with less-restrictive gun laws and much lower rates of firearm violence. If Handgun Control Inc. is wrong and John Lott is correct in observing that increased regulation of legal possession of firearms generates increased firearm violence, federal imposition of D.C.-style restrictions would push the rest of the nation toward the level of firearm violence now common in the District of Columbia. One of the beauties of the federalist system is that the states can act as laboratories for assessing different legal regulations. Further, variation between states also provides citizens the freedom to choose whether to reside in a highly regulated state or a freer one.

Troubling Federal Proposals

The flood of gun-control proposals that bespeak a desire for the expansion of federal power raise another federalist issue. Gun-control advocates have called, for example, for increased federal prosecution of certain types of firearm possession cases. Although firearms-rights advocates protest this increased federal role in traditionally local criminal matters, at least this intrusion is restricted to people who have committed violent crimes and to convicted felons who have forfeited their inherent freedom to possess a firearm.

The more troubling proposals are those to extend federal jurisdiction over traditionally legal behaviors, such as proposed federal laws to require gun owners to obtain a license and register their firearms with the federal government, and proposed federal provisions defining and mandating "safe" storage of personal, legally owned firearms. Many gun owners believe that the right to bear arms is the society's protection against state tyranny and an individual's only sure means of self-defense, and it is therefore clear that many otherwise law-abiding citizens will refuse to reg-

> *"The expansion of laws makes it less likely that federal enforcement will focus on policies that have demonstrated the most potential for reducing firearms violence."*

ister their firearms. Thus the main effect of such laws would be to create a new class of criminals among the 99 percent of gun owners who would never use a gun in a crime nor allow the gun to be used in an accidental shooting.

To clarify these issues, let's consider the . . . Soros Foundation report on gun control (see http://www.soros.org/crime/gunreport.htm). The report begins by noting that "a 12-year-old in North Carolina needs parental permission to play Little League Baseball, but not to possess a rifle or shotgun." What the report refuses to mention is the fact that federal laws prohibit all twelve-year-olds in the United States from purchasing firearms. Further, under North Carolina state law, adults who allow a minor access to a firearm that is used by the minor as a threat, causes personal injury, or is used in a crime are guilty of a crime. North Carolina law allows twelve-year-olds to be in possession of a rifle or shotgun where a parent or guardian allows possession for activities such as firearms training, shooting at a target range, competitive shooting, or other adult-supervised activities. A federal law criminalizing a parent and child shooting at the local firing range is clearly overwrought and utterly unnecessary.

The proliferation of federal regulations on firearms possession not only threatens to criminalize currently legal behavior but also carries important opportunity costs. The more federal laws that are passed, the more widely the targets for federal enforcement activities expand beyond the relatively small pool of convicted felons to a broad pool of otherwise law-abiding citizens. Moreover, the expansion of laws makes it less likely that federal enforcement will focus on policies that have demonstrated the most potential for reducing firearms violence—aggressive enforcement of felons in possession of firearms and of people using firearms in crimes. This is particularly troubling given trends in federal law enforcement during the 1990s. A Syracuse University study found that Bureau of Alcohol, Tobacco, and Firearms (BATF) referrals to federal prosecutors declined from 9,885 in 1992 to 5,510 in 1998, a 44 percent drop. Making more instances of firearm possession illegal, however, would increase the number of potential cases for the BATF to investigate. With more targets than can ever be investigated, the likelihood of arbitrary application of the law increases. This, in turn, threatens the legitimacy of the rule of law. Requiring the BATF and U.S. attorneys to prosecute offenders more vigorously would be far more effective than asking them to handle more and more federal laws and regulations regarding possession, sale, and storage of firearms.

The gun-control issue, then, is heated precisely because it represents a fundamental disagreement over whether current circumstances should ever override the nation's commitment to its fundamental principles. America's founders were committed to the ideas of rule of law, individual liberty, individual responsibility, and limited federal government. Advocates of increased enforcement of existing gun laws against those who use firearms to commit crimes draw on these principles. The Second Amendment makes it clear that an American citizen has an inherent right to bear arms unless he forfeits it through egregious criminal behavior. Violators of the social contract lose that right and should be held accountable. Advocates of increased federal gun regulation, by contrast, seek to restrict liberty a priori and to extend the reach of the federal government. As the nation confronts the gun control versus firearms-crime-enforcement debate, we are struggling not only with the question of saving lives but also with our nation's commitment to its fundamental governing principles.

Gun Control Does Not Reduce Youth Gun Violence

by Timothy Brezina and James D. Wright

About the authors: *Timothy Brezina is an associate professor of sociology at Tulane University, and James D. Wright is a professor of sociology and anthropology at the University of Central Florida.*

Heightened media attention, especially to homicides with multiple victims, has led the public to believe that school violence is a growing problem. In fact, the total number of school-related violent incidents, including suicides and homicides, has steadily declined since the 1992–1993 school year, as have overall incidents of youth violence. The chance of dying a violent death at school is still less than one in a million.

Although the levels of serious school violence—including homicide, robbery, rape, sexual assault, and aggravated assault—remain unacceptably high, most serious violence occurs outside schools, on neighborhood streets or in the home. Students are three times more likely to be victims of a violent crime away from school than on school property, at a school-sponsored event, or on the way to or from school.

To be sure, the number of multiple-victim homicides has increased in recent years, but fortunately the incidence of such acts remains extremely rare. Since August 1995, an average of just five such acts has occurred each year. Considering the number of children that attend school in the United States—50 million or more—and the number of hours they spend in school each year, multiple-victim homicides at school are "the statistical equivalent of a needle in a haystack."

Because school-related violent deaths are rare and isolated, we must be very cautious about drawing conclusions or generalizations from them. Nevertheless, recent incidents raise many questions about kids and guns, specifically about the likely impact of popular gun-control proposals. The first question is how violent youths gain access to firearms.

Guns Are Easy to Obtain

How do kids get their hands on guns? This question is often posed as if there were some mystery about it. In fact, guns are easy to obtain. An estimated 200 million firearms are currently in circulation in the United States, and some 40 percent of all households own at least one gun.

In 1991, criminologists Joseph Sheley and James Wright interviewed more than 800 incarcerated juvenile offenders to gauge how hard it would be for them to get a gun when they were released from jail. Even though these juveniles couldn't legally purchase a gun because of their age and criminal record, 70 percent said they would have "no trouble at all" obtaining one. For inner-city high school students answering a similar question, 41 percent believed they could get a gun with no trouble at all; an additional 24 percent said getting a gun would be "only a little trouble." Adolescents in the general population, when asked about the availability of guns, provide somewhat smaller estimates, but the data confirm rather than challenge the fact that guns are not difficult for youths to obtain.

In the same study, juvenile inmates and high school students were asked how they would obtain guns. These respondents reported that family, friends, and street sources are the main sources of guns for juveniles. Evidently, perpetrators of school gun violence obtain guns in the same manner. In the school shooting sprees of the past decade, most of the perpetrators obtained guns from their own households or from the usual sources—parents and grandparents, occasionally from friends, and sometimes from street sources or theft. The shooters in Littleton[1] obtained all of their guns illegally through straw purchases—that is, using older friends and acquaintances to buy the guns for them.

Current Laws Can Be Circumvented

For many people, it is shocking that guns are so easily accessible to youths. This state of affairs, however, is not the result of a large gap in the law. Moreover, the passage of additional legal restrictions will do little to rectify the situation, since most of the avenues through which youths obtain guns are already against the law.

Federal law already prohibits juveniles from purchasing guns through normal retail outlets. The legal age for purchasing firearms at such outlets is 18 for rifles and shotguns and 21 for handguns. Federal and state laws also prohibit persons of any age from carrying guns without a permit and bringing a gun onto school property. And most municipalities have local ordinances that ban the discharge of a firearm within city limits.

---

1. In April 1999 Eric Harris and Dylan Klebold killed twelve classmates and a teacher at their Colorado high school and then committed suicide.

Although age restrictions are readily circumvented through the use of inter-mediaries and straw purchases, this too is illegal. Friends, acquaintances, and drug dealers who provide juveniles with firearms are at the least contributing to the delinquency of a minor and probably violating a dozen other laws as well. For example, Mark E. Manes—the 22 year-old man who provided the Columbine killers with a semiautomatic handgun—was charged with several felony counts: one for supplying a handgun to a minor and one for possession of a sawed-off shotgun. He was sentenced to six years in prison.

Nevertheless, the 1991 survey found that 32 percent of juvenile inmates and 18 percent of inner-city high school students had asked someone else to purchase a gun for them in a gun shop, pawnshop, or other retail out-let. And, as the Columbine shooters explained in a home-video tape, had it not been for Mark E. Manes they "would have found someone else."

> *"Guns are not difficult for youths to obtain."*

So long as guns are available to anyone, they will also be available to any juvenile with the means and motive to exploit his network of family, friends, and acquaintances for the purpose of obtaining a firearm. However much we wish it to be otherwise, there is no plausible way to limit juvenile access to guns except to limit general access to guns, just as there is no plausible way to approach the problem of child poverty except by addressing the poverty of parents. There is, in turn, no practical way to limit general access to guns without doing some-thing about the 200 million firearms already in circulation. It is by no means obvious how that could or should be accomplished. We are forced to ask, then, whether more or different laws will provide a solution.

Evaluating Several Proposals

After the Columbine incident, state and federal lawmakers proposed a variety of gun-control measures. Much of the attention focused on bills that would place further restrictions at the point of sale—measures such as extending back-ground checks to all buyers at gun shows and extending the waiting period for background checks. Other bills would ban the manufacture or importation of certain additional types of firearms and high-capacity ammunition clips, require trigger locks or other safety devices on all guns sold, and create liability for gun owners who do not store their firearms in a safe and secure manner.

Given the ease of acquiring guns through intermediaries and straw purchases, the potential impact of further point-of-sale restrictions is not at all clear. Additional bans on specific types of guns and ammunition, moreover, would do nothing to curb access to guns already in circulation. For example, the manu-facture of the combat-style TEC-9 semiautomatic handgun—one of the weapons used by the Columbine shooters—was outlawed in 1994, but that gun remains widely available.

Laws that encourage the safe and secure storage of firearms appear promising at first glance. Many gun owners keep and store firearms in irresponsible ways, a point that gun enthusiasts acknowledge and lament.

But safe-gun technologies—trigger locks and smart guns—are no panacea. The principal aim of safe-gun technologies is to reduce the incidence of accidental discharge of firearms. Yet most of the gun violence that befalls young people is intentional, not accidental. Fatal gun accidents have always been the least important component in the annual death toll. Thus, even if successful, safe-gun technologies will have little effect on the death toll from firearms.

There is a second and more fundamental reason safe-gun technologies are unlikely to have a substantial impact: "safe gun" is an oxymoron. The entire point of a firearm is that it be able to inflict grave harm and to do so reliably, efficiently, and decisively. The only real gun safety consists of well-trained, responsible users.

Ultimately, by passing more laws, and failing to understand the limits of the law, we may fool ourselves into believing that something important has been done about the problems of violence and youth. For example, legislators who promoted similar restrictions in the past, and who saw them become federal law under the Gun Control Act of 1968, believed they would "substantially alleviate" the problem of gun use by juvenile delinquents.

Aggressive Law Enforcement

Since existing gun laws already have considerable scope, we must ask whether greater enforcement of existing laws would bring us closer to solving the problem of youth violence.

There is some evidence that aggressive law enforcement can reduce gun-related crime, at least in certain areas and for certain periods of time. Beginning in July 1992, Kansas City led a 29-week experimental crackdown on gun violence. Police intensively patrolled high-crime areas and seized illegally carried guns through plain-view sightings, frisks, and traffic stops. An evaluation of the crackdown indicated a drop in gun crime

> *"From the concrete view of risk offered by public health officials, it is surprising that more youths do not engage in gun violence."*

within the target area, while such crimes did not decrease in a similar non-target area. A replication of the experiment in Indianapolis, however, produced only mixed results.

Although the potential of such efforts is not yet clear, it would be surprising if they did not produce some positive effects. Aggressive law enforcement will surely be a component of successful gun-violence reduction efforts, and when integrated into a comprehensive violence-prevention strategy, positive results may be especially likely. It remains to be seen, however, whether innovative crackdowns can avoid the decay effect—a gradual reduction in effectiveness over time due to adaptive criminal behavior—that so often plagues law enforcement efforts.

Little Effect on Violent Crime

Gun-control opponents and advocates alike share great faith that the criminal justice system can prevent and deter crime through legal restrictions or crackdowns and punishment. The criminal justice system has an obvious and critical role to play. But as criminologist Marcus Felson warns, "It is easy to exaggerate the importance of the police, courts, and prisons as key actors in crime production or prevention."

First, most crimes do not come to the attention of officials, in part because victims fail to report them. Even when victims report a crime to the police, the prospect of apprehending a suspect is not very good. For example, less than half of all reported violent crimes end with an arrest, and the figure is much lower for property crimes. As the criminal justice funnel narrows, fewer cases are deemed suitable for prosecution, and fewer still lead to conviction and punishment. Thus official punishment, while it can be extreme, tends to be rare and uncertain. This, of course, is not the fault of criminal justice personnel. They are merely subject to the practical limits of law and law enforcement "in society as we know it."

Moreover, most research indicates that legal sanctions are not particularly effective or meaningful deterrents, most likely because punishment is uncertain at best, and when it does happen, it is delayed. People are deterred from criminal involvement mainly because of informal and nonlegal sanctions such as the anticipation of a negative reaction from significant others, the expectation of guilt or shame for violating personal moral standards, and other stakes in conformity.

It is, therefore, not surprising that gun-control laws typically have little or no effect on rates of violent crime. At best, the effects are modest and short-term. According to the results of a recent evaluation published in the *Journal of the American Medical Association*, the 1994 Brady Law—which requires a background check and waiting period for the purchase of handguns from licensed dealers—is no exception.

In short, uncritical faith in the criminal justice system is part of the problem. The cops-and-courts fallacy leads us to place unrealistic demands on the criminal justice system in hopes that some fine-tuning of the system here or there will produce dramatic effects on behavior. The cops-and-courts fallacy also contributes to severe dependence on the law and discourages the consideration of non-legal and possibly more-effective responses to crime.

The Relationship Between Guns and Crime

No one engaged in the gun-control debate disputes the fact that youth violence is a serious national problem or that guns contribute to the annual death toll. These facts alone, however, do not support the conclusion that guns are a root cause of the violence.

The language of "risk" promoted by the public health movement encourages us to see guns as being inherently destructive, putting gun owners at risk of destroying themselves or others regardless of their intentions or disposition to violence. This view of the problem, however, relies on a logical sleight of hand that strips violent acts of human agency and intentionality. Gun violence, unlike physical illness or disease, is a willful act.

From the concrete view of risk offered by public health officials, it is surprising that more youths do not engage in gun violence and that the problem is not more demographically widespread. It bears repeating that some 40 percent of all households have at least one firearm. Moreover, a national survey reveals that just under 30 percent of adolescents claimed personal ownership of a gun, and 39 percent reported using firearms for recreational purposes such as hunting and target shooting. Yet few of these adolescents had engaged in acts of violent crime.

In fact, no relationship was observed between recreational firearm use and criminal involvement. If we acknowledge that most crimes involving guns are committed intentionally by a handful of violent individuals, the problem becomes not so much getting guns out of the hands of juveniles, but reducing the motivations for juveniles to arm themselves and use guns against each other in the first place.

Responding to Danger

When asked to explain why they carry guns for reasons other than recreation, youths overwhelmingly reply they do so for protection and self-preservation. In other words, there is a direct relationship between gun carrying and perceived environmental dangers such as fear of neighborhood violence, past threats of violence, and known victimization of friends and family members.

In the inner city, where the rates of gun carrying by juveniles are particularly high, the attraction to guns is not difficult to understand. Just under half of the inner-city students in the 1991 study knew someone at whom shots had been fired, many had been the targets of gunshots themselves, and just under 15 percent described themselves as scared in school most of the time.

In this environment, gun carrying is readily interpreted as a response to the daily threat of victimization and intimidation. This threat not only presents itself at school, but pervades so-

"Additional gun-control laws will not necessarily prevent determined youths from obtaining firearms."

cial life and serves as a constant reminder of the powerlessness of inner-city residents. Wracked by poverty and severe social disorganization, these communities provide relatively few incentives for long-term investment in the future, nor do they offer the certainty of the police protection that people in more affluent neighborhoods expect. From afar, the attraction to guns may seem pathological, since the proliferation of firearms only serves to increase the threat of violence within such communities. But from the standpoint of individuals caught in the middle, a gun must seem a bargain at nearly any price, transforming otherwise powerless people into forces to be reckoned with.

> *"[Gun-control] laws fail to address the immediate conditions of life that lead youths to carry guns."*

Instead of focusing on neighborhoods that statistically are the most dangerous—the inner-city killing fields where violence and despair are rampant—media coverage has focused on multiple-victim homicides occurring in unsuspecting communities, involving white, suburban, or rural school children from apparently good homes. This type of coverage has contributed to the impression that youth violence of today is not only increasing, but that it is more or less random in nature and divorced from the immediate conditions of life. This is a seriously distorted view of the problem, since definite patterns exist. For example, while suburban schools are obviously not immune from violence, rates of serious violence are as much as 15 times higher in some poor, urban schools.

In the highly publicized suburban school incidents of recent years, bullying, harassment, rejection, and long-standing grievances among classmates have been commonplace. While these problems were present in the details of the Columbine incident, this particular shooting spree was atypical in almost all other respects. While school violence is an extensive problem, only a tiny fraction involves guns, and this is especially true of schools in suburban communities.

Responding to Youth Violence

The gun-control response to school violence illustrates some of the problems that arise when social policy is driven by extreme and unusual cases. Additional gun-control laws will not necessarily prevent determined youths from obtaining firearms. More important, such laws will do nothing to address violence that is not gun-related. Yet this type of violence—the bullying, harassment, fist fights, and knife wielding that can occur at any school—is much more typical and undoubtedly contributes to much of the gun-related violence that does occur.

A better response to school and youth violence is to address the problems that confront youths in their immediate environment, including obstacles to conventional success and the social strains and personal antagonisms that can provoke or escalate aggression. A number of prevention and early-intervention programs have demonstrated positive long-term effects on behavior in rigorous evaluations and might serve as models for other communities. Such programs include "anti-bullying" campaigns, the implementation of anger-management, impulse-control, and problem-solving curricula at schools, and the provision of early-childhood education and family support services for urban, low-income families.

It remains to be seen whether such programs can be replicated successfully on a wide scale, especially since many people believe that the problems of crime and violence can be solved by creating new laws and applying tougher penalties. When asked to identify the main source of blame for the crime problem, the majority of respondents in a 1994 national survey blamed the criminal justice system and, presumably, its lenient treatment of offenders. This exaggerated dependence on the law helps explain why, to date, so little effort has been spent getting to the root of the problem.

It also remains to be seen whether prevention and early intervention programs will receive adequate funding in the future. The number of dollars currently allocated to prison construction and get-tough measures far exceeds the number allocated to the type of programs described above. Regardless, it is difficult to see how more gun-control laws will alleviate the problem of youth violence, because such laws fail to address the immediate conditions of life that lead youths to carry guns and to break the law in the first place.

Lawsuits Against the Gun Industry Are Baseless

by Robert A. Levy

About the author: *Robert A. Levy is a senior fellow in constitutional studies at the Cato Institute, a libertarian think tank.*

[A] major claim of cities suing the gun industry is that firearms are "defective and unreasonably dangerous" as they are currently manufactured. How are the firearms defective? Do they misfire? Do they fire inaccurately? Not at all. Even the *Washington Post* has editorialized: "As a legal matter, it is hard to see how companies making lawful products can be held liable when those products perform precisely as intended." No matter. First New Orleans, then other cities, insisted that guns are defective if they are sold without devices that prevent discharge by unauthorized users. On that ground, the cities hope to drag gun makers to the settlement table—turning the law of product liability on its head.

In order to hold gun makers liable for selling an unsafe product, tort law requires a true defect, not merely that a product is dangerous when it does what it is designed to do. True enough, some guns have features that are particularly attractive to criminals. But that may be because criminals value many of the same features that appeal to law enforcement officers. Legislatures across the nation have regulated virtually every aspect of gun design and distribution. If a determination is to be made that guns are unreasonably dangerous, the legislature, constrained by the Constitution, must make that determination, not the courts. Here's how a federal judge in Massachusetts put it in a 1996 case, *Wasylow v. Glock:* "Frustration at the failure of legislatures to enact laws sufficient to curb handgun injuries is not adequate reason to engage the judicial forum in efforts to implement a broad policy change."

Even Brooklyn's Jack Weinstein, the favorite federal judge of the plaintiffs' bar, had this comment about the safety of guns: "Whether or not . . . products liability law would require an anti-theft safety mechanism as part of the design of handguns requires a balancing of the risk and utility. . . . Plaintiffs have not shown that such a device is available, nor have they asserted the possibility of showing at trial that such a device would satisfy the . . . risk-utility test." Weinstein added, "The mere act of manufacturing and selling a handgun does not give rise to liability absent a defect in the manufacture or design of the product itself."

Hypocritical Lawsuits

When it comes to guns, New Orleans city officials are singularly unsuited to be the guardians of public safety. In 1998 the city's police department traded more than 8,000 confiscated weapons—40 percent of which were semiautomatic—to a commercial dealer in return for Glocks. Nearly half of the traded guns would have been characterized as "unsafe" in the city's lawsuit against gun makers—including TEC9s, AK47s, and Uzis, banned since 1994. Only a quarter of the guns had safety locks. Still, Mayor Marc Morial signed and approved the deal, paving the way for resale of those guns across the nation. Ironically, New Orleans could end up as defendant in other cities' suits.

Under pressure, Morial suspended the swap program. But New Orleans wasn't the only hypocritical plaintiff. Police departments in Boston, Detroit, Oakland, Miami, St. Louis, and Bridgeport also traded in "unsafe" guns, which are now back on the street, even while suing gun makers for marketing a defective product. Undoubtedly sensitive to the bad publicity, several police departments announced that they would explore a lease program, rather than trade-ins, with Glock. Yes, that might relieve the city of direct responsibility for providing unsafe guns for commercial resale. But the revised contractual arrangement is mere camouflage for what is basically the same deal—that is, a so-called defective product is first used by the police and then recycled by Glock for sales to private citizens.

Whether the claim is a defective product, negligent marketing, or public nuisance, these lawsuits are rubbish. Five of them have reached final judgment and all five were fully or partially dismissed. In October 1999 an Ohio state judge threw out Cincinnati's claims. He wrote that gun makers are not responsible for the criminal misconduct of customers. "The city's complaint is an improper attempt to have this court substitute its judgment for that of the legislature." The "design, manufacturer and distribution of a lawful product" is not a public nuisance.

> *"Whether the claim is a defective product, negligent marketing, or public nuisance, these lawsuits are rubbish."*

Bridgeport's and Miami's suits were also dismissed, in December 1999. Miami's judge observed that the city cannot use the courts to regulate; that's the job of the legislature. A Florida appeals court upheld the Miami ruling, calling the lawsuit "an attempt to regulate firearms . . . through the . . . judiciary." "Clearly this round-about attempt is being made because of the County's frustration at its inability to regulate firearms," the appeals court wrote. "The County's frustration cannot be alleviated through litigation."

In Chicago on September 15, 2000, a judge threw out that city's negligent-marketing claim saying that statistical evidence of causation wasn't good enough and that individual instances of illegal sales were a matter for the police to counter.[1] Most recently, on December 21, 2000, a federal judge dismissed Philadelphia's claims, describing the city's charge of public nuisance as "a theory in search of a case," and rejecting the negligence claim "for lack of proximate cause."

The Litigation Continues

Nevertheless, the trial lawyers press forward. Sooner or later they're likely to find a sympathetic judge who's willing to ignore the law in favor of his personal policy preferences. It's called "forum shopping," and it's a favorite tactic of the plaintiffs' bar. In fact, the major reason each city has sued its local dealers as well as the gun manufacturers is so the plaintiff and at least one defendant reside in the same jurisdiction. That way the case cannot be removed to federal court, where the rule of law generally prevails over provincial prejudices.

While the search for friendly forums moves ahead, pending lawsuits are having predictable effects. Smaller gun makers are going out of business; two California dealers have declared bankruptcy; and Colt announced a layoff of 300 workers, then said it would withdraw from the consumer handgun business and focus instead on military weapons and collectibles. Prospective litigation costs are showing up in higher gun prices. Top quality handguns are now priced in the $350 to $550 range, and fewer guns are available for less than $100. Not surprisingly, higher prices have less impact on criminal demand than on the demand from price-sensitive, law-abiding citizens, especially those from the inner city.

On a parallel track, threatened litigation by the federal government and actual litigation by dozens of cities were used as a bludgeon to force the industry's largest manufacturer, Smith & Wesson, into a settlement. Despite countervailing pressure from its customers and other gun makers, Smith & Wesson threw in the towel—explaining that the $100 million or more in damages sought by several of the larger cities exceeded the company's profits for the entire past decade. Moreover, the company protested, it cost $1 million to defend against each government-sponsored claim. Smith & Wesson simply didn't have the resources to fight multiple lawsuits across the country. Accordingly, on March 17, 2000, it surrendered.

The Smith & Wesson Settlement

Essentially, the Smith & Wesson deal is no better than a shakedown. Various government entities—HUD [Department of Housing and Urban Development] at the federal level, New York and Connecticut at the state level, and 13 cities—

1. In November 2002 the Illinois Appellate Court reinstated the action.

agreed not to pursue their baseless but costly litigation against the company. Other cities and counties offered to review their suits but made no formal commitment to exclude Smith & Wesson. In return, the gun maker pledged, first, to impose the following restrictions on its dealers and distributors: (a) No sales of any manufacturer's guns unless the buyer has passed a safety course and cleared a background check—even if the check takes longer than the three-day period required by law. (b) No sales at any gun show unless all sales at the show are subject to a background check. (c) No sales of Smith & Wesson guns if a "disproportionate number of crimes" is traced to guns sold by a dealer or distributor. (d) No purchase by one person of more than one gun at a time unless the buyer is willing to wait 14 days before picking up the rest.

Second, Smith & Wesson agreed to childproof all of its handguns within a year, presumably by using features like a heavier trigger pull or a magazine disconnect, which prevents a gun from firing once the magazine is removed. Under terms of the settlement, every Smith & Wesson handgun would also be equipped with an external lock within 60 days and an internal lock within 24 months.

Third, each gun would have a hidden serial number to facilitate tracing the weapon if it is used in a crime. Fourth (reminiscent of the tobacco settlement that forced manufacturers to fund anti-smoking programs), Smith & Wesson promised to "work together to support legislative efforts to reduce firearm misuse" and contribute 1 percent of its revenue toward an "education trust fund" to inform the public about the risk of firearms. The specific content of the anti-gun campaign will be determined by a five-member oversight committee in each settling city. That same committee—comprising one Smith & Wesson official and one representative each from the city, county, state, and federal government—will monitor and supervise all provisions of the settlement.

The Real Story Behind the Settlement

Those terms and conditions obscure what is actually driving the settlement. From the government's perspective, the settlement was a means of bypassing state and federal legislatures that had been singularly unresponsive to a variety of gun control proposals. Moreover, the settlement circumvents court review in many jurisdictions. Judicial approval would be required only in jurisdictions where lawsuits had already been filed and were to be dismissed as a condition of the settlement. That excludes the suits threatened but not filed by HUD and various cities and states.

From the company's perspective, the settlement represented an opportunity to avoid the cost, time, and uncertainty of pending litigation. That opportunity took on special meaning in the case of Smith & Wesson, which is owned by a United Kingdom company that was looking to sell its investment. The market for acquisitions is materially diminished, of course, when lawsuits lurk menacingly in the background.

To sweeten the deal further, President [Bill] Clinton sought to form an alliance of local governments and HUD—the Communities for Safer Guns Coalition—which would refrain from buying police firearms manufactured by any company that didn't sign the settlement. That commitment to favor Smith & Wesson was not embedded in the text of the settlement agreement but communicated informally by Clinton. Perhaps that's because he knew that a refusal to deal might violate local and federal procurement regulations, discriminate against law-abiding gun makers, and deny disfavored companies the right to pursue a legitimate business.

> *"Unprincipled politicians are more than willing to use the antitrust laws as a club."*

In June 2000 the House of Representatives attempted, unsuccessfully, to pass a bill prohibiting enforcement of the Smith & Wesson settlement. But the House did approve a provision that would prevent spending in support of Clinton's coalition, which ultimately comprised 600 localities that agreed, first, not to sue Smith & Wesson and, second, to favor the company in police gun buys. That was followed a month later by Senate approval of a bill barring federal procurement preferences for Smith & Wesson. With a change in administration, the settlement probably will not attract other gun makers as co-signers, nor is the settlement likely to benefit Smith & Wesson, which announced this past June [2000] that it was closing two of its plants for a month, in part because angry customers were buying fewer guns.

As the real terms of the settlement (including preferential contracting) became clear, seven gun makers and their trade association, the National Shooting Sports Foundation [NSSF], filed suit against HUD secretary [Andrew] Cuomo, New York attorney general Eliot Spitzer, Connecticut attorney general Richard Blumenthal, and 14 mayors for conspiring to violate the constitutional right of the gun makers to engage in trade. The plaintiffs asked a federal court to forbid new gun regulations that were not authorized by Congress. By August 2000, however, it was apparent that the buying preferences had not materialized. Police departments wanted the best weapons available for obvious reasons. Even HUD bought guns from Glock, which did not sign the settlement yet continued to supply roughly two-thirds of police weapons nationally. In January of this year [2001], NSSF and the seven gun makers dropped their suit.

On another front, to intensify the pressure for a settlement, Cuomo, Spitzer, and Blumenthal threatened an antitrust suit against Smith & Wesson's rivals for organizing a boycott against that company's products. Blumenthal issued subpoenas for documents, despite no "solid evidence" other than a post-settlement industry meeting attended by a number of gun makers, who expressed criticism of Smith & Wesson and the settlement. Spitzer pulled no punches. The goal, he gloated, is to "squeeze [gun] manufacturers like a pincers"—proving once again that unprincipled politicians are more than willing to use the antitrust laws as a club to force conformity by companies that refuse to play ball. . . .

The Lawsuits Must Be Stopped

There is a lesson to be learned from all of this. If we do nothing to rein in baseless, government-sponsored lawsuits, private attorneys and their accomplices in the public sector will continue to invent legal theories to exact tribute from friendless industries. In the latest rounds of litigation, law-abiding gun manufacturers may be forced to pay for the actions of criminals. That outcome will likely entice politicians unwilling to make tough choices and enrich trial lawyers, but there can be no pretense that litigation of that sort has any basis at all in the rule of law.

Handguns Cannot Be Made to Recognize Authorized Users

by Massad Ayoob

About the author: *Massad Ayoob is a police officer and the director of the Lethal Force Institute in New Hampshire.*

A handgun which can instantly recognize authorized users is the Holy Grail of today's R&D departments, but is this a quantum leap in firearm safety or just a technological disaster waiting to happen.

A Repeated Failure

"Smart guns" has become the latest buzzword cliche among opponents of the civil right of private gun ownership. Colt's (with a subsidiary called iColt), Smith & Wesson and Sandia Labs are all firmly on the bandwagon, having put significant funding into the research and development of such a gun.

None, however, have been able to field a working model for potential end-users to test. Colt's was embarrassed when they showed their prototype to a reporter from a major newspaper and it failed to work. An Eastern Seaboard governor who was pushing for a bill that would limit people to "smart guns" was humiliated when the model he was demonstrating locked up solid and wouldn't work when it was supposed to.

All this has left a foul taste in the mouths of legitimate gun users, in the private and police sectors alike. Those who have seen the reality of self-defense know that a protection gun must be available for use instantly. The gun-banners' "model legislation" mandating "smart guns" has been written to expressly exempt police from the requirement. This tells you cops don't trust it. If they don't, then perhaps neither should you.

The concept of the smart gun sounds great. It's a gun you can fire instantly but only you can fire at all. Imbedded technology keeps the bad guy from harming you or someone else if he gets control of your gun. You could leave your gun where you could quickly reach it, but an irresponsible child or other unauthorized person would be unable to fire it if they found it.

If it worked. . .

The concept, as sold to the public, breaks down into three categories: fingerprint recognition, electronic recognition and magnetic action. Let's look at all three.

I have yet to meet a working street cop who likes the idea of fingerprint recognition technology. The sellers say that it will instantly recognize the user's fingerprint, which is programmed in, and be capable of firing immediately soon as the authorized hand takes a firing grasp.

We potential buyers have some grave concerns. What about cold weather when we will be wearing gloves? Fingerprint recognition potential is now totally blocked, and in a fast-breaking emergency there won't be time to rip the glove off the shooting hand.

If the legitimate user has been injured in the attack, viscous blood will quickly fill up the areas between the ridges of the fingerprints, probably rendering them unreadable by the device, and thus causing an "access denied" reaction when the user needs the gun most. The same could happen in a scuffle that leaves the legitimate user's hands covered with mud or whatever.

Problems with Electronic Technology

Electronic transponder technology raises even more concerns. The theory is that the gun will be activated when it is within a certain proximity to a transponder the intended user wears on the belt or wrist. When the gun is outside this range, it will "go dead."

Where, then, shall we draw the line of the transponder's range? I've heard a distance of three feet postulated. Now, I'm only an average size man, but when I drop down into a rollover prone firing position, the grip-frame of my handgun is a measured 41.5 [inches] from my hip holster, presumably the location of the transponder. Thus, I've put my own gun out of reach of its activator.

The same could happen with a long-armed officer or citizen firing with arm extended, or anyone firing straight up at a sniper in a high vantage-point or a wildcat about to pounce from a tree limb. Therefore, the transponder would have to reach more than four feet away from itself to activate the gun to reliably be of use to the legitimate user.

> *"Most of the people who theorize about 'smart guns' have never actually carried one."*

The purpose, however, is to keep you from getting shot with your own gun. Virtually anyone who gets your gun out of your hand or holster is going to be within three or four feet of you. In any case, a disarmed cop will instinctively lunge toward the attacker to retrieve the snatched weapon, again putting the responder into "activation range." Therefore, the belt-mounted transponder doesn't offer much promise in the real world.

What about a wrist-mounted transponder? Of course, you'll need one for each wrist in case you have to fire with the weak hand only due to an injury to the gun hand.

But things on the wrist can be torn off in a struggle. If it happens all the time in fights, the kind of fights that escalate to deadly force situations. This is why experienced cops and bouncers are seen to take off their wristwatches and ID bracelets and slip them into a pocket when they think a brawl is in the offing. This factor makes the wrist-mounted transponder also seem impractical.

> *"[The 'smart gun'] may be the sneakiest trick yet to deprive the American public of its right to own firearms."*

A ring on each hand is more promising—in theory. We are, however, still waiting patiently for one to be shown to us that might actually work, given the limited space a ring offers for electronics without getting in the way of hand function in normal daily activities.

With any sort of electronic technology, you have to worry about jamming. We live in a world where scofflaw "techies" pay big bucks for devices that block police radar. How long would it be before the first "gangland geek" came up with a device that would block the transponder of any nearby officer (or armed citizen), rendering the good guy's weapon inoperable?

Magnetic Smart Gun Technology

The third smart gun safety mechanism postulated is magnetic technology. This is the one least often discussed by the gun-banners. That's because a magnetism-based smart gun actually exists, and has been working for some 25 years.

A full-time inventor named Joe Davis designed something he called Magna-Trigger in 1975, and patented it shortly thereafter. It was a modification of a S&W revolver with leaf-type mainspring (i.e., K-frame or larger) so that it could only be fired by someone wearing a magnetic ring on their middle finger.

The front strap of the S&W's grip-frame is cut away and replaced with a module that holds what looks like a little steel flag and flagpole. The flag blocks the rebound slide, allowing the trigger to be drawn back only far enough to drop the bolt and allow a cylinder rotation check. It prevents the gun from firing. When the hand wearing the magnetic ring closes into a firing grasp, reverse polarity between the ring magnet and the one mounted at the base of the "flagpole" spins the latter unit. The metal flag is now clear of the rebound slide, and the gun can instantly be fired in double-action mode.

A ring should be worn on each hand, to allow for shooting back if wounded in the gun arm. The gun should be modified to double action only, since if the gun is taken away in a cocked condition, anyone can fire one shot from the single-action position before the rebound slide is blocked again. The rings are interchangeable, allowing spouse, partner or other authorized person to use the "proprietary" gun.

Downsides? You cannot handle computer disks, videotapes, audiotapes or any other of the magnetically-sensitive things we come into contact with daily without ruining those things. The rings are ugly—plain steel bands—though they can be styled to look like class rings or other ordinary jewelry for an extra cost. The technology is limited to K-through N-frame S&W revolvers. I've seen attempts to use the magnetic principle differently to modify revolvers with coil mainsprings (J-frame S&W, Colt Trooper, Ruger) but they were not as reliable and therefore not as successful.

Attempts were made by another inventor to modify the Beretta DA auto pistol and the Colt 1911 to work this way, but test samples were finicky, and in any case would work only in the right hand. For all practical purposes, "magnetic smart gun technology" does not exist at this time for the semiautomatic pistols that are overwhelmingly preferred by the police community and largely favored by today's private citizen handgun purchasers.

Personal Experiences with "Smart Guns"

Most of the people who theorize about "smart guns" have never actually carried one on police duty or as an armed citizen, or relied on one as a home defense weapon. For almost five years, I carried a Magna-Trigger equipped six-gun. The experience was instructive.

The gun was a S&W Model 66, the stainless steel .357 Combat Magnum model. Its action had been tuned by famed revolver-smith Andy Cannon.

My first child was three years old when I had the 66 modified by Joe Smith. It allowed me to have a loaded revolver at my bedside that the toddler couldn't harm herself or anyone else with if she stumbled across it while I was asleep. At the time, I was teaching classes involving officer survival, handgun retention and awareness for armed citizens. It made sense for me to have a MagnaTrigger gun along to show the students, and using it as my personal defensive weapon was convenient as there was simply one less gun to carry on trips.

The rings were no more inconvenient than any other piece of jewelry. The gun always worked, so long as it wasn't fitted with finger-groove grips. The flanges between the grooves could turn the flat, inward facing magnetic portion of the ring to an angle where it might not work.

While teaching officer survival with Ray Chapman at Chapman Academy, we discovered one weakness in the design. Cutting away the front of the frame to install the module weakens the overall structure of the grip-frame. This is not a problem in routine shooting, even with lots of magnum ammo going downrange. (The K-frame revolver had to be rebuilt once or twice from the constant pounding of 125 gr. .357 rounds, but the function of the Magna-Trigger was never impaired.)

The Potential for Disarming

What we did find was that a certain disarming technique popularly taught in prisons would lever the gun in such a way that the cutaway frame of the S&W could bend back and outward. This caused the Magna-Trigger module to slip just enough that it would no longer block the rebound slide, which allowed the gun to be fired by anyone.

There was a silver lining to this cloud, however; both Chapman and I could now testify as expert witnesses in court that if your gun was ripped out of your hand, it was possible that this action would make it fire despite the Magna-Trigger, warranting your use of your backup gun to shoot the person who had unlawfully disarmed you. Prior to that, the concern had been expressed that if someone got such a "smart gun" away from you, the courts might hold you liable if you harmed him, since even though in theory he had a gun, he would be armed with a nonfunctioning weapon.

In the mid-'80s, however, I regretfully put this gun into semi-retirement. Our teaching format had gone heavily toward videotapes, and handling them with magnetic rings could have wiped them out. Our students and the cops I trained at my department were increasingly trending toward semiautomatic pistols, and the technology of the MagnaTrigger did not translate.

Joe Smith died some years ago. Rick Devoid acquired the rights to the product from the estate, and today offers conversions (and already converted revolvers) through Tarnhelm Supply. The conversion of your revolver costs around $350 and includes two magnetic rings.

The True Intention of the Anti-Gun Movement

Why do those handgun prohibitionists who push for the "mandatory smart gun legislation" pointedly ignore magnetic ring technology? For the simple reason that it actually exists. For one side of the anti-gun movement, the "smart gun" is a Trojan Horse. Their plan is simple.

The first step is to pass a law that says the only guns people can carry, or even possess, are "smart guns." The second step is to raise a glass of champagne with [gun control advocates] Sarah Brady and Al Gore and toast their own cleverness. They have now banned all existing firearms, with the false promise that citizens can only possess something that doesn't exist.

The fact that the MagnaTrigger does exist mightily nettles those in the anti-gun community. Interestingly, another wing of the anti-gunners is against the whole concept. They see the smart gun as a gun, after all, and absolutely refuse to "endorse" any gun of any kind.

It will be interesting to see how the prototype "smart guns" from S&W, iColt, etc., perform, if they ever actually reach the point where those who hype them will let them out of the factory for independent testing.

In the meantime, a true smart gun that has stood the test of time does in fact exist. However, the MagnaTrigger revolver is a special purpose tool that cannot possibly replace the conventional defensive handgun for many purposes. The one man on earth who knows the most about it, Rick Devoid, has said so himself. In fact, he has said so publicly, which irks the anti-gunners enormously. But then, those people never did handle the truth very well.

The "smart gun" is just pie in the sky. At best, it's an immature technology a great distance away from proving itself applicable to the guns used daily by police officers and law-abiding armed citizens. At worst, it may be the sneakiest trick yet to deprive the American public of its right to own firearms.

Chapter 3

Is Gun Control Constitutional?

Overview: The Second Amendment and Gun Control

by Deborah Homsher

About the author: *Deborah Homsher is the author of* Women & Guns: Politics and the Culture of Firearms in America, *from which the following viewpoint was excerpted.*

Article I, Section 8 of the United States Constitution, introduced by the pragmatist Alexander Hamilton and eventually ratified by the states, granted Congress the right to "provide for organizing, arming and disciplining the Militia, and for governing such Part of them as may be employed in the Service of the United States." Simply put, this meant that the U.S. Congress would have the power to muster its own standing army. But a number of influential patriots distrusted standing armies, which they pictured as mercenary, parasitic hordes dispatched against the people by a despotic monarch. So in 1789 James Madison proposed a set of twelve amendments—the Bill of Rights—to reinforce the powers of the people against centralized authority. Pared down to ten amendments, the Bill of Rights was adopted in 1791. Its second amendment assured the states that their citizens would retain their weapons and so maintain the power to revolt against a federal government should it turn tyrant.

It states: "*A Well regulated militia, being necessary to the security of a free State, the right of the people to keep and bear Arms shall not be infringed.*"

A Much Different Society

This single sentence was composed more than two hundred years ago by men who lived in a different world—before repeating rifles, before the infected, intestinal rending of the Civil War and the liberation of the nation's slaves, before the enfranchisement of women, before anesthesia, antibiotics, electrical outlets, photographic film, automobiles . . . add to the list all technological advances in medicine, communications, transportation, and weaponry developed in the last two hundred years. And when these men wrote referring to the "people"—"*the right of the people to keep and bear Arms shall not be infringed*"—they did not mean to include servants, slaves, vagabonds, or females. No skirts interrupted the hedge of trousered legs standing in queue for exercises on the drilling field.

The fact that the Constitution was composed in a such different time, and that it named entities that have altered drastically since that time—the states, the government, the people—challenges, but never completely defeats, those who use the document as a guide for contemporary government. Wonderfully, it turns out that this last entity, the people, has from the first been difficult to pin down. The Founding Fathers themselves quickly discovered that America's general population failed to live up to their expectations when it came to virtue. The most articulate revolutionaries, who identified with one another as genteel men, found that their newly enfranchised fellow citizens sometimes neglected to respect or even elect them, and voted instead for noisy upstarts who promised favors and local improvements. "Effrontery and arrogance, even in our virtuous and enlightened days, are giving rank and Importance to men whom Wisdom would have left in obscurity," mourned John Jay, revolutionary and political theorist. By the 1790s, political thinkers had already learned that "the people were not an order organically tied together by their unity of interest but rather an agglomeration of hostile individuals coming together for their mutual benefit to construct a society," according to Gordon Wood. The people were already a ragtail mystery.

And there were other mysteries. The Constitution did not explain how a "well regulated" militia would be created from such a disparate collection of male gun owners. It would require a people practiced in devotion to the common good, but already the people were showing themselves to be head-strong, diverse, and unreliable. The regiments of American patriots mustered against England most nearly approximated such a universal militia, and the authors of the 1789 Bill of Rights were doubtlessly recalling their own experiences as armed and principled rebels when they penned the Second Amendment. But they were also borrowing from similar bills in a number of the states' constitutions, bills that defended the people's right to bear arms and located the abiding source of security in an armed, trained (male) populace, rather than in a standing army. These bills were themselves modeled after a portion of the English Bill of Rights, which had been introduced by Parliament a century earlier in response to the aggressions of the Catholic King James II and his standing army. In all these cases, it was understood that a citizens' militia was meant to unite against tyranny. This honorable goal gave the volunteer militia, as defined, its authority; without such an honorable goal, any restive

> *"The Second Amendment shows itself to be . . . a perplexing document for the late twentieth century."*

collection of armed American rebels would be nothing more than pack of traitorous rabble. The propertied Founding Fathers had little use for traitorous rabble. George Washington's forceful suppression of the Whiskey Rebellion of 1794, a citizens' armed protest against a federal excise tax on homemade whiskey, indicated as much. After crashing the Pennsylvania rebellion with a force of 15,000 armed militiamen mustered by the federal government, Washington addressed Congress and spoke against "self-created societies" that prompted small groups of citizens to resist the authority of the federal government.

The Gap Between Public and Private

The authors of the Constitution had been scrupulous in designing a governmental machine that relied on the people for its power and could be altered by the people when they chose. This made it very difficult to imagine when and how such a government could ever be judged despotic—it was much easier to judge an individual king to be despotic—so that a collection of U.S. citizens might justifiably arise, challenge the central government or the United States' standing army through force of arms and, after the dust had cleared, be judged as virtuous, patriotic militiamen . . . not "irregular" riffraff excited by "specious pretexts."

Somewhere between the vision of a mustered regiment marching in step outdoors and the vision of a single Kentucky rifle slung from a nail indoors, the Second Amendment presents us with deep obscurity. This gap between the public, outdoor

> *"The Second Amendment . . . appears to have been written by men who valued the people's right to keep their own firearms."*

mustering of arms and the private, indoor keeping of arms creates a fertile ground for conflicting interpretations of the amendment's central meaning. Did the authors of the Constitution intend for the government to regulate the number and kinds of weapons a citizen could keep in his own home, or would they have defined that intrusion as an infringement of the citizen's rights? It seems clear that James Madison and his illustrious colleagues had little fear of guns as poisonous, infectious, or immoral objects, as pathogens. These men did not think of firearms in the way gun-control advocates do now. Their perspective was more plainly masculine and militant. At the same time, it is also clear that the Founding Fathers lived in a young nation where unwritten gun-control laws were at work. Madison and Jefferson equated *freedom* with *regulation*, just as George Washington equated "true liberty" with duty. A well *regulated* militia, being necessary to the security of a *free* state. . . . What's more, they did not grant a universal right to "self-defense." Reviewing eighteenth-century debates about the Bill of Rights, the legal scholar David Williams found that "the references to a popular right of resistance are countless; in contrast, the references to a popular right to arms for self-defense are quite rare." It is clear that Thomas

Jefferson, a sterling representative of the people as defined then, would have expected to defend himself and his own extensive property with firearms. But he would not have been ready to grant his slaves, male and (more tellingly) female, the right to bear arms for their own self-defense . . . against him, for instance.

> *"We the People of the United States speak the same language as Thomas Jefferson . . . with some difficulty."*

In the late nineteenth and twentieth centuries, the Supreme Court has interpreted the Second Amendment with some consistency by concluding that the American right to keep and bear arms is inextricably linked to a stated purpose—the establishment of a militia to defend the freedom of the state—and this right is empty when divorced from that purpose. A landmark case, *United States v. Miller*, was decided in 1939, after a citizen challenged the National Firearms Act of 1934 prohibiting possession of sawed-off shotguns. In their 1939 ruling, members of the Court judged that the purpose of the Second Amendment was "to assure the continuation and render possible the effectiveness of (militia) forces." The Court said it found no evidence to show that "possession of use of a [sawed-off shotgun] has some reasonable relationship to the preservation or efficiency of a well-regulated militia." But at the same time the justices acknowledged that in the eighteenth century, when the Constitution and the Bill of Rights were written, the militia included "all males physically capable of acting in concert for the common defense" and agreed that "when called for service, these men were expected to appear bearing arms supplied by themselves." Interpreted in this way, the Second Amendment not only accepts, but condones, the existence of a substantial arsenal of privately owned weapons. But the brief amendment does not specify which styles of weapons meet the criteria as firearms appropriate to be used for the common defense (only nonrepeating guns, flintlocks, and pistols would have been available at the time), nor does it make clear whether citizens who would be unlikely to act for the common defense, that is, reprobates and British sympathizers and their ilk, could be stripped of their weapons. At last, it does not make clear whether the public purpose described in the amendment could be used to regulate private ownership of firearms.

A Complicated Document

Viewed from these many angles, the Second Amendment shows itself to be a problematic document for the eighteenth century and a perplexing document for the late twentieth century. Some critics, notably feminist critics, have argued that it ought to be scrapped. One such author, Wendy Brown, writing in the *Yale Law Journal*, contended the Founding Fathers' "republican intellectual tradition includes a militarism, elitism and machismo that is past due for thoughtful critique and reworking." Even the scholar David Williams, who generally defends the republican tradition, concluded: "The absence of a universal militia is now severe and chronic, and self-deception about its existence has become impossible. . . . As a result, for judges trying to interpret the Second Amendment, republicanism suggests that the Amendment, as worded, is meaningless." Alert to feminist criticism, he acknowledged that the Founding Fathers' eloquence was powered by age-old masculine enthusiasms:

> Republicans' use of metaphors of masculinity to describe militia members, and the centrality of guns, danger, physicality and male-bonding themes in recollections of militia service suggest that, for many, the militia may have offered rich emotional rewards for the same reasons that hunting trips and team sports do.

Yet the Second Amendment remains in the Constitution, and it appears to have been written by men who valued the people's right to keep their own firearms. The legal scholar Sanford Levinson, a self-described "card-carrying member of the ACLU [American Civil Liberties Union]," has studied the Second Amendment and concluded that the Founding Fathers did mean to insure that law-abiding individual citizens would have the right to own and keep firearms untroubled by the state, for they recognized the people as an arm of government. He says: "Arguments on behalf of a 'strong' Second Amendment are stronger than many of us might wish were the case." He moves on to consider the core reason for liberal opposition to the Second Amendment, based on a calculation and measurement of gun deaths in the United States: "It appears almost crazy to protect as a constitutional right something that so clearly results in extraordinary social costs." But Levinson wonders if those who would happily discard the Second Amendment have looked hard enough at contemporary examples of people effectively resisting—or failing to resist—a massively armed state. He cites the situations in Northern Ireland and Palestinian territories occupied by Israel, "where the sophisticated weaponry of Great Britain and Israel have proved almost totally beside the point . . ." and mentions Tiananmen Square. His conclusion: "A state facing a totally disarmed population is in a far better position, for good or ill, to suppress popular demonstrations and uprisings than one that must calculate the possibilities of its soldiers and officials being injured or killed."

This ongoing analysis of the very brief Second Amendment—and of the much longer Constitution to the United States—illuminates how history *works*. Not only do the words and actions of our forebears continue to influence us in significant ways, but our own changing lives alter our perceptions of our forebears, so that even dead men and women may be given new voices through historical studies, through efforts to rediscover individuals who had been neglected and forgotten, or to reassess individuals who previously had been revered without question as national heroes. In this way we begin to hear what our predecessors have to say to us. Again, when we try to understand the meanings of these familiar, resounding texts, we must take into account not only what they signified to the original authors and their audiences, but how their meanings have changed over time as they have been newly interpreted, again and again, in an effort to make them fit a growing, protean nation of people. Our attempts to grapple with these inherited texts, to guard and to adapt them, make history.

We the People of the United States speak the same language as Thomas Jefferson . . . with some difficulty. Our modern cities would shock him, as a blood-spattered eighteenth-century surgeon's theater would shock us, but time-travel visitors from both centuries would recognize elemental American traits in the people they encountered. We are occupied with many of the same political questions: How can order be maintained in a democratic republic when such a wide range of people have been invited to share in the power of the state? Is it possible to educate citizens in virtue so that order can be maintained by agreement, by cooperation, and not by coercion? How can the majority of the people be prevented from dealing unjustly with a misfit minority? Which is the more trustworthy body, a collection of distant federal representatives who may be better able to judge national issues impartially, or a collection of local, states' representatives who understand the territory? This is all our heritage—a markedly masculine, thoughtful, democratic heritage. It is always necessary to sort out and refine it, for The Enfranchised People continues to expand to include those who were "Not-People" just yesterday. Which of the Founding Fathers' gifts will we keep, discard, or alter? We debate to decide that question.

The Second Amendment Allows for Gun Control Regulations

by Charles L. Blek Jr.

About the author: *Charles L. Blek Jr. is an attorney and the chairman of the Million Mom March Orange County, California, chapter.*

For too long, our elected officials have hidden behind the phrase "our Second Amendment rights" in order to defend the status quo with regard to guns. Guns are not the root cause of violence; but their widespread usage dramatically increases the lethality of the violence. The news channels overflow with the tragedies: Springfield, Oregon; Littleton, Colorado; Granada Hills, California; poor, inner city communities across the nation, too numerous to mention, and on and on!

Clearly, these issues must be addressed. We must challenge and move beyond the mistaken belief that creating responsible gun laws in some manner offends our constitutional rights.

Misinterpretation of the Second Amendment

The Second Amendment reads, "A well regulated Militia being necessary to the security of a free state, the right of the people to keep and bear arms shall not be infringed." In *United States v. Miller*, 307 U.S. 174 (1939), the Supreme Court discusses the purpose and the limit of the Second Amendment and tells us that the "obvious purpose" of the Amendment was "to assure the continuation and render possible the effectiveness" of our state militia forces (our present day National Guard). The right to bear arms was not extended to each and every individual, but rather was expressly limited to maintaining effective state militia.

The National Rifle Association's (NRA) continuous omission of the "well-regulated militia" language in its literature speaks volumes. It even prompted former U.S. Supreme Court Chief Justice Warren Burger to comment:

Charles L. Blek Jr., "Our Second Amendment," *Human Rights*, vol. 26, Fall 1999, pp. 3–4. Copyright © 1999 by the American Bar Association. All rights reserved. Reproduced by permission.

It's the simplest thing: a well-regulated militia. If the militia—which is what we now call the National Guard—essentially has to be well-regulated, in heaven's name why shouldn't we regulate 14-, 15-, and 16-year old kids having handguns or hoodlums having machine guns? I was raised on a farm, and we had guns around the house all the time. So I'm not against guns, but the National Rifle Association has done one of the most amazing jobs of misrepresenting and misleading the public. (*USA Today*, December 16, 1991.)

The NRA uses our First Amendment right of freedom of speech to repeat their misinformed rhetoric. In comparing First and Second Amendment rights that we all recognize that freedom of speech, as broadly as it is interpreted, still has limitations. For example, we are not allowed to yell "fire" in a crowded theater when none exists. However, if we are to believe the NRA, the Second Amendment grants an unconditional right to individuals to possess arms. The NRA's questionable analysis prompted Erwin N. Griswold, former dean of Harvard Law School who served as U.S. Solicitor General to comment:

> . . . to assert that the Constitution is a barrier to reasonable gun laws, in the face of the unanimous judgment of the federal courts to the contrary, exceeds the limits of principled advocacy. It is time for the NRA and its followers in Congress to stop trying to twist the Second Amendment from a reasoned (if antiquated) empowerment for a militia to a bulletproof personal right for anyone to wield deadly weaponry beyond legislative control. (*Washington Post*, November 4, 1990.)

History tells us that the Second Amendment is based on the colonist's fear of the military forces sent by [England's] King George III to compel obedience to cruel and burdensome laws and taxes. Federalist James Madison drafted a Bill of Rights for presentation at the first Congress. His draft of the Second Amendment was ultimately restructured into its present form in order to place greater emphasis on the militia purpose in dealing with the right to keep and bear arms. Ironically, the

> *"The Second Amendment does **not** guarantee any individual the unconditional right to own a handgun."*

New Hampshire convention suggested far broader language—that being: "Congress shall never disarm any citizen unless such as are or have been in actual rebellion." It is indeed significant that our first Congress rejected this broad language in order to adopt the present version with its more restrictive language.

Not an Unrestricted Right

Our federal appellate courts, in interpreting the application of our Second Amendment, have created a well-settled principle of law—that the Second Amendment does *not* guarantee any individual the unconditional right to own a handgun or to bear arms. Beginning with the decision in *United States v. Miller*, the court held that a firearms statute is unconstitutional only if it adversely affects a state's ability to maintain a militia. Numerous other cases uphold laws that regulate private ownership of firearms, such as *Eckert v. City of Philadelphia*, 695 F.2d 261 (7th Cir. 1982) ("The right to keep and bear arms is not a right given by the United States Constitution"); *Stevens v. United States*, 440 F.2d 144 (6th Cir. 1971) ("There can be no serious claim to any express constitutional right of an individual to possess a firearm"); and *Quilici v. The Village of Morton Grove*, 477 F.2d 610 (3rd Cir. 1973), wherein the NRA attempted to challenge a handgun ban, and the U.S. Supreme Court, by refusing to hear the case, allowed a lower appellate court ruling to stand that stated "there is no individual right to keep and bear arms under the Second Amendment."

> *"The Second Amendment is completely compatible with responsible gun laws."*

The appellate courts agree—the Second Amendment is completely compatible with responsible gun laws affecting the private possession of firearms. The logic involved in these cases is clear and consistent; however, the NRA attempts to distort the true significance and meaning of the Second Amendment. Fortunately, in California, we need look no further than to a court case that arose in 1996 involving the City of West Hollywood and the National Rifle Association/California Rifle and Pistol Association for a local case that upholds the true meaning of the Second Amendment. (See *California Rifle and Pistol Ass'n, Inc. v. City of West Hollywood*, 66 Cal. App. 4th 1302 [1998].)

The City of West Hollywood was the first city in California to create a local ordinance specifically banning the sale of Saturday Night Special handguns. The ordinance created certain guidelines describing what constituted a Saturday Night Special. Based on these guidelines, the city developed a list setting forth specific models of handguns that could no longer be sold within its city limits. If we are to believe the NRA's rhetoric, then this ordinance would easily be set aside and voided by a Second Amendment challenge.

The California Rifle and Pistol Association (CRPA) initiated a lawsuit against the City of West Hollywood requesting the court to find that the city's ordinance was void because: 1) the State of California had pre-empted this legislative area; 2) the local ordinance was simply a duplicate of current state criminal statutes; 3) the local ordinance violated our First Amendment commercial free speech rights; 4) the local ordinance violated the due process clause; and 5) the local ordinance violated the equal protection clause.

Each of these theories was thrown out of court without even reaching trial. The city presented a motion for summary judgment, which was successful. On appeal, the trial judge's decision to dismiss was upheld. . . . The California Supreme Court issued an order declining to review the court of appeals decision. Accordingly, the decision is now final and binding on all lower California courts.

Interestingly, but not surprisingly, the pro-gun lobby did not raise the Second Amendment in their lawsuit against the City of West Hollywood. Their lawyers know that the Second Amendment is not applicable in court; however, this well-funded special interest group continues to argue otherwise and we, the general public, continue to be manipulated.

The Damage Caused by Gun Violence

We must not allow the NRA's distortion of the Second Amendment to distract us from the health and safety risks associated with gun violence. We experience tragedy upon inexcusable tragedy, but fail to recognize firearms as the lethal consumer products that they are. Unfortunately, there are no federal agencies to which we can turn for regulation of the gun industry. The Bureau of Alcohol, Tobacco, and Firearms has no warrant to regulate firearm safety and is not empowered to protect us from the dangers of firearm use. The Consumer Product Safety Commission, the agency charged with overseeing the use and manufacture of most household products, is specifically *prohibited* from regulating firearms in any way. Therefore, we must regulate through legislation.

It is amazing that although we readily acknowledge that safety measures like automobile seatbelts save lives, we are unable or unwilling to connect this same philosophy with the handgun. We all understand that an automobile not only affects the driver but all who are within close proximity of the car. The same is true of a handgun. Therefore, we should no longer allow any regulatory exceptions when it comes to these weapons.

When our policymakers are allowed to misuse the Second Amendment as a shield against supporting responsible gun policy, what are the results? Well, the result is a 15-year old armed with a 50-round magazine, opening fire at his Oregon high school, shooting off the entire magazine in less than one minute in the crowded school cafeteria, and killing four and injuring twenty. Simple math tells us if, at the very least, we had laws limiting the capacity of magazines to ten rounds or less that it would have been physically impossible for more than twenty people to have been injured or killed during his rampage. We now know that the two young men responsible for the carnage in Littleton, Colorado,[1] had no difficulty obtaining the high-capacity assault weapons that were used in their rampage.

A few weeks after the Littleton tragedy, I had an opportunity to talk with Tom Mauser, the father of Daniel Mauser, one of the victims in the Littleton shootings. Tom described what happened to his son: "Daniel was in the school library during the lunch period and was confronted with a Tek DC9 semi-automatic assault weapon with a 30-round magazine. The assault weapon was pointed into Daniel's face and then exploded into action."

When will we say "Enough?" We must focus on policies that will reduce the lethality of gun violence rather than continuously lament its deadly results.

---

1. Two teenagers killed thirteen people and then committed suicide at their high school in April 1999.

The Founding Fathers and Supreme Court Do Not Support the Individual Right to Bear Arms

by the Violence Policy Center

About the author: *The Violence Policy Center is an educational foundation that conducts research on gun violence.*

On May 17, 2001, Attorney General John Ashcroft shook the foundation of the U.S. Justice Department's enforcement of federal gun laws, writing to National Rifle Association (NRA) chief lobbyist James Jay Baker on official Department of Justice stationery to proclaim a 180-degree shift in the Department's position regarding the Second Amendment to the U.S. Constitution. The timing of Attorney General Ashcroft's letter coincided with the NRA's annual meeting of members, where Baker touted the letter as evidence that "[i]n John Ashcroft, we have an Attorney General who agrees with us." In his letter, . . . Attorney General Ashcroft detailed a position on the Second Amendment—interpreting it to explicitly protect an individual right to privately possess firearms—that directly conflicts with longstanding legal precedent, historical evidence, and established policy of the Department of Justice. By seeking to elevate firearms ownership to the status of a fundamental constitutional right, Attorney General Ashcroft has placed his NRA membership before his responsibility as the nation's chief law enforcement officer, jeopardizing the Department's ability to vigorously enforce this nation's gun laws and keep guns out of the hands of felons, fugitives, stalkers, and other prohibited persons.

The Violence Policy Center (VPC) was the first gun control organization to obtain a copy of the Ashcroft letter, which was made available at the NRA's annual meeting. . . .

Deconstructing Ashcroft's Assertions

Attorney General Ashcroft: "This view of the [Second Amendment] comports with the all but unanimous understanding of the Founding Fathers. . . ."

Ashcroft Deconstructed: Attorney General Ashcroft identifies [three] sources as evidence of the "all but unanimous" position regarding the right to keep and bear arms that he ascribes to the Founding Fathers. However, this conclusion rests upon an extremely creative and liberal reading of the writings that he cites. Also, it is mystifying how Attorney General Ashcroft can claim that these statements, even if they did support his assertions in substance (which they do not), reflect the understanding of the Founders regarding the Second Amendment. Not one of the statements he cites was made in connection with the debates over the ratification of the Bill of Rights and the Second Amendment in 1791. Rather,

> *"Attorney General [John] Ashcroft has placed his [National Rifle Association] membership before his responsibility as the nation's chief law enforcement officer."*

every single statement was made at least two years earlier—and in one case at least 15 years earlier—in connection with either the ratification debate on the Federal Constitution or a state constitution.

Ashcroft cites *Federalist 46*, written by James Madison, which discusses the relative powers of the federal and state governments, not individual rights. It addresses the subject of an armed citizenry only in conjunction with the possible need to protect the political power of the states from the reach of the federal government. *Federalist 46* states:

> Let a regular army, fully equal to the resources of the country be formed; and let it be entirely at the devotion of the Federal Government; still it would not be going too far to say, that the State Governments with the people on their side would be able to repel the danger. The highest number to which, according to the best computation, a standing army can be carried in any country, does not exceed one hundredth part of the whole number of souls, or one twenty-fifth part of the number able to bear arms. This proportion would not yield in the United States an army of more than twenty-five or thirty thousand men. To these would be opposed a militia amounting to near half a million citizens with arms in their hands, officered by men chosen from among themselves, fighting for their common liberties, and united and conducted by governments possessing their affections and confidence. It may well be doubted whether a militia thus circumstanced could ever be conquered by such a proportion of regular troops. Those who are best acquainted with the late successful resistance of this country against the British arms will be most inclined to deny the possibility of it. Besides the advantage of being armed, which the Americans possess over

the people of almost every other nation, the existence of subordinate governments to which the people are attached, and by which the militia officers are
appointed, forms a barrier against enterprizes of ambition, more insurmountable than any which a simple government of any form can admit of.

According to Madison, the people are to be armed so that they can form a
state-regulated militia in order to defend the political powers enjoyed by the
state. *Federalist 46* is completely silent on whether the people should have the
right to own weapons for individual self-protection, whether they should be
able to conceal weapons on their person, or even whether they should be permitted to store them in their homes.

The essay continues, stating that the right to bear arms exists in relation to
service in a militia that is formed to represent the will of local governments.
According to *Federalist 46:*

> Notwithstanding the military establishments in the several kingdoms in Eu-
> rope, which are carried as far as the public resources will bear, the govern-
> ments are afraid to trust the people with arms. And it is not certain that with
> this aid alone, they would not be able to shake off their yokes. But were the
> people to possess the additional advantages of local governments chosen by
> themselves, who could collect the national will, and direct the national force;
> and of officers appointed out of the militia, it may be affirmed with the great-
> est assurance, that the throne of every tyranny in Europe would be speedily
> overturned, in spite of the legions which surround it.

Arming and training the people to defend their government through a disci-
plined militia cannot be accomplished solely by a militia that is unconnected to
any local government entity. Nowhere does this essay discuss arming people for
individual self-defense: Madison limits his remarks to the discussion of arming
people so that they may defend the governments of their respective states.

Alexander Hamilton and Militias

Attorney General Ashcroft also cites *Federalist 29*, which was penned by
Alexander Hamilton. Like *Federalist 46*, this essay does not discuss the right to
bear arms for individual self-protection. Instead, Federalist 29 offers a justifica-
tion for the existence and regulation of state militias, as provided for in the
Constitution. *Federalist 29* is wholly an argument regarding the necessity and
feasibility of disciplining the militia to become a useful military force. The general argument of *Federalist 29* is summarized by Hamilton:

> It requires no skill in the science of war to discern that uniformity in the orga-
> nization and discipline of the militia would be attended with the most benefi-
> cial effects, whenever they were called into the service for the public defense.
> It would enable them to discharge the duties of the camp and of the field with
> mutual intelligence and concert; an advantage of peculiar moment in the oper-
> ations of the army: And it would fit them much sooner to acquire the degree of
> proficiency in military functions, which would be essential to their usefulness.

This desirable uniformity can only be accomplished by confiding the regulation of the militia to the direction of the national authority. It is therefore with the most evident propriety that the plan of the Convention proposes to empower the union "to provide for organizing, arming and disciplining the militia, and for governing such part of them as may be employed in the service of the United States, reserving to the states respectively the appointment of the officers and the authority of training the militia according to the discipline prescribed by Congress."

Thus, the right of a citizen to be part of the militia carries with it substantial responsibility. In order to bear arms in the militia, a citizen must submit to rigorous military training and discipline, as required by Congress. Hamilton does suggest in *Federalist 29* that the militia should be formed from the general population, which would extend his earlier reasoning to mean that large parts of the population should undergo strict training in military tactics. *Federalist 29*'s vision of the bearing of arms arose wholly within the context of militia membership, carrying with it responsibilities and restrictions. If anything, this essay highlights the importance of the first clause of the Second Amendment—which is often omitted by proponents of the individual-rights view—making it determinative in understanding the overall meaning and purpose of the provision. To cite *Federalist 29* as support for the proposition that the Founding Fathers endorsed an individual right to bear arms demonstrates a wholesale misinterpretation and distortion of the document.

A Collective Right

After misrepresenting Madison and Hamilton, Attorney General Ashcroft proceeds to quote a line from Thomas Jefferson: "No freeman shall ever be debarred the use of arms." Unlike the *Federalist Papers*, which were written following the drafting of the Constitution in 1787 to support the document's ratification, Jefferson's statement was written during consideration of the proposed constitution for the Commonwealth of Virginia. It was not written in connection with the U.S. Constitution and Bill of Rights. Moreover, Jefferson unveiled it as early as 1776, 15 years before the ratification of the Bill of Rights.

> **"Federalist 46** *is completely silent on whether the people should have the right to own weapons for individual self-protection."*

Jefferson's seemingly broad statement suggests that the Framers knew how to describe the right to bear arms in more expansive terms if they had wanted to. They did not choose to. The Federalist Papers reinforce the view that the contemporaneous thinking around the Constitution envisioned a collective right to bear arms that was related exclusively to the maintenance of state militias as permitted by Congress, and that the Second Amendment is the product of that thinking. . . .

Quoting Out of Context

Thus, the actual texts that Attorney General Ashcroft cites fail to support his claim that the Founding Fathers had an "all but unanimous" view mirroring his own. In addition, there are other texts that further undermine his claim. For example, in contrast with documents cited by Ashcroft, Hamilton addressed private possession of arms in a report on how duties should be calculated for firearms:

> There appears to be an improvidence, in leaving these essential instruments of national defence to the casual speculations of individual adventure; a resource which can less be relied upon, in this case than in most others; the articles in question not being objects of ordinary and indispensable private consumption or use.

Such language from Hamilton, downplaying the importance of privately held arms, fails to appear in Attorney General Ashcroft's letter. Instead, the Attorney General quotes language regarding armed militias out of context while declining to acknowledge statements by the Founding Fathers that would refute his views.

Inaccurate Supreme Court Interpretations

Attorney General Ashcroft: "In early decisions, the United States Supreme Court routinely indicated that the right protected by the Second Amendment applied to individuals."

Ashcroft Deconstructed: Not one of the cases cited by the Attorney General establishes that the Second Amendment protects an individual right of the kind he advocates—i.e., the possession of guns absent any connection to a state militia.

The first case cited by Attorney General Ashcroft, *Logan v. United States*, defines the scope of a federal prisoner's constitutional right to be protected from physical violence while in the custody of the United States Marshal. In fact, the page Attorney General Ashcroft cites is not actually a page from the Court's opinion. It is a page from the lengthy summary that appears before the beginning of the Court's opinion in Logan, and it contains no discussion of the Second Amendment. It is quite possible that the Attorney General intended to cite text appearing 10 pages later, where the Court referred to a discussion of the first two amendments in an earlier case:

> 1st. It was held that the First Amendment of the Constitution, by which it was ordained that Congress should make no law abridging the right of the people peaceably to assemble and to petition the government for a redress of grievances, did not grant to the people the right peaceably to assemble for lawful purposes, but recognized that right as already existing, and did not guarantee its continuance except as against acts of Congress; and therefore the general right was not a right secured by the Constitution of the United States. But the court added: "The right of the people peaceably to assemble for the purposes of petitioning Congress for a redress of grievances, or for anything else connected with the powers or the duties of the national government, is an attribute of the national citizenship, and, as such, under the protection of, and

guaranteed by, the United States. The very idea of a government, republican in form, implies a right on the part of its citizens to meet peaceably for consultation in respect to public affairs and to petition for a redress of grievances. If it had been alleged in these counts that the object of the defendants was to prevent a meeting for such a purpose, the case would have been within the statute, and within the scope of the sovereignty of the United States."

2d. It was held that the Second Amendment of the Constitution, declaring that "the right of the people to keep and bear arms shall not be infringed," was equally limited in its scope.

The extent of this case's treatment of the Second Amendment is limited to a restatement of the latter portion of that amendment's text, as part of a series of examples of cases interpreting various provisions in the Bill of Rights that constrain government action in some fashion. At the same time, however, the federal government does not have an affirmative obligation to enforce these constitutional provisions unless additional authority exists for it to do so. Logan notes that this limitation applies to the Second Amendment and does not otherwise define the scope of the amendment, other than to state that the right "was equally limited in its scope."

> *"Not one of the cases cited by the Attorney General establishes that the Second Amendment protects an individual right of the kind he advocates."*

Miller v. Texas

The next case Attorney General Ashcroft cites, *Miller v. Texas*—not to be confused with *United States v. Miller*—does address the Second Amendment, but not in a way that supports Ashcroft's view. In that case, the defendant unsuccessfully challenged a law that prohibited persons from carrying weapons. The Court rejected the Second Amendment challenge on the grounds that the provision does not apply against the states through the Fourteenth Amendment:

> Without, however, expressing a decided opinion upon the invalidity of the writ as it now stands, we think there is no Federal question properly presented by the record in this case, and that the writ of error must be dismissed upon that ground. The record exhibits nothing of what took place in the court of original jurisdiction, and begins with the assignment of errors in the Court of Criminal Appeals. In this assignment no claim was made of any ruling of the court below adverse to any constitutional right claimed by the defendant, nor does any such appear in the opinion of the court, which deals only with certain alleged errors relating to the impanelling of the jury, the denial of a continuance, the admission of certain testimony, and certain exceptions taken to the charge of the court. In his motion for a rehearing, however, defendant claimed that the law of the State of Texas forbidding the carrying of weapons and authorizing the arrest without warrant of any person violating such law, under which cer-

tain questions arose upon the trial of the case, was in conflict with the Second and Fourth Amendments to the Constitution of the United States, one of which provides that the right of the people to keep and bear arms shall not be infringed, and the other of which protects the people against unreasonable searches and seizures. We have examined the record in vain, however, to find where the defendant was denied the benefit of any of these provisions. . . .

The Court only discussed the language of the Second Amendment to show how it may be constitutionally limited and to demonstrate how a prohibition on firearm possession outside the home would be constitutional.

Attorney General Ashcroft also relies on *Robertson v. Baldwin*, a decision which reaffirms *Miller v. Texas*. In *Robertson*, several sailors, having been convicted of a crime, were sent back to their ship and forced to work against their will. The sailors claimed their rights under the Fifth and Thirteenth Amendments were infringed. The opinion refers to the Second Amendment to make the point that there are limitations on the scope of the rights secured by the Bill of Rights:

> The law is perfectly well settled that the first ten amendments to the Constitution, commonly known as the Bill of Rights, were not intended to lay down any novel principles of government, but simply embody certain guarantees and immunities which we had inherited from our English ancestors, and which had from time immemorial been subject to certain well-recognized exceptions arising from the necessity of the case. In incorporating these principles into the fundamental law there was no intention of disregarding the exceptions, which continued to be recognized as if they had been formally expressed. Thus . . . the right of the people to keep and bear arms (art. 2) is not infringed by laws prohibiting the carrying of concealed weapons.

Not a Private Right

As in *Logan*, the Court discusses the Second Amendment without specifying what the right actually is, beyond a recitation of a portion of the amendment's language. And as in *Miller v. Texas*, the Court points out how the right secured by the Second Amendment constitutionally may be limited. This case is useful primarily in the support that it lends to gun control legislation, and does not elucidate the nature of the actual right which the Second Amendment secures.

> *"The [Supreme] Court points out how the right secured by the Second Amendment constitutionally may be limited."*

The final case cited by Attorney General Ashcroft is *Maxwell v. Dow*. As in *Miller v. Texas*, the Court refused to apply the Second Amendment against the states through the Fourteenth Amendment:

> In *Presser v. Illinois*, 116 U.S. 252 [1886], it was held that the Second Amendment to the Constitution, in regard to the right of the people to bear

arms, is a limitation only on the power of Congress and the National Government, and not of the States. It was therein said, however, that as all citizens capable of bearing arms constitute the reserved military force of the National Government, the States could not prohibit the people from keeping and bearing arms, so as to deprive the United States of their rightful resource for maintaining the public security, and disable the people from performing their duty to the General Government.

Maxwell, which dealt primarily with the right to a trial by jury, interpreted the right to bear arms with the end of maintaining an effective military. Since citizens have a duty to protect their government, the right to keep and bear arms should not be infringed so as to limit their ability to fulfill that duty. As in the other cases, *Maxwell* does not provide any support for Attorney General Ashcroft's claim that the Supreme Court recognized a private right to bear arms independent of service in a militia. The right which this opinion discusses as constitutionally protected is the same one which *United States v. Miller* and The Federalist Papers indicate, and nothing more—namely, the limited right to keep and bear arms in a militia in the service of the government.

Giving Individuals the Right to Bear Arms Has a Negative Effect on Society

by Robin West

About the author: *Robin West is an author and law professor.*

The NRA (National Rifle Association), right-wing militias, gun sellers, owners, their lawyers, and assorted political pundits all now quite routinely argue, and with growing success, that every individual has a constitutional right to own guns under the Second Amendment. This argument, which [in the late 1980s] was regarded as the rantings of the lunatic fringe, is now widely accepted not only by gun owners and advocates but also by a handful of respected liberal constitutional scholars and, more ominously, by at least one federal district court judge.

The claim has serious consequences. First of all, simply as a matter of law, were the courts ever to accept the proposition that an individual has a constitutionally protected right, under the Second Amendment, to possess firearms (as a lower federal district court in Texas has), such a right could invalidate even limited gun control legislation. Like all rights, the "right to bear arms," if it exists, expresses a constitutional commitment to protect the ownership of guns regardless of the severity of social consequences or costs: rights exist, fundamentally, to protect the rights holder against precisely the sort of emotional and political intensity occasioned by events like [the school shooting at Columbine High School].

Although rights are never absolute, nevertheless it is the nature of a constitutional right to "trump" laws that unduly infringe upon it, and to do so even if that law represents perfectly sound policy desired by solid majorities. In other words, if the right to own guns is pitted against nothing but a policy in favor of laws that control gun ownership, the policy will very likely lose.

Chapter 3

The Costs of Gun Rights

But there is a deeper, less visible cost exacted by this new controversial right, and it is a cost borne directly by our politics of meaning. Asserted constitutional rights—even contested rights—create as well as rest on a cross-generational social consensus about the meaning of civic and individual life, a consensus that runs so deep that it trumps conflicting democratic judgments of policy. A claim that a right exists, then, essentially claims the existence of such a meaning, and such a consensus. The "right to bear arms" is no different. When gun advocates assert a right to own guns, and the courts, the pundits, scholars, and the public listen, something profound has occurred: gun ownership has been invested with constitutional authority, and hence constitutional meaning. The gun owner becomes, by virtue of the claimed constitutional right, the embodiment of a mythic-constitutional vision of our nature, ourselves, our community, and our state. We must protect his rights, because he has become, in essence, a symbol; he represents a way of being in the world—lone, idiosyncratic, and self-sufficient, defiantly bucking the ties of community and state control that in our wisest and longest vision of ourselves, we can and should ideally be. The gun owner becomes an ideal, and an ideal which is constitutional. Her defiance defines us. Even if their legal claim ultimately fails, in other words, the NRA's depiction of our

> *"We cannot forge loving connections between people . . . when we simultaneously, through our shared constitution, valorize the gun owner."*

nature, and of what it means to be an American, remains, with respect to guns and gun ownership, the only constitutional story being told.

But is the NRA's the only constitutional story that should be told, or that could be told? Of course, one can without difficulty find, in American mythology and constitutional history both, support for the social vision implied by the community of gun advocates now urging a Second Amendment right to bear arms; one can find in our histories plenty of support for the proposition that we are, fundamentally, a loose confederation of borderline, anti-social, and paranoid individuals, united only in our shared perpetual rage against the demands of community life, each and all of us bent on protecting our individual rights against the smothering embrace of social obligation. Indeed, as "rights critics" have argued over the past thirty years, it is fair to say that this is only a slight exaggeration of the hyper-individualistic constitutional rhetoric that monotonously repeats itself in volumes of utterly mainstream constitutional case law, scholarship, and folklore, and it is for precisely that reason that they urge us to abandon talk of individuating rights altogether, if we wish to create a world of connection. Rights talk, however, is not the only mythology, the only meaning, or the only social history compatible with our constitutional language and history. There are other stories to be told as well, and other constitutional visions to paint. Rather than abandon rights, rights-talk, and the constitution to the monopolistic rhetorical powers of free marketeers, rugged individuals, and gun zealots, we should be telling those other stories and filling in the details of the visions they suggest. The gun debate is an opportunity to do so.

Rights stem, minimally, from our constitutional history, as read through the lens of our highest political ideals, and as informed by our best understanding of our human and social nature. All three sources strongly imply the existence, not of an individual right to bear arms, but, to the contrary, of a right to mutual disarmament. First, as an historical matter, the Reconstruction amendments in general, and the Fourteenth Amendment's Equal Protection Clause in particular, were written in part to ensure that all citizens (not just whites) received the state's protection against private acts of violence. The Amendments' framers understood that unless the freed slaves were granted a right to enjoy this "first duty of government"—the duty to protect citizens against violence—the promise of equality and liberty, given the reality of persecution, threats, and lynchings, would remain illusory. Second, that we have such a right to protection against violence flows directly from the liberal, Hobbesian, and Lockean political ideals[1] that underlie our constitutional framework. The Leviathan[2] exists, so said Hobbes, to protect us against the violence of others, in exchange for our agreement to give up "self help" and enter civil society. A right to that protection, then, and to the private disarmament required to achieve it, is at the very heart of even a "minimalist" understanding of the liberal state.

The Need to Disarm

But most important, a right to disarmament, and the gun control legislation that would require it, would affirm something true and important about both our individual and our civic nature. We cannot forge loving connections between people, or reward ecological and spiritual sensitivity, when we simultaneously, through our shared constitution, valorize the gun owner and his "rights" and disparage the victim of gun violence. More to the point, we cannot ourselves connect with people, live in awe and wonder, or nourish our own spirit, when we live in fear of each other; many of us—disproportionately poor people and women and children—live with that fear daily. Fear destroys trust—it is its antithesis—and pervasive distrust destroys the spirit. As every battered woman, rape survivor, or harassed school child knows, one can neither spiritually grow nor form loving connections when one lives in fear of intimates, neighbors, or co-citizens: the inner self deadens, precisely so as to ward off attack. A right to the equal protection of the state against the lethal violence that triggers that

1. referring to the political philosophers Thomas Hobbes and John Locke   2. In Hobbes' book *Leviathan*, he argued in favor of government and society. The leaders of these societies are Leviathans, authority figures named for a biblical sea monster.

spirit-deadening fear, as well as the state's affirmative obligation—indeed, its "first duty"—to legislate in such a way as to control the flow of private weapons that threatens the right's enjoyment, can be readily derived from our constitutional sources. Rather than turn our backs on these constitutional sources of political and moral meaning—as left and progressive rights critics have urged us to do—we should embrace and seek to transform them.

Some Gun Control Regulations Are Unconstitutional

by Nelson Lund

About the author: *Nelson Lund is a law professor.*

Timothy Joe Emerson is a Texas physician who lawfully bought a pistol in 1997. About a year later, Emerson's wife filed for divorce and sought a temporary injunction containing 29 separate prohibitions, most of them aimed at protecting Mrs. Emerson's financial interests. The proposed order also prohibited various sorts of interference with the couple's child, and it forbade Emerson to threaten or injure his wife or to communicate with her in vulgar or indecent language.

At a hearing on whether to grant the injunction, the state divorce court judge explored the financial circumstances of the couple and decided on the amount of temporary child support Emerson should provide. In her testimony, Mrs. Emerson reported that her husband had threatened her new boyfriend but denied that Emerson had threatened her. The judge issued the injunction, but he made no findings that Emerson was likely to commit any of the 29 separate acts prohibited in the temporary restraining order, many of which were not alluded to in any way during the hearing.

Nothing in the story so far is unusual. It is apparently routine for Texas courts to issue such prophylactic restraining orders in divorce cases, without evidence that the acts prohibited in those orders would otherwise be likely to occur. The story became less commonplace when Mrs. Emerson subsequently accused her husband of brandishing the pistol, and federal prosecutors took up the case. A federal grand jury indicted Emerson in December 1998 for violating an obscure portion of the 1994 Violent Crime Control Act, which is better known for its prohibition of certain so-called assault weapons. The provision used against Emerson appears on its face to impose a ban on firearms possession by any person who is subject to a court order that prohibits him from using or threatening physical violence against an "intimate partner" or that partner's child.

The Initial Ruling

This was too much for Judge Sam R. Cummings, a federal trial judge in Texas, who [in 1999] declared the indictment unconstitutional. Cummings reasoned that if the federal statute had been triggered by a court order based on a finding of danger to Mrs. Emerson or her child, forbidding Mr. Emerson to own a gun might be a reasonable regulation. But because the prosecution was based on a boiler-plate order that was unsupported by any such finding, it violated Emerson's Second Amendment right to keep and bear arms.

Had this case concerned any other part of the Bill of Rights, Cummings's analysis would have bordered on the obvious. The law, for example, forbids us to libel other people. But this doesn't mean that anyone who has been officially told to refrain from breaking the libel laws can also be told to remain completely silent, or be barred from possessing a printing press. If it did, a legislature could simply outlaw speech, or printing presses, on the ground that this would help prevent libel. While this sort of sweeping prior restraint might be very effective in preventing libel, it would violate the First Amendment.

Judge Cummings thought that the same kind of analysis should apply to Emerson's case. The law forbids people to cause or threaten bodily injury to others. But how can people be deprived of their right to possess runs merely because they have been told to obey the law? If they could, it would seem to follow that Congress could choose to promote obedience to the laws against murder and assault by forbidding everyone to possess weapons. And the Second Amendment would then mean only that the right of the people to keep and bear arms shall not be infringed unless the government decides to infringe it.

Despite the obvious logic in Cummings's opinion, his decision has created a stir, and rightly so. The federal courts had never before invalidated any gun control statute for violating the Second Amendment. What's more, almost every court of appeals in the country has concluded that this part of the Bill of Rights means nothing at all, or so close to nothing that it might as well not exist.

Emerson in the Fifth Circuit

Cummings's decision, however, is not doomed to inevitable reversal. Unlike most lower courts, the Supreme Court has never decided to boot the Second Amendment out of the Constitution, and neither has the Fifth U.S. Circuit Court of Appeals (which covers Judge Cummings's northern Texas jurisdiction). Those two courts have decided only a handful of Second Amendment cases and always on narrow grounds. It is therefore possible that the long pattern of judicial hostility to the Second Amendment could soon be broken.

The Fifth Circuit heard oral arguments in the government's appeal of Cummings's decision on June 13, [2000]. The session featured a number of humorous exchanges, including comments by the judges about their own personal arsenals, and an embarrassing display of ignorance by the government's lawyer about the statutory definition of the term "militia." But the most promising aspect of the argument was how little interest the judges showed in joining the many other courts that have treated the Second Amendment as a kind of enemy alien within the Bill of Rights.

Though it is always dangerous to predict what courts will do on the basis of judges' questions at oral argument, the following possibilities seem most likely. The court may simply avoid the Second Amendment issue by holding that the 1994 Violent Crime provision exceeds congressional authority under the Supreme Court's recent federalism decisions. Another way of avoiding serious Second Amendment questions would be to dismiss the indictment of Emerson on the ground that the federal statute includes an implied limitation to cases where there has been a judicial finding of dangerousness to the "intimate partner" or child. But it is also possible that the Fifth Circuit will conclude Cummings was right, and that the statute violates the Second Amendment.

> *"Unlike most lower courts, the Supreme Court has never decided to boot the Second Amendment out of the Constitution."*

If the court goes down this last road, the *Emerson* case could be headed for the Supreme Court. And whether in this case or some other, the Supreme Court will eventually have to decide whether the Second Amendment is going to remain in the Constitution. It is therefore worth understanding why expunging it would require a level of sophistry and willfulness on a par with such disastrous instances of high court usurpation as *Dred Scott* and *Roe v. Wade.*[1]

Militia or Individuals

For much of the twentieth century, there were two schools of thought about the meaning of the Second Amendment. Virtually the entire legal establishment, from the professoriate to most appeals courts, asserted that it protects only the right of state governments to maintain military organizations like the National Guard. On the other hand, people who read English in the normal way thought that it protects the right of individual citizens to keep and bear arms.

If the framers of the Second Amendment had simply provided that "the right of the people to keep and bear arms shall not be infringed," even a lawyer would have trouble denying that it creates an individual right like the other "rights of the people" described in the Bill of Rights. But that's not what they did. Instead, they appended an explanatory introduction, so that the constitu-

---

1. In June 2002 the U.S. Supreme Court decided not to review the *Emerson* case, which had been appealed to the Court after the Fifth Circuit declined to rehear motions.

tional text says: "A well-regulated militia, being necessary to the security of a free state, the right of the people to keep and bear arms, shall not be infringed."

The introductory phrase, however, does not change the meaning of the operative clause, and the Second Amendment means exactly what it would have meant had the preface been omitted. To see why that's so, and also why such an explanatory preface makes perfect sense, one needs to grasp two interrelated arguments. The first is based on the text of the Second Amendment and its relationship with other clauses in the Constitution. The second focuses on the immediate political problem that the preface was meant to address.

Let's start with the text of the Second Amendment. The operative clause protects a "right of the people," which is exactly the same terminology used in the First Amendment and the Fourth Amendment. Those two provisions indubitably protect individual (not states') rights, and so does the Second Amendment.

Absent Words

What the introductory phrase tells us is that this individual right is protected, at least in part, because doing so will foster a well-regulated militia. Before asking how it can do that, it's worth emphasizing what the Second Amendment does *not* say.

It emphatically does not protect the right of the *militia* to keep and bear arms. The people and the militia were and are two very different entities. Nor does the Second Amendment say that the people's right to arms is *sufficient* to establish a well-regulated militia, or that a well-regulated militia is *sufficient* for the security of a free state.

Nor does the Second Amendment say that the right of the people to keep and bear arms is protected *only to the extent* that such a right fosters a well-regulated militia or the security of a free state.

In order to see why the introductory phrase cannot be interpreted as qualifying the right of the people to keep and bear arms, one need only consider the Patent and Copyright Clause, which is the Constitution's nearest grammatical cousin to the Second Amendment. That clause gives Congress the power "to promote the progress of science and useful arts, by securing for limited times to authors and inventors the exclusive right to their respective writings and discoveries."

Nobody thinks the prefatory language limits the reach of the granted power. It doesn't mean Congress must stop granting copyrights to racists or pornographers or Luddites, who are hardly promoting the progress of science. And yet the grammatical case for this interpretation would be much stronger than the legal establishment's reading of the Second Amendment's militia phrase as a limitation on the right to arms. Moreover, state constitutions from the founding period were littered with explanatory prefaces like the one in the Second Amendment, which were never construed to change the meaning of the operative clauses to which they were appended.

How, then, can the individual right to keep and bear arms contribute to fostering a well-regulated militia? To answer that question, we have to look at the original Constitution, which allocates responsibility for governing the militia. It tells us five things that are crucially important in understanding the Second Amendment.

Five Important Lessons

First, *the militia is not the army.* The Constitution has separate provisions for each and it never confuses or blends the two.

Second, *Congress is given almost plenary authority over the army and the militia alike.* The only powers reserved to the states are the rights to appoint militia officers and to train the militia according to rules prescribed by Congress.

Third, *the Constitution nowhere defines the militia.* There is abundant historical evidence that the founding generation saw a fundamental difference between armies (usually composed of professional soldiers) and the militia (consisting of civilians temporarily summoned to meet public emergencies). But there is also abundant evidence that the founding generation was acutely aware the militia could be converted into the functional equivalent of an army. There had been examples of this in England, and we have an example today in the National Guard.

Fourth, *the Constitution imposes no duties whatsoever on the federal government, either with respect to armies or with respect to the militia.* Congress is not required to organize the militia in any particular way, or to keep it well regulated, or indeed to do anything at all to secure its existence.

Fifth, *the Constitution expressly prohibits the states from keeping troops without the consent of Congress.*

Turning back to the Second Amendment with these facts in mind, it becomes apparent why the Second Amendment cannot possibly have been a states' rights amendment—meant to constitutionalize a right of *states* to keep up military organizations like the National Guard. That theory implies that the Second Amendment silently repealed or amended two separate provisions of the Constitution: the clause giving the federal government virtually complete authority over the militia, and the clause forbidding the states

> *"The Second Amendment forbids [the federal government] from disarming citizens under the pretense of regulating the militia."*

to keep troops without the consent of Congress. These provisions have allowed the federal government essentially to eliminate the state militias as independent military forces by turning them into adjuncts of the federal army through the National Guard system. Under the states' rights theory of the Second Amendment, this takeover of the National Guard would represent an unconstitutional usurpation of state power by Washington.

Congress Cannot Disarm Citizens

But of course the Second Amendment is not about states' rights, and the relationship between its introductory phrase and its operative clause turns out to be deceptively simple. A well-regulated militia is not one that is heavily regulated, but rather one that is not inappropriately regulated. Recall that the original Constitution gives Congress almost unlimited authority to regulate the militia. As the operative clause of the Second Amendment makes perfectly clear, its purpose is simply to forbid one kind of inappropriate regulation (among the infinite possible regulations) that Congress might be tempted to enact. What is that one kind of inappropriate regulation? *Disarming the citizenry from among whom any true militia must be constituted.*

Congress is permitted to do many things that harm the militia, and to omit many things that are necessary for a well-regulated militia. Congress may pervert the militia into the fictional equivalent of an army, or even deprive it completely of any meaningful existence. A lot of those things have in fact been done, and many members of the founding generation would have strongly disapproved. But the original Constitution allowed it, and the Second Amendment did not purport to interfere with congressional latitude to regulate the militia. The one and only thing the Second Amendment does is expressly forbid a particular, and particularly extravagant, extension of Congress's authority over the militia. Whatever the federal government does or fails to do about the militia, the Second Amendment forbids it from disarming citizens under the pretense of regulating the militia. . . .

Suggestions for the Courts

What the courts should do, starting with the *Emerson* case, is subject federal gun control laws to the same close scrutiny they apply to other statutes that are challenged under the Bill of Rights. That undertaking will leave room for many debates in which reasonable minds can differ, as is true with other provisions of the Bill of Rights. But anarchy will not descend upon the land.

Indeed, most existing federal regulations of gun ownership would probably survive such scrutiny because they are sufficiently well tailored to achieve sufficiently important government purposes. It is not constitutionally problematic, for instance, to limit the Second Amendment rights of exceptionally dangerous people, such as violent felons and adjudicated mental defectives.

Even the statute at issue in *Emerson* could be applied constitutionally in cases where a court has reasonably found that someone represents a real threat to the physical safety of his family. Just as a divorce court judge may forbid an abusive husband to continue subjecting his wife to hateful late-night telephone tirades, so a judge should be able to deprive a genuinely threatening man of the right to acquire convenient tools for murdering his wife.

But the *Emerson* case itself is different. An injunction was issued with no evidence that the defendant had ever threatened his wife, and no court had ever found that he was a danger to her. By its literal terms, the 1994 Violent Crime Control statute purports to impose gun controls on citizens like Emerson who have never been convicted of a crime and who have never been shown to be any more dangerous than anyone else. If these individuals can lose their Second Amendment rights merely because a divorce court judge has entered a routine order instructing them to obey the law, it becomes difficult to imagine that any civilian disarmament statute could violate the Constitution.

> *"The purpose of the Second Amendment is to protect the fundamental right of self-defense."*

The courts have no legitimate authority to adopt an "interpretation" of the Second Amendment that renders it nugatory. Nor should one suppose that this provision of the Constitution has lost its value because we lack the founding generation's intense fear of standing armies and federal oppression. The Second Amendment makes no sharp distinction between the use of guns to resist oppression by the government and their use to resist oppression from which the government fails to protect us.

An Amendment That Protects Citizens

The purpose of the Second Amendment is to protect the fundamental right of self-defense, and thereby to protect the interests of a free political community. For the Framers, those interests were at stake whether the threat took the form of a foreign invasion, a political coup, marauding Indians, or a simple highwayman. It was for this reason natural that the Constitution authorized the militia to be used "to execute the laws of the Union, suppress insurrections and repel invasions."

Even if one supposes that civilians will never need arms to resist political oppression, the Second Amendment will thus continue to serve an important constitutional purpose. The government has neither the obligation nor the ability to offer its citizens reliable protection from murder, rape, and robbery. The police almost always arrive at the scene of a crime well after the crime has been committed, and no one would want to have police officers stationed everywhere that crime might occur. These fundamental aspects of American society have *not* changed since the eighteenth century, and an armed citizenry continues to have great value both to those who choose to be armed and to their fellow citizens.

In fact, armed resistance to criminal violence is very common. It occurs on the order of two million times each year, and in most of these cases a mere display of the weapon scares off the attacker. Furthermore, armed resistance is much more often successful than passive acquiescence in preventing injuries to the victim, especially when a woman is the target of an attack.

An armed citizenry is also an extremely powerful *deterrent* to violent crime. Burglary rates of occupied dwellings, for example, are much lower in America than in England [where private gun ownership is banned]. Similarly, states adopting laws that allow civilians to carry concealed weapons have seen significant drops in violent crime rates. The huge number of crimes that are invisibly deterred by America's armed citizenry constitute an important private and public benefit. Congress has no more right to take away this benefit than it does to deprive us of the benefits of a free press or the free exercise of religion. It is true that these freedoms, like the right to arms, have costs as well as benefits. But it is also true that in all three cases the framers of our Constitution rightly calculated that the benefits outweigh the costs. It is time for the courts to stop substituting ill-considered policy preferences for the legally binding wisdom embodied in the Constitution.

The Supreme Court Supports the Individual Right to Bear Arms

by Dave Kopel

About the author: *Dave Kopel is an author and gun rights advocate.*

"A well regulated Militia, being necessary to the security of a free State, the right of the people to keep and bear Arms, shall not be infringed." The Second Amendment is only 31 words. But the meaning of those 31 words has been the subject of considerable debate.

There are four main interpretations of the Second Amendment. The Standard Model is that the right to bear arms belongs to individual American citizens. The states' rights view is that the right belongs to state governments, to control their National Guards. The collective view is that the right to bear arms belongs collectively to all the people, but in practice may be exercised only by the government—like collective property in a communist country. Another interpretation—propounded by Gary Wills—is that the Second Amendment means nothing at all.

Key Supreme Court Decisions

The overwhelming weight of Supreme Court precedent supports the Standard Model. A few ambiguous cases could be read as consistent with the Standard Model or with the states' rights theory. The collective rights and nihilist views can find no support in Supreme Court jurisprudence. Let's look at some of those Supreme Court cases, starting with the Court's most important decision, the 1939 *Miller* case, and working our way back to the very beginning.

United States v. Miller (1939)

Miller grew out of a 1938 prosecution of two bootleggers (Jack Miller and Frank Layton) for violating the National Firearms Act by possessing a sawed-off shotgun without having paid the required federal tax. The federal district court dismissed the indictment on the grounds that the National Firearms Act violated the Second Amendment. Freed, Miller and Layton were never heard from again, and thus only the government's side was heard when the case was argued before the Supreme Court.

The key paragraph of the Supreme Court's Miller opinion is this:

> In the absence of any evidence tending to show that possession or use of a "shotgun having a barrel of less than eighteen inches in length" at this time has some reasonable relationship to the preservation or efficiency of a well regulated militia, we cannot say that the Second Amendment guarantees the right to keep and bear such an instrument.

This paragraph has been read to support either the Standard Model or the states' rights theory. By the states' rights theory, the possession of a gun by any individual has no constitutional protection; the Second Amendment only applies to persons actively on duty in official state militias.

In contrast, the Standard Model reads the case as adopting the "civilized warfare" test of 19th-century state supreme court cases: individuals have a right to own arms, but only the type of arms that are useful for militia service; for example, ownership of rifles is protected, but not ownership of Bowie knives (since Bowie knives were allegedly useful only for fights and brawls). The main case cited as authority by the *Miller* Court, *Aymette v. State*, is plainly in the Standard Model, since it interprets the Tennessee Constitution's right to arms to protect an individual right to own firearms, but only firearms suitable for militia use; Aymette states that the Second Amendment has the same meaning.

Hamilton v. Regents (1934)

Two University of California students, the sons of pacifist ministers, sued to obtain an exemption from participation in the University of California's mandatory military training program. The two students did not contest the state of California's authority to force them to participate in state militia exercises, but they argued, in part, that the university's training program was so closely connected with the U.S. War Department as not really to be a militia program. A unanimous Court disagreed, and stated that California's

> *"The 'right of the people' to arms is listed in a litany of other rights which are universally acknowledged to be individual rights."*

acceptance of federal assistance in militia training did not transform the training program into an arm of the standing army. States had the authority to make their own judgments about training.

The Court used the Second Amendment to support a point about a state government's power over its militia. *Hamilton* used the Second Amendment as a reminder of the expectation by all the Founders that states would supervise the militia. This reminder would be consistent with the states' rights theory and with the Standard Model.

United States v. Schwimmer (1929)

A divided Supreme Court held that a female pacifist who wished to become a United States citizen could be denied citizenship because of her energetic advocacy of pacifism. The Court majority found the promotion of pacifism inconsistent with good citizenship because it dissuaded people from performing their civic duties, including the duty to bear arms in a well-regulated militia. Since it is agreed by Standard Modelers and their critics alike that the federal and state governments have the authority to compel citizens to perform militia service, the *Schwimmer* opinion is consistent with the Standard Model and the states' rights model.

Early Twentieth-Century Rulings

Stearns v. Wood (1915)

After World War I broke out in Europe, the U.S. War Department sent "Circular 8" to the various National Guards, putting restrictions on promotion. Plaintiff [Daniel C.] Stearns, a major in the Ohio National Guard, was thereby deprived of any opportunity to win promotion above the rank of Lieutenant Colonel. Stearns argued that Circular 8 violated many parts of the Constitution, including the Second Amendment.

Writing for a unanimous Court, Justice [James C.] McReynolds contemptuously dismissed Stearns' claim without reaching the merits. Since Stearns' present rank of major was undisturbed, there was no genuine controversy for the Court to consider, and the Court would not render advisory opinions.

Twining v. New Jersey (1908)

In *Twining*, the Supreme Court refused to make the Fifth Amendment self-incrimination guarantee in the Bill of Rights applicable to state trials, via the 14th Amendment. In support of this result, the majority listed other individual rights which had not been made enforceable against the states, under the Privileges and Immunities clause.

The Second Amendment here appears—along with Seventh Amendment civil juries, Sixth Amendment confrontation, and Fifth Amendment grand juries—as a right of individuals, but a right only enforceable against the federal government.

Maxwell v. Dow (1900)

Maxwell was the majority's decision not to make the right to a jury in a criminal case into one of the Privileges or Immunities protected by the 14th Amendment. Regarding the Second Amendment and *Presser* (discussed below), the Court wrote:

> In *Presser v. Illinois*, 116 U.S. 252, it was held that the Second Amendment to the Constitution, in regard to the right of the people to bear arms, is a limitation only on the power of the Congress and the National Government, and not of the States.

Maxwell used *Presser* only to show that the Second Amendment does not in itself apply to the states.

Trono v. United States (1905) and *Kepner v. United States* (1904)

After the United States won the Spanish-American War, the Philippines were ceded to the United States. Congress in 1902 enacted legislation imposing most, but not all of the Bill of Rights on the Territorial Government of the Philippines. The *Trono* case and the *Kepner* case both grew out of criminal prosecutions in the Philippines in which the defendant claimed his rights had been violated.

In *Trono*, at the beginning of Justice [Rufus] Peckham's majority opinion, the congressional act imposing the Bill of Rights was summarized: "The whole language [of the Act] is substantially taken from the Bill of Rights set forth in the amendments to the Constitution of the United States, omitting the provisions in regard to the right of trial by jury and the right of the people to bear arms. . . ." *Kepner* had similar language.

> *"Only if the Second Amendment is an individual right does the Court's invocation of a concealed carry exception make any sense."*

As with other cases, the "right of the people" to arms is listed in a litany of other rights which are universally acknowledged to be individual rights, not states' rights.

Robertson v. Baldwin (1897)

The Court refused to apply the 13th Amendment to merchant seamen who had jumped ship, been caught, and been impressed back into maritime service without due process. The Court explained that 13th Amendment's ban on involuntary servitude, even though absolute on its face, contained various implicit exceptions. In support of the finding of an exception to the 13th Amendment, the Court argued that the Bill of Rights also contained unstated exceptions:

> The law is perfectly well settled that the first ten Amendments to the constitution . . . [are] subject to certain well-recognized exceptions arising from the necessities of the case. . . . Thus, the freedom of speech and of the press (article 1) does not permit the publication of libels, blasphemous or indecent articles, or other publications injurious to public morals or private reputation; the right of the people to keep and bear arms (article 2) is not infringed by law prohibiting the carrying of concealed weapons; the provision that no person shall be twice put in jeopardy (art. 5) does not prevent a second trial, if upon the first trial the jury failed to agree, or the verdict was set aside upon the defendant's motion. . . .

In 1897, state laws which barred individuals from carrying concealed weapons were common, and usually upheld by state supreme courts; the laws did not forbid state militias from carrying concealed weapons. The prohibitions on concealed carry are the exceptions that prove the rule. Only if the Second Amendment is an individual right does the Court's invocation of a concealed carry exception make any sense.

Considering Other Amendments

Brown v. Walker (1896)

When a witness before an Interstate Commerce Commission investigation invoked the Fifth Amendment to refuse to answer questions under oath, the majority of the Supreme Court ruled against his invocation of the privilege against self-incrimination.

Dissenting, Justice Stephen Field (perhaps the strongest civil liberties advocate on the Court during the 19th century) carefully analyzed English and early American precedent, reflecting his vivid appreciation of the long Anglo-American struggle for liberty against arbitrary government. All Constitutional rights ought to be liberally construed, for:

> As said by counsel for the appellant: "The freedom of thought, of speech, and of the press; the right to bear arms; exemption from military dictation; security of the person and of the home; the right to speedy and public trial by jury; protection against oppressive bail and cruel punishment,—are, together with exemption from self-incrimination, the essential and inseparable features of English liberty."

As one of the "essential and inseparable features of English liberty," the right to arms was obviously a right of free individuals, not a power of state governments.

The *Miller* Decision

Miller v. Texas (1894)

Franklin P. Miller was a white man in Dallas who fell in love with a woman whom local newspapers would later call "a greasy negress." In response to a rumor that Miller was carrying a handgun without a license, some Dallas police officers invaded Miller's store with guns drawn. A shoot-out ensued, and the evidence was conflicting as to who fired first, and whether Miller realized that the invaders were police officers. Miller killed one of the intruders during the shoot-out.

During Miller's murder trial, the prosecutor asserted to the jury that Miller had been carrying a gun illegally.

Appealing to the Supreme Court in 1894, Miller alleged violations of his Second Amendment, Fourth Amendment, Fifth Amendment, and 14th Amendment rights. Regarding the Second Amendment, Miller claimed that it negated the Texas statute against concealed carrying of a weapon.

A unanimous Court rejected Miller's contentions: A "state law forbidding the carrying of dangerous weapons on the person . . . does not abridge the privileges or immunities of citizens of the United States." This statement about concealed weapons laws was consistent with what the Court would say about such laws three years later, in the *Robertson* case.

Moreover, the Second Amendment, like the rest of the Bill of Rights, only operated directly on the federal government, and not on the states.

But did the 14th Amendment make the Second, Fourth, and Fifth Amendments applicable to the states? Here, the *Miller* Court was agnostic: "If the Fourteenth Amendment limited the power of the States as to such rights, as pertaining to the citizens of the United States, we think it was fatal to this claim that it was not set up in the trial court."

Just eight years before, in *Presser*, the Court had said that the Second Amendment does not apply directly to the states; Miller reaffirmed this part of the *Presser* ruling. Another part of *Presser* had implied that the right to arms was not one of the "privileges or immunities" of American citizenship, although the *Presser* Court did not explicitly mention the 14th Amendment.

In *Miller v. Texas*, the Court suggested that Miller might have had a 14th Amendment argument, if he had raised the issue properly at trial. Miller was a private citizen, and never claimed any right as a member of the Texas Militia. But according to the Court, Miller's problem was the Second Amendment was raised against

> *"The First and Second Amendments recognize preexisting fundamental human rights."*

the wrong government (Texas, rather than the federal government), and at the wrong time (on appeal, rather than at trial). If the states' rights theory were correct, then the Court should have rejected Miller's Second Amendment claim because Miller was an individual rather than the government of Texas. Instead, the Court treated the Second Amendment exactly like the Fourth and the Fifth, which were also at issue: all three amendments protected individual rights, but only against the federal government; while the 14th Amendment might, arguably, make these rights enforceable against the states, Miller's failure to raise the issue at trial precluded further inquiry.

The Second Amendment in the Nineteenth Century

Logan v. United States (1892)
The issue before the Court was whether the prisoners in federal custody, who were injured by a mob, had been deprived of any of their federal civil rights.

Logan affirmed the position of *Cruikshank* (below) that the First and Second Amendments recognize preexisting fundamental human rights, rather than creating new rights.

Presser v. Illinois (1886)
In the late 19th century, many state governments violently suppressed peaceful attempts by workingmen to exercise their economic and collective bargaining rights. In response to the violent state action, some workers created self-defense organizations. In response to the self-defense organizations, some state governments, such as Illinois', enacted laws against armed public parades.

Defying the Illinois statue, a self-defense organization composed of German working-class immigrants held a parade in which one of the leaders carried an unloaded rifle. At trial, the leader—Herman Presser—argued that the Illinois law violated the Second Amendment.

The Supreme Court ruled against him unanimously. First, the Court held that the Illinois ban on armed parades "does not infringe the right of the people to keep and bear arms." This holding was consistent with traditional common law boundaries on the right to arms, which prohibited terrifyingly large assemblies of armed men.

Further, the Second Amendment by its own force "is a limitation only upon the power of Congress and the National Government, and not upon that of the States."

Race and the Right to Bear Arms

United States v. Cruikshank (1875)

An important part of Congress' work during Reconstruction was the Enforcement Acts, which criminalized private conspiracies to violate civil rights. Among the civil rights violations which especially concerned Congress was the disarmament of freedmen by the Ku Klux Klan and similar gangs.

After a rioting band of whites burned down a Louisiana courthouse which was occupied by a group of armed blacks (following the disputed 1872 elections), the whites and their leader, Klansman William Cruikshank, were prosecuted under the Enforcement Acts. Cruikshank was convicted of conspiring to deprive the blacks of the rights they had been granted by the Constitution, including the right peaceably to assemble and the right to bear arms.

In *United States v. Cruikshank*, the Supreme Court held the Enforcement Acts unconstitutional. The 14th Amendment did give Congress the power to prevent interference with rights granted by the Constitution, said the Court. But the right to assemble and the right to arms were not rights granted or created by the Constitution, because they were fundamental human rights that pre-existed the Constitution:

> The right of the people peaceably to assemble for lawful purposes existed long before the adoption of the Constitution of the United States. In fact, it is, and always has been, one of the attributes of citizenship under a free government. . . . It is found wherever civilization exists.

A few pages later, the Court made the same point about the right to arms as a fundamental human right:

> The right . . . of bearing arms for a lawful purpose . . . is not a right granted by the Constitution. Neither is it in any manner dependent on that instrument for its existence. The second amendment declares that it shall not be infringed; but this . . . means no more than it shall not be infringed by Congress . . . leaving the people to look for their protection against any violation by their fellow citizens of the rights it recognizes [to state and local governments].

According to *Cruikshank*, the individual's right to arms is protected by the Second Amendment, but not created by it, because the right derives from natural law. The Court's statement that the freedmen must "look for their protection against any violation by their fellow citizens of the rights" that the Second Amendment recognizes is comprehensible only under the individual rights view. If individuals have a right to own a gun, then individuals can ask local governments to protect them against "fellow citizens" who attempt to disarm them. In contrast, if the Second Amendment right belongs to the state governments as protection against federal interference, then mere "fellow citizens" could not infringe that right by disarming mere individuals.

Scott v. Sandford (1856)

Holding that a free black could not be an American citizen, the *Dred Scott* majority opinion listed the unacceptable consequences of black citizenship: black citizens would have the right to enter any state, to stay there as long as they pleased, and within that state they could go where they wanted at any hour of the day or night, unless they committed some act for which a white person could be punished. Further, black citizens would have "the

> *"Until the 1960s, the United States Department of Justice acknowledged the Second Amendment as an individual right."*

right to . . . full liberty of speech in public and private upon all subjects which [a state's] own citizens might meet; to hold public meetings upon political affairs, and to keep and carry arms wherever they went."

Thus, the "right to . . . keep and carry arms" (like "the right to . . . full liberty of speech," and like the right to interstate travel without molestation, and like the "the right to . . . hold public meetings on political affairs") was an individual right of American citizenship. The plain source of the rights listed by the Court is the United States Constitution.

Another part of the Court's opinion began with the universal assumption that the Bill of Rights constrained Congressional legislation in the territories:

> No one, we presume, will contend that Congress can make any law in a territory respecting the establishment of religion, or the free exercise thereof, or abridging the freedom of speech or of the press, or the right of the people of the territory peaceably to assemble and to petition the government for redress of grievances. Nor can Congress deny to the people the right to keep and bear arms, nor the right to trial by jury, nor compel anyone to be a witness against itself in a criminal proceeding.

The Taney Court [led by Chief Justice Roger Taney] obviously considered the Second Amendment as one of the constitutional rights belonging to individual Americans. The "states' rights" Second Amendment could have no application in a territory, since a territorial government is by definition not a state government. And since Chief Justice Taney was discussing individual rights which Congress could not infringe, the only reasonable way to read the Chief Justice's reference to the Second Amendment is as a reference to an individual right.

The First Major Second Amendment Case

Houston v. Moore (1820)

The Houston case grew out of a Pennsylvania man's refusal to appear for federal militia duty during the War of 1812. The failure to appear violated a federal statute, as well as a Pennsylvania statute that was a direct copy of the federal statute. When Mr. Houston was prosecuted and convicted in a Pennsylvania court martial for violating the Pennsylvania statute, his attorney argued that only the federal government, not Pennsylvania, had the authority to bring a prosecution; the Pennsylvania statute was alleged to be a state infringement of the federal powers over the militia.

When the case reached the Supreme Court, both sides offered extensive arguments over Article I, section 8, clauses 15 and 16, in the Constitution, which grant Congress certain powers over the militia.

Responding to Houston's argument that Congressional power over the national militia is plenary (and therefore Pennsylvania had no authority to punish someone for failing to perform federal militia service), the State of Pennsylvania lawyers retorted that Congressional power over the militia was concurrent with state power, not exclusive. In support of this theory, they pointed to the Tenth Amendment, which reserves to states all powers not granted to the federal government.

If, as some writers claim, the only purpose of the Second Amendment were to guard state government control over the militia, then the Second Amendment ought to have been the heart of the State of Pennsylvania's argument. But instead, Pennsylvania resorted to the Tenth Amendment to make the "state's right" argument.

Justice Bushrod Washington delivered the opinion of the Court, holding that the Pennsylvania law was constitutional, because Congress had not forbidden the states to enact such laws enforcing the federal militia statute.

Justice Joseph Story, a consistent supporter of federal government authority, dissented. He argued that the congressional legislation punishing militia resisters was exclusive, and left the states no room to act.

Deep in the lengthy dissent, Justice Story raised a hypothetical: what if Congress had not used its militia powers? If Congress were inert, and ignored the militia, could the states act? "Yes," he answered: the Second Amendment "may not, perhaps, be thought to have any important bearing on this point. If it have, it confirms and illustrates, rather than impugns, the reasoning already suggested."

Justice Story's dissent is inconsistent with the states' rights theory that the Second Amendment somehow reduces Congress' militia powers. Immediately after the Second Amendment hypothetical, Justice Story wrote that if Congress actually did use its Article I powers over the militia, then congressional power was exclusive. There could be no state control, "however small." If federal militia powers, when exercised, are absolute, then the theory that the Second Amendment limits federal militia powers is incorrect.

Second Amendment case law from 1820 to 1939 is consistent with only one interpretative model, the Standard Model of an individual right to keep and bear arms. That is one reason why, until the 1960s, the United States Department of Justice acknowledged the Second Amendment as an individual right, and why Attorney General [John] Ashcroft was correct in returning the Department of Justice to its long-standing, original position regarding the Second Amendment.

The Founding Fathers Supported the Right of Individuals to Own Guns

by Gary Lantz

About the author: *Gary Lantz is a writer for* America's 1st Freedom, *a monthly publication of the National Rifle Assocation.*

Jefferson and his fellow constitutional framers might be stunned to learn that the right to keep and bear arms currently generates so much furor. While we argue the pros and cons of individual gun ownership in our coffee shops, courts and halls of Congress, the crafters of the Constitution, according to their recorded testimony, could not envision a truly free nation with prohibition of arms in place.

George Washington, America's first president and the man many wanted as a king, insisted publicly in 1790 that a free people ought to be armed. Washington swelled with pride at the sight of the armed citizenry he served.

In 1794 he told Congress that "it has been a spectacle displaying the highest advantage of republican government to behold the most and the least wealthy of our citizens standing in the same ranks as private soldiers, preeminently distinguished by being the army of the Constitution."

Considering these words, it would seem that the man we refer to as the father of our country would roll over in his grave upon hearing the demands of those demanding disarmament of all Americans other than police or military.

Such pride in seeing the "most and least wealthy" armed and ready to serve a free nation is revealing when you consider that Washington was the son of landed gentry, the well bred and well fed of colonial America's upper economic and social crust.

The benefits and pleasures of plantation life apparently didn't dampen Washington's desire to be outdoors, to remain active and involved in the exploration of the vast wilderness at his doorstep. He joined a survey party at 16 and

Gary Lantz, "The Founding Fathers Speak Out: Our Panel of Constitutional Experts Speak Out on the Second Amendment," *America's 1st Freedom*, September 2003, pp. 32–35. Copyright © 2003 by the National Rifle Association of America. Reproduced by permission.

combed the countryside of both Virginia and West Virginia for several years be-fore receiving an appointment as a major in the militia in 1753.

A year later Washington had risen to the rank of colonel and was fighting the French along the Ohio River. However, the arrival of the British regular troops di-luted the stature of the colonial militia, and Washington resigned his commission.

Washington reentered military service in 1755. His courage and skill under fire while fighting the French and their Indian allies as they completed with the British for control of North America once again earned Washington the rank of colonel and command over all the Virginia militia forces.

Yet the Virginia colonel soon grew disillusioned with British contempt for the colonial militia, and once again resigned. Over the years his relationships with England grew increasingly strained, while his political influence among the colonists grew. Washington's intelligence, patience and dignity as leader of the revolutionary army did not go unnoticed and paved the way to the new nation's first presidency.

Washington's popularity was such that he could have reigned as a monarch. Instead he chose to manage the nation's affairs within the framework of the Constitution, to work closely with Congress and thus allow a new system of government ample time to mature. He died after several years of retirement at his Mount Vernon home. At the end of his political career this brilliant yet hum-ble man urged his fellow Americans to overcome their political and philosophi-cal differences and to avoid entanglements in the wars and domestic policies of other nations. At the same time he wrote out a will granting freedom of his slaves—an act of conscience focusing attention on the inherent self worth of all men, no matter their wealth, status or social station.

Jefferson's Stance

The noted eloquence of Thomas Jefferson came to a point when discussing the Right to Keep and Bear Arms. Jefferson made it clear during the debate over the proposed Virginia Constitution that as far as he was concerned, "No freeman shall ever be debarred the use of arms. . . ."

Jefferson was another founding father who had everything to lose and little in the way of materialism to gain by advancing libel. Born in 1743 in Albermarle County, Va., he inherited a prime Virginia acreage and considerable social standing. Jefferson studied at William & Mary and took a law degree.

Never a fiery orator, Jefferson instead relied upon his pen to deliver beauti-fully crafted and heartfelt communication. The 33-year-old Virginian wrote the Declaration of Independence, and later penned legislation establishing freedom of religion.

Jefferson served as minister to France and, as president of the United States, was responsible for the Louisiana Purchase. A man of marvelous intellect and vision, Jefferson retired from public service to, as a French nobleman noted, boost his mind to "an elevated situation, from which he might contemplate the universe."

Jefferson and many other men of station placed their personal stature and fortunes in peril by speaking out against British rule. As Jefferson spelled out in a private letter, "I have sworn upon the altar of God eternal hostility against every form of tyranny over the mind of man." Born into wealth, he sought the universal common ground of liberty, including the right of every individual to be armed.

Patrick Henry and Samuel Adams

Few among the framers were more passionate than the fiery libertarian Patrick Henry. Born in 1736, the Virginia attorney caused a political conflagration in 1763 when he told a colonial court that any king who would veto a good and necessary law made by a local representative body was not a father to his people but a tyrant who should forfeit the people's allegiance.

Henry tiptoed around charges of treason far too often for comfort, yet threats didn't deter him. In March of 1775 the impassioned orator urged fellow Virginians to arm in self-defense, closing his appeal with the now famous words, "I know not what course others may take, but for me, give me liberty or give me death."

Henry's call for self-armament rose over the protests of more conservative Virginia lawmakers and prompted the royal British governor to remove gunpowder from local magazines. Referred to as a "Quaker in religion yet the very devil in politics," Henry's call for armed resistance is said to have led to the British march on Concord Bridge and, within hours, the Shot Heard Round the World.

"Guard with jealous attention the public liberty," Henry cautioned in 1788. "Suspect every one who approaches that jewel. Unfortunately, nothing will preserve it but downright force. Whenever you give up that force, you are ruined."

Few among the founding fathers were more concise in their convictions concerning the Second Amendment than Samuel Adams.

"Among the natural rights of the colonists are these." Adams said. "First, a right to life. Secondly, to liberty. Thirdly, to property, together with the right to support and defend them in the best manner they can. These are evident branches of, rather than deductions from, the duty of self-preservation, commonly called the first law of nature."

> *"Obviously by their own words the founding fathers decided that real liberty could not be handed down by any form of government."*

Adams was born in Boston and graduated from Harvard with a master's of art degree. Upon election to the Massachusetts legislature he fought the laws imposed by the British Parliament designed to wring revenue from the sweat and toil of colonists.

Adams urged a boycott against trade with Britain and was a Massachusetts delegate to the first Continental Congress. He summed up his sentiments thusly: "If ye love wealth greater than liberty the tranquility of servitude greater than the animating contest for freedom, go from us in peace. We seek not your

156

counsel, nor your arms. Crouch down and lick the hand that feeds you; may your chains set lightly upon you, and may posterity forget that ye were our countrymen."

Madison's View

President James Madison mistrusted a government that raised a large standing army to the detriment of an armed militia drawn from among the nation's rank-and-file citizens. During his first inaugural address, he pointed out that the nation should "keep within the requisite limits a standing military force, always remembering that an armed and trained militia is the firmest bulwark of republics—that without standing armies their liberty can never be in danger, nor with large ones safe."

Obviously by their own words the founding fathers decided that real liberty could not be handed down by any form of government. Instead it had to well up from the roots like an artesian spring, and would rest in the hands of the self-ruled, the self-armed, the self-determined.

The founding fathers cautioned that the system would collapse if the people failed to question, relaxed their commitment, grew indifferent, or allowed leaders, parties and armies too much power over a society that has lost the capacity and capability to act in its own behalf.

Men like Madison, [George] Mason or Jefferson wouldn't appreciate today's tendencies to replace personal responsibility with bureaucratic mandates. They would be ashamed of leaders who insist that police or professional soldiers are available for public protection. As Madison pointed out, it is also necessary sometimes for the private citizen to protect himself from the professional bearer of arms.

Thomas Paine

Another eloquent wordsmith, Thomas Paine was born in England and came to America in 1774 at the urging of Ben Franklin.

Paine served as a magazine editor, launched a crusade against slavery and sympathized with the colonists' desire to rid themselves of British rule. His eagerly read pamphlet *Common Sense* said that independence for the colonies was inevitable because America had lost touch with the mother country.

Paine observed that "those who expect to reap the blessings of freedom, must, like men, undergo the fatigues of supporting it." Like a good evangelist, Paine could turn a phrase into flint and steel capable of igniting passion: "These are the times that try men's souls. The summer soldier and the sunshine patriot will, in this crisis, shrink from the service of their country; but he that stand it now, deserves the love and thanks of man and woman. Tyranny, like hell, is not easily conquered; yet we have this consolation with us, that the harder the conflict, the more glorious the triumph. What we obtain too cheap, we esteem too lightly: it is dearness only that gives every thing its value. Heaven knows how to put a proper price upon its goods; and it would be strange indeed if so celestial an article as freedom should not be highly rated. Britain, with an army to enforce her tyranny, has declared that she has the right (not only to tax) but 'to bind us in all cases whatsoever,' and if being bound in that manner is not slavery, then is there such a thing as slavery upon earth."

While Paine was rallying farmers to take up arms against the king, a fledgling nation's leaders were deliberating how to break away from the social and political mentality that had kept much of humanity enslaved in some form for thousands of years.

> *"The right of each free individual to keep and bear arms was symbolic as well as practical."*

A basic tenet of the new order would be the previously unthinkable notion that all men are created equal—laborers, shopkeepers, soldiers sharing equality, even with aristocrats. Therefore the right of each free individual to keep and bear arms was symbolic as well as practical.

Certainly there were flaws: we would have to fight a civil war to extend even the simplest liberties to people of color. But, in the case of the constitutional framers, the right to own a gun seemed, within the context of their culture, self evident in a free society, for as George Mason remarked, "To disarm the people (is) the best and most effectual way to enslave them."

Of course, even then slaveholders were freeing their oppressed human property, and men like Paine were warning us that the American dream could never be complete and the Constitution would be doomed to remain little more than ink-stained parchment as long as slavery, racism and other unconscionable sins were rationalized for economic or political convenience. The construction of a truly free nation would take time, but at least the framers provided the perfectly hewn cornerstone in the form of the Bill of Rights.

A Slow Destruction

Not everyone agrees with every detail of the framers' intent, yet in a free society that is as it should be. With this in mind they provided legal means to deal with portions of the Constitution that might no longer serve the nation's best interest in a future they could not envision. Through an arduous, precise process, we can repeal any of the constitutional amendments that the majority feels no longer suits their needs. But as we've seen in recent years, those who fight to abolish individual firearm ownership would rather make backdoor inroads to deceitfully whittle away at freedom a little at a time.

They've adopted a strategy of legal nicks and cuts: pushing laws to ban certain kinds of guns, outlawing certain kinds of bullets, mounting public relations campaigns that promote the voluntary surrender of firearms, poisoning young minds about traditional gun uses.

Enemies of the Second Amendment say that we no longer need a gun over the mantle to defend ourselves from Indians or bears. One might counter that in our highly flammable modern world, far more Americans are harmed by street thugs, thieves and other violent social parasites than were ever killed by bears, big cats or marauding Indians.

More than anything else, it appears that the founding fathers sensed the glaring, self-evident truth that times and names may change, but the frailties of the human condition revolve through the ages as an act of seemingly perpetual motion. Today, doors still get smashed in, and we still reach for the only existing, workable form of instantaneous self-protection. Is that wrong?

From their speeches and writings it is clear that the constitutional framers would say no—not if life matters. And according to the essence of the Constitution the answer is yes, ALL of life matters, because all of it is equal. And worth protecting at all costs.

Chapter 4

Is Gun Ownership an Effective Means of Self-Defense?

Chapter Preface

Any American adult who passes a background check can legally purchase guns to keep in the home. Often these guns are intended to be used to defend homeowners and their families from criminals breaking into the home. However, the right to carry guns in public as a way of defending oneself against crimes committed outside the home is not as common. Thirty-two states allow any adult who is not a felon to obtain a "carry concealed weapons" (CCW) license (although four other states have similarly liberal laws). All other states disallow the carrying of concealed weapons. The first state to pass a "shall-issue," or liberalized concealed-carry, law was Florida, in 1987. Thus, Florida quickly became a test case in determining whether guns are an effective means of self-defense.

Supporters of Florida's shall-issue law assert that it has led to a significant decline in gun crime. According to Marshall Lewin, a writer for *America's 1st Freedom*, a magazine published by the National Rifle Association, Florida's murder rate was 36 percent higher than the national average in 1987. Four years later, after the passage of the law, the rate had declined to 4 percent below the national average. Other reports have indicated that the U.S. homicide rate has risen 12 percent since 1987 while Florida's has decreased by 21 percent.

Studies conducted from the mid-1990s and beyond also appear to suggest that adults who possess CCW licenses are overwhelmingly law abiding. Lewin states that only 160 of the 846,841 carry permits that had been issued in Florida as of summer 2003 were revoked because of an incident involving a firearm. Meanwhile, a report by the gun rights organization GunCite declares that only one permit holder in the first ten years of issuing CCW licenses was convicted of homicide. Gun rights advocate Dave Kopel observes, "What we can say with some confidence is that allowing more people to carry guns does not cause an increase in crime."

However, the gun control organization Brady Campaign to Prevent Gun Violence casts doubt on these conclusions. The organization asserts that violent crimes have increased in Florida and insists that permits are frequently issued to people who should not be allowed to possess concealed weapons. According to its report "Carrying Concealed Weapons," "between 1987 and 1992, the violent crime rate in [Florida] increased 17.8%. In every year since 1987, Florida has had the highest rate of violent crime in the nation according to the FBI's Uniform Crime Report." While the campaign acknowledges that Florida's handgun homicide rate has experience a slight decline of late, it contends that this decrease is the result of stricter gun laws.

Furthermore, the Brady Campaign asserts that more CCW licenses have been revoked than has been claimed by Lewin and other shall-issue advocates. They also argue that law-abiding citizens are not the only people carrying hidden weapons. The organization states that more than five hundred licenses have been revoked; approximately 60 percent of those revocations "were for convictions of crimes committed by the licensee after issuance." In addition, the organization maintains that while people who have been convicted of a felony cannot receive a license, the law does not bar people who have a violent misdemeanor conviction or whose felony conviction has not been finalized from getting a license.

A large number of Americans have turned to guns as a way of protecting themselves against crime. Unfortunately, Florida's experience with concealed-carry laws has not put to rest the question of whether guns truly are the best way to protect oneself and one's family from crime. In the following chapter the authors consider whether gun ownership is the best approach to self-defense.

Allowing Private Citizens to Carry Guns Reduces Crime and Protects Gun Owners

by Patrick Mullins

About the author: *At the time this article was written, Patrick Mullins was a PhD student in the history department at the University of Kentucky.*

In the wake of the tragic shootings at Columbine High School on April 20, 1999, the relation of gun availability to violent crime was furiously debated in the media.

One highly visible scholar in the media debate is economist and social scientist, John Lott, Jr., the John M. Olin Visiting Law and Economics Fellow at the University of Chicago. The title of his 1998 book, *More Guns, Less Crime*, may at first strike the reader as provocatively counterintuitive. Lott argues that states' issuance of permits allowing private citizens to carry concealed handguns has *not* caused crime to rise, but has in fact dramatically *reduced* violent crimes.

How is this possible?

Nondiscretionary concealed-carry permits deter crimes against persons because criminals—fearing for their own lives—don't know which potential victims in a right-to-carry state are armed and which are not. National polls suggest that there are as many as 3.6 million defensive uses of handguns by private citizens each year. There are no hard numbers available, because these incidents are rarely reported to the authorities and because 98% of them consist merely of brandishing the gun rather than discharging it. Lott's landmark study now confirms the bountiful anecdotal evidence for deterrence.

An In-Depth Analysis

In the last two and a half years since Lott first published his findings in the *Journal of Legal Studies*, he has vanquished all attempts by political and academic opponents to undermine his thesis.

Lott's statistical analysis of crime in the U.S. remains unsurpassed in its depth and thoroughness. While other crime studies look at a small area over a long period of time or a broad area over a short period, Lott's study examines the data on crime rates from the FBI's *Uniform Crime Reports* for all 3,054 counties in the United States, from 1977 to 1992. He supplemented this evidence with other FBI data for 1993 and 1994.

Lott cross examined this data on crime rates with U.S. Census data on population density per square mile, total county population, breakdowns of county population according to race, sex, age, real per-capita income, etc. He also took care to distinguish changes in the crime rates produced by concealed-carry laws from changes associated with long-term trends and with changes in the rates of other deterrents such as arrest, conviction, length of sentences, etc. While other crime studies look only at aggregate, state-level data, Lott went county by county, noting differences between rural, sparsely populated counties and urban, densely populated counties, poor and rich counties, etc.

Lott's conclusions shattered the conventional wisdom about the correlation of crime to gun ownership by responsible citizens.

"National crime rates have been falling at the same time as gun ownership has been rising. Likewise, states experiencing the greatest reductions in crime are also the ones with the fastest growing percentages of gun ownership."

"Allowing citizens to carry concealed handguns reduces violent crimes, and the reductions coincide very closely with the number of concealed-handgun permits issued. Mass shootings in public places are reduced when law-abiding citizens are allowed to carry concealed handguns."

The Effects of Discretionary Rules

Nondiscriminatory concealed-handgun laws require law enforcement officials to issue, without subjective discretion, concealed-weapons permits to all qualified applicants. State requirements generally include lack of a criminal record, lack of mental illness, a minimum age restriction of 18 or 21, various fees, and training in proper usage. Discretionary state laws empower law enforcers or judges to make case-by-case decisions as to whether an applicant has a "compelling need" for a permit.

> *"Allowing private citizens to carry concealed handguns has* **not** *caused crime to rise, but has in fact dramatically reduced* **violent crimes.**"

As of 1996, 31 states have nondiscretionary rules or no permit requirements at all.[1] Twelve states have discretionary rules while seven, plus the District of Columbia, forbid the carrying of concealed handguns altogether.

---

1. As of 2004, that number had reached thirty-six.

"When state concealed-handgun laws went into effect in a county," Lott found, "murders fell by about 8 percent, rapes fell by 5 percent, and aggravated assaults fell by 7 percent." Prohibition states have murder rates 127% higher than those states with the most liberal carry laws.

States with discretionary rules or outright prohibition of concealed weapons have dramatically higher rates in violent crimes [than] states with nondiscretionary rules or no requirements. In such states murder is 86% higher, rape 25% higher, aggravated assault 82% higher, and robbery 105% higher.

> *"Populous, urbanized counties, women, and racial minorities benefited most from nondiscretionary carry laws."*

Lott found that populous, urbanized counties, women, and racial minorities benefited most from nondiscretionary carry laws.

The deterrence of violent crime by these laws was offset, though, by lower decreases in property crimes, as criminals shifted from violent crime to auto theft or burglaries to avoid contact with potentially armed victims. Deterrence in violent crime is further indicated by the movement of criminals out of right-to-carry states. The adoption of a nondiscriminatory carry law in one state corresponds with a large increase in violent crimes in the counties of neighboring states without the right to carry (although those increases prove to be short-lived).

Permit Holders Are Not a Threat

When many states began debating the merits of a concealed-carry law in the late 1980s and 1990s, gun-control advocates warned that the proliferation of concealed weapons would result in an explosion of gun fatalities, if only as a result of arguments over car accidents, drunken quarrels, mistaken identity, and the like. Although there are, as of January 2001, 31 right-to-carry states (and some of the concealed-carry laws are decades old), there exists only one recorded instance of a permitted, concealed handgun being used in a shooting after a traffic accident (and that shooting was in self-defense).

No permit holder in the U.S. has ever shot a police officer, and there have been occasions in which permit holders used their guns to save officers' lives. About 30 persons are killed annually by private citizens mistaking them for intruders, by contrast with 330 accidental killings by police officers each year.

As part of his study, Lott made a telephone survey of the top law enforcement officials in all 50 states. He learned some telling facts.

From 1 October 1987, when Florida's concealed-carry law went into effect, until the end of 1996, over 380,000 permits were issued to qualifying applicants. Only 72 permits were revoked because of crimes committed by the permit holders (and most of these crimes didn't involve the permitted weapon). Between September 1987 and August 1992, only 4 crimes involving permitted handguns occurred in Dade County (Greater Miami), and none of those resulted in injury.

Multnomah County, Oregon, issued 11,140 permits from January 1990 to October 1994. In that time, only 5 permit holders were involved in shootings. Three of these were found to be justified by grand juries. Neither of the remaining two produced a fatality (one was domestic dispute, the other a loading accident).

In Virginia, no permit holder has been involved in a crime. In the first year following the enactment of a concealed-carry law in Texas, 114,000 permits were issued and only 17 were revoked (for reasons not specified). After Nevada's first year, law enforcers could not document a single instance of a fatality resulting from misuse of a gun by a permit holder. The same is true of Kentucky.

North Carolina has not revoked a single permit as a result of the misuse of a permitted weapon. Since 1989, only one person holding a gun permit in South Carolina has been indicted for a felony. (The felony had nothing to do with the gun and the indictment was later dropped.) These stories go on and on. . . .

An Irrational Belief

Private citizens carrying handguns in public places may evoke terrifying images of shoot-outs over gambling disputes in the dusty streets of Dodge City (a legendary image demonstrated to be historically inaccurate by the scholarship of Old West historian, Roger McGrath).

But a man with a concealed-carry license who walks along a crowded sidewalk, carrying a pistol in a shoulder holster under his coat, no more poses an objective threat to the lives of pedestrians than a man with a driver's license who drives his car down that same street. Indeed, a one-ton Oldsmobile could kill a lot more people if the driver accidentally swerved onto that crowded sidewalk than a 9mm Beretta could kill even if fired into the crowd deliberately by a cool-headed marksman.

It is no more rational or moral to prohibit the bearing of concealed handguns by law-abiding citizens in public so as to reduce murders, than it would be to prohibit the driving of automobiles down public streets to reduce hit and runs. If "gun control" advocates were really concerned with saving lives, and reducing violent crime, they would demand states introduce concealed gun permits rather then viciously opposing them.

Gun Ownership Helps Protect Women

by Richard W. Stevens, Hugo Teufel III, and Matthew Y. Biscan

About the authors: *Richard W. Stevens, Hugo Teufel III, and Matthew Y. Biscan are lawyers.*

Since 1968 Americans who face criminal attack have been advised to "dial 911" and rely upon the emergency police response for protection. Indeed, according to a study of 911 calls, "the public has built up extraordinary levels of expectation and reliance on the [911] system's effectiveness." Meanwhile, a story in *U.S. News & World Report* magazine in 1996, headlined, "This is 911, please hold," reported that "in recent years, many law enforcement executives have questioned the entire foundation on which 911 is built—the idea that police can stop crimes by responding rapidly to citizens' 'emergency' calls."

In practice, does dialing 911 actually protect crime victims? Fewer than 5 percent of all calls dispatched to police are made soon enough for officers to stop a crime or arrest a suspect. Even when it functions at its best, the 911 system cannot adequately protect crime victims. When citizens rely solely on 911 and police protection from imminent criminal attacks, their risks of harm increase because of slow police response times, clogged emergency telephone lines, and occasional partial or total 911 system outages. More striking is the position of the law in nearly every state: The police have no legal obligation to protect citizens from crime.

The Ruth Bunnell Case

In one landmark California case, a woman separated from her husband, and he retaliated with threats and violence. Over a period of a year, Ruth Bunnell had called the San Jose police at least twenty times to report that her estranged husband, Mack, had violently assaulted her and her two daughters. Mack had even been arrested for one assault.

One day Mack called Ruth to say that he was coming to her house to kill her.

Ruth called the police for immediate help. The police department, according to court documents, "refused to come to her aid at that time and asked that she call the department again when Mack Bunnell had arrived." Forty-five minutes later Mack arrived and stabbed Ruth to death. Responding to a neighbor's call, the police eventually came to Ruth's house—after she was dead.

Ruth's estate sued the police for negligently failing to protect her. The California appeals court held that the city of San Jose was shielded from the suit because of a state statute and because there was no "special relationship" between the police and Ruth—the police had not started to help her, and she had not relied on any promise that the police would help. Case dismissed.

A Lack of Police Protection

In a particularly brutal Washington, D.C., case, three women discovered that the law promises them no protection against brutal attack by strangers. All three women were sleeping in their rooms during the early morning hours when two men broke down the back door of their three-floor house in northwest Washington. The men first entered the second-floor room and violently assaulted one woman there.

From the third-floor room they shared, the other two women heard the screams and commotion and called the police. The call was dispatched as "Code 2" priority, which has a lower priority than "Code 1" given to crimes in progress. Four police cruisers responded to the call within a few minutes. One of the police cars drove through the alley without stopping to check the back door and then went around to the front of the house. A second police officer knocked on the front door but left when he got no answer. All officers left the scene just five minutes after they had arrived.

The two women, who had escaped to an adjoining roof, then climbed back into their room and called the police a second time because they still heard screams. The duty officer assured them that help was on the way. That second call was logged as "investigate the trouble," but no officers were dispatched.

> "A woman with a firearm ... can credibly threaten and deter an attacker of any size, shape, or strength."

Minutes later, the women thought the police were in the house and called down for them. There were no policemen there, but the attackers heard the screams and came upstairs. All three women were kidnapped, taken to one of the attacker's houses, and raped, robbed, beaten, and sexually abused.

The three women sued the District of Columbia and the officers for negligently failing to provide police protection, but their complaint was dismissed. Under D.C. law, "official police personnel and the government employing them are not generally liable to victims of criminal acts for failure to provide adequate police protection." This rule "rests upon the fundamental principle that a government and its agents are under no general duty to provide public services, such as police protection, to any particular individual citizen." Many state courts follow and apply this same rule.

The city of Sonoma, California, recently settled a federal civil rights lawsuit by paying one million dollars to the children of a battered and murdered woman whom the police failed to protect against her violent ex-husband. This lawsuit alleged that the police denied the woman her civil rights by failing to protect her. Although this settlement does not create a legal precedent, it does signal that city governments may see holes forming in their legal immunity.

The Advantages of Self-Defense

But the inadequacy of the 911 system (and also of the protective orders that many women seek against abusers) suggests that self-defense may be a better option for many women and other potential victims of crime.

On average, men are physically bigger and stronger than women are. Male batterers of women, for example, are on average forty-five pounds heavier and four to five inches taller than their female victims. With serious martial arts training, a woman can fight off an unarmed man in many cases, but she likely still faces a disadvantage if attacked by more than one man or an armed man.

A woman with a firearm, however, can credibly threaten and deter an attacker of any size, shape, or strength. Even though weaker and unskilled in the use of firearms, she can sometimes protect herself with a sidearm without firing a shot. In more than 92 percent of defensive gun uses, the defender succeeds by firing only a warning shot or never firing the gun at all.

A sidearm can "equalize" physical disparity between a woman and her attacker. For a battered woman, the equalization can make all the difference, because such a woman is likely to be prepared for an abuser's attack. Typically the battered woman can sense cues of impending violence from her male partner (in the home) more quickly and accurately than a person who has not been abused. Because she can prepare, she can more effectively use the sidearm to deter and prevent a looming violent episode.

Although a woman can overcome a male attacker's physical advantages with a firearm, social and psychological factors can weaken her willingness to prepare and defend herself by using force. Some argue that American women generally have a victim mentality because of sex-role stereotyping. In our society, nonaggressiveness is characteristic of what is supposed to be "normal" heterosexual femininity. Male rapists look for the weak and fearful "damsel in distress." The more stereotypically feminine and passive a woman is, the more likely that she will be a victim of aggression. The same nonaggressive woman is unlikely to learn self-defense techniques and obtain defense tools.

Self-defense instructors have reported seeing "physically strong women who are at first so frightened of violence and of fighting that they cower and cry uncontrollably even in a simulated self-defense situation." Even female police officers sometimes need extra training to be willing to fight back against aggressors. This apparently widespread fear of conflict makes women targets of rape and violence.

"Crime prevention" programs that teach only nonviolent resistance actually reinforce the weak/passive female stereotyping. The Maryland Community Crime Prevention Institute, for example, reportedly has told women that martial arts training would not decrease the chances of injuries in an attack. Instead, the institute has advised women to struggle, cry hysterically, and pretend to faint, be sick, pregnant, or insane. Sexual stereotyping that discourages women from defending themselves can be deadly. Studies have shown that women who resist and fight back are less likely to be harmed than those women who submit passively.

Some might admit that firearm ownership could have prevented the attacks discussed above, yet they may nevertheless oppose ownership of firearms in general because of their belief that gun ownership increases the total level of violence in society. We must ask, therefore, whether self-defense through firearms is beneficial not only for battered women or women under imminent threat of violence but also for society as a whole.

Opponents of the private possession and use of firearms for defense assert that greater numbers of firearms mean more unlawful killings. Put another way, they claim that any increase in gun ownership results in an increase in murders. The facts show otherwise: The overwhelming majority of gun owners never hurt anyone with their firearms. Increasing the number of firearms available to peaceable, nonviolent citizens—the vast majority of the population—will not convert these citizens into criminals.

> *"Potential crime victims who are in imminent danger of violence are better protected by individual self-defense options."*

Homicide studies dating back to the nineteenth century show that murderers, far from being normal people who "lost control," are extreme aberrants whose life histories feature prior felonies, substance abuse, and/or psychopathology. "The vast majority of persons involved in life-threatening violence," wrote Delbert S. Elliott in the *University of Colorado Law Review*, "have a long criminal record and many prior contacts with the justice system." These facts appear in homicide studies so consistently that, according to an article in *Homicide Studies*, they "have now become criminological axioms" about the "basic characteristics of homicide." In short, everyday people don't commit homicide—violent criminals do.

While gun ownership rates increased substantially and the number of privately owned guns nearly doubled between 1973 and 1992, the homicide rate in 1992 was 10 percent lower than the 1973 rate. It is even lower today despite an increase in gun ownership. The homicide rates over this period rose and fell with no correlation with gun ownership rates. Despite the increase in firearms, there was no correlation with homicide rates in general nor an increase in the percentage of murders committed specifically with firearms. In 1973, 68.2 percent of all murders were committed with guns. In 1992, the figure was 68.2 percent. Contrary to the gun control rhetoric, more guns do not equal more murders.

Sexist Arguments

Some of the arguments for gun control and against armed self-defense play directly on sex-role stereotypes of women. One argument is that using a sidearm requires a lot of training, so the gun is more dangerous to the average citizen than a deterrent to the criminal.

This argument emphasizes incompetence and lack of training as a reason not to be armed. Women are more likely to be considered incompetent and untrained with firearms. Some women may also see themselves as incompetent and physically weak. This argument points to leaving the job of protecting women to the men (typically) in uniform who are experts. Yet Lee J. Hicks noted in *Police Chief* magazine that he found that civilian women with two hours of instruction could learn to shoot a gun as accurately as could police academy cadets in simulated real-life situations.

Another argument concerns fears of gun "take-away." According to this rationale, the criminal can wrest the gun out of the hands of the physically weaker woman. The armed woman can too easily be converted into an unarmed woman at the mercy of her now-armed attacker. The statistics that back up this argument come from cases where police officers in the line of duty have lost their guns to criminals. But the analogy is faulty. Police officers must approach, subdue, and take suspects into custody. The officers must therefore come close enough for the suspects to be able to grab the guns. Personal- and home-defense situations are quite different; they do not require the defender to get close to the attacker. Indeed, the opposite is true: The defender wants to keep the attacker at a distance, and that requires no special strength except the gun. A woman strong enough to shoot is strong enough to keep an attacker out of reach of her gun.

Sayoko Blodgett-Ford, author of an article headlined "Do Battered Women Have a Right to Bear Arms?" in the *Yale Law and Policy Review*, recounts the story of a California woman whose husband shattered her jaw while she held their baby. After she had her jaw rebuilt at the hospital, she tried to press charges against him, but police and county mental health workers persuaded her not to because the husband had agreed to get counseling. After two sessions, even the counselor refused to meet with him because of death threats.

Despite a restraining order, the estranged husband continued to prowl around his wife's house, sleeping in her yard and calling her constantly by phone. When the police refused to arrest him for violating the restraining order, she decided to buy a gun. While she waited the fifteen days required by California law to get the gun, he repeatedly assaulted her at home and at work. Once she obtained the sidearm, however, and her abuser knew she was armed, the assaults stopped. He continued lesser insults, such as stealing her mail and harassing her by phone, but the physical attacks stopped.

To decide whether to support or oppose private ownership of firearms, individualist feminists should consider the options for self-defense, particularly in the case of domestic violence. The data, logic, and human experience all show that potential crime victims who are in imminent danger of violence are better protected by individual self-defense options than by government laws and centralized police response. Individual women in peril quite frequently fare better when they develop skill and confidence in the carrying and using of defensive firearms. Victim disarmament ("gun control") laws that discourage women from developing the skills and using defensive firearms actually heighten the risks of criminal violence that women face. Such laws place women at a disadvantage against violent men and run against the feminist goal of equal treatment under the law.

Keeping a Gun in the Home for Self-Defense Is Not Dangerous

by Gary Kleck and Don B. Kates

About the authors: *Gary Kleck is a professor at the School of Criminology and Criminal Justice at Florida State University, and Don B. Kates is a criminological policy analyst with the Pacific Research Institute.*

That defensive gun uses are common is not surprising in light of how many Americans own guns for defensive reasons and keep them ready for defensive use. A 1994 national survey found that 46 percent of gun owners have a gun *mainly* for protection, while in a 1989 survey, 62 percent said that protection from crime was at least *one* of the reasons they owned guns. A December 1993 Gallup poll indicated that 49 percent of U.S. households contained a gun, and 31 percent of U.S. adults personally owned a gun. With 97,107,000 households and 192,323,000 persons age eighteen or over in 1994, these figures translate into about 47.6 million households with guns, 59.6 million adults who personally owned a gun, 27.4 million adults who owned guns mainly for protection, and about 37.0 million who owned them at least partly for protection. Thus, the 2.55 million people using guns defensively each year are only 4 percent of all who personally own guns and less than 7 percent of those who have guns for defensive reasons.

Further, many gun owners, and almost certainly a majority of those who own guns primarily for protection, keep a household gun loaded. The 1994 Police Foundation survey found that 16.4 percent of all guns, and 34.0 percent of handguns, were kept loaded and unlocked, i.e., ready for immediate use (referred to hereafter as "the ready status"). Applied to the national gun stock at the end of 1994 of 84.7 million handguns, 150.0 million long guns, and 235.7 million total guns, these figures imply 28.8 million handguns, 9.9 million long guns, and 38.7 million total guns kept loaded and unlocked at any one time.

Thus, three quarters of the guns kept in this status are handguns, which are most commonly kept in the bedroom, where they are ready for nighttime use.

Reanalysis of these data indicates that of handguns kept loaded and unlocked, 83.3 percent were owned by persons who said their most important reason for owning a handgun was "self-defense or protection." Very likely most, and probably nearly all, of the remaining 16.7 percent also owned handguns for self-defense, as a secondary reason (secondary motives were not addressed in this survey). It is a common failing of studies of gun storage practices that they do not separately identify gun owners for whom protection is a secondary reason for owning a gun, or fail to determine reasons for ownership at all. This flaw conceals or obscures the fact that virtually everyone who keeps a gun in the ready status owns the gun at least partly for defensive reasons, thereby blurring the extent to which gun owners have what they would regard as a rational reason for storing guns this way.

Irrelevant Arguments

Some scholars have claimed that, by storing guns loaded and unlocked, many gun owners keep guns in violation of safety rules promulgated by gun owner organizations such as the National Rifle Association (NRA). They then profess to be puzzled by their finding that this "unsafe" storage pattern is as common, or more common, among those who have received formal firearms safety training. This is misleading because the NRA in fact supports keeping guns unloaded and locked, *except* when the gun is kept for defensive reasons, stating that "a gun stored primarily for personal protection must be ready for immediate use. It may be kept loaded, as long as local laws permit and every precaution is taken to prevent careless or unauthorized individuals from gaining access." Some writers misrepresent the NRA's position by not mentioning the exception for defensive guns. Since nearly all of the guns kept in this ready status are owned for defensive reasons, this means that in fact very few gun owners violate the safety rules concerning gun storage that are promulgated by the NRA.

The most common argument against keeping guns in the ready status for self-defense is that it could lead to accidents or other violence involving guns because unauthorized persons, especially small children, could gain access to the gun. This argument is of limited relevance for several reasons. First, it is common for adolescents, especially in small towns and rural areas, to personally own guns with their parents' knowledge and approval.

> *"Virtually everyone who keeps a gun in the ready [loaded and unlocked] status owns the gun at least partly for defensive reasons."*

A member of this group would not be an "unauthorized person," but rather would be the gun's owner and thus would often be the person with the key or combination to any lock on the gun. And among adolescents who possess their own gun without a parent's knowledge (e.g., an urban gang member), access to these guns obviously could not be affected by their parents' locking and storage practices. The failure of gun owners in other households to secure their guns against theft is more likely to play a role in such an adolescent obtaining a gun.

Excluding accidents among preadolescent children (under age thirteen), there is no evidence that any significant number of misuses of guns are committed by persons gaining unauthorized access to guns. More than 99 percent of all suicides and homicides are committed by persons age thirteen or over, that is by persons old enough to own their own guns. As far as we know, virtually everyone who commits an assaultive act of violence or attempts suicide with a gun, and virtually every adult or adolescent who accidentally shoots someone, had "authorized" access to the gun that was used, most commonly because it was the shooter's own gun.

Second, gun accidents among preadolescent children, which *are* likely to involve unauthorized users, are extremely rare. In the entire United States in 1996, there were only 78 FGAs [fatal gun accidents] involving victims under age thirteen (compared to 855 accidental deaths in this age group due to drowning, 724 due to fire, and 2,415 due to motor vehicle accidents). Analysis of 1979–1994 Mortality Detail File data indicates that 36.35 percent of FGAs involving victims under age thirteen involved a handgun (among cases

> *"Gun accidents among preadolescent children . . . are extremely rare."*

with a known gun type). Thus, for 1996, an estimated twenty-eight FGAs with preadolescent victims involved handguns, the type of gun that accounts for at least three quarters of guns kept in the ready status.

Third, most gun-owning households have neither children nor adolescents (and probably rarely or never have visits from youngsters). More specifically, the practice of keeping guns in the ready status is largely confined to households without children or adolescents. Data from a large-scale 1994 national survey indicated that 79 percent of U.S. households that kept at least one gun unlocked and either loaded or stored with ammunition had no children under the age of eighteen (and data from another 1994 national survey put this figure at 76 percent). Data from the 1994 Police Foundation survey indicate that only 5.4 percent of households with children under age eighteen owned guns and kept at least one gun loaded and unlocked.

Further, data indicated that households with preadolescent children are only about half as likely to keep guns in the ready status as those with only adolescents. Thus, perhaps 4 percent of households with preadolescent children, and perhaps 8 percent of households with only adolescents (which would roughly average out to the aforementioned 5.4 percent for households with children of any age), have guns kept loaded and unlocked. In the Police Foundation survey, among households with a gun in the ready status, 16.6 percent had children under eighteen, so a reasonable rough estimate would be that perhaps 10–14 percent had preadolescent children. Thus, the risk of a resident preadolescent child obtaining access to a gun is irrelevant for 86 to 90 percent of households with guns in the ready status.

Finally, the argument is one-sided in not taking account of deaths and injuries that are prevented because a crime victim had quick access to a gun and was able to use it effectively for self-protection. We do not know how many of the 2.55 million annual defensive gun uses, or the nearly one million defensive gun uses in the home, were only possible because the victim had quick access to a gun. The number is not, however, likely to be zero, in light of the fact that criminals rarely give their victims advance warning of their criminal plans, and thus time to make preparations.

Keeping Guns Loaded and Secured

To describe storing a gun in the ready status as "unsafe" implies a one-sided focus on danger to household members from the household gun, and effectively prejudges the question of whether the harm of shootings committed with the household gun by unauthorized users outweighs the benefit of quick access to guns for self-protective purposes. This is unreasonable, given that it would require only a tiny fraction of the one million home defensive gun uses to involve a life saved due to quick access to a gun to counterbalance the subset of twenty-eight deaths of preadolescent children in handgun accidents that might have been caused by the gun being stored in the ready status.

In any case, there are compromise modes of storage that permit guns to be safely kept loaded, yet secured in some way—storage modes that provide both security against unauthorized access and quick access by authorized users for defensive purposes. For those who can afford to spend $150 or more, a handgun can be safely stored, in a loaded condition, inside a lockbox that can be quickly opened, but only by persons with the correct combination or key. With the better variants of these products, the user can gain access to the gun in under ten seconds, yet unauthorized users cannot gain access at all. I know of no documented case where a person was killed in an act of gun violence as a result of a lockbox being defeated. Further, the lockbox, if securely fixed to a relatively immovable object, can strongly discourage gun theft.

For those who cannot afford a lockbox, locks that are placed on the gun, such as trigger locks, cable locks, and various other gun locks offer cheap, next-best alternatives. These cost as little as $10 and are also effective in preventing unauthorized use of the gun. They also have various shortcomings that could theoretically allow, or cause, accidents when used on loaded guns. In the absence of evidence on whether these risks have actually resulted in real-world injuries or deaths, about all that can be said is that there is a potential risk to storing a gun loaded using the less expensive security alternatives. Nevertheless, they are clearly better than not securing the gun at all, and for many gun owners may be the only security measure that they can afford. Further, locks that go on a gun, even if they in fact render the gun unusable for unauthorized persons, may nevertheless fail to deter some gun thieves, and some gun locks do nothing to make theft physically difficult or impossible.

Given that most gun criminals acquire their guns directly or indirectly as a result of theft, probably the strongest rationale for keeping guns stored in a secure manner of some sort is to reduce gun theft and thereby reduce acquisition of guns by criminals. It is far more common for violence to be committed by criminals using stolen guns than for it to be committed by persons gaining unauthorized access to guns in their own home. Therefore, arguments for keeping guns stored more securely are more sensibly grounded in efforts to reduce gun theft than in dubious efforts to persuade people of the dangers of guns kept in their own homes.

Perhaps the most prominent example of such dubious efforts is the case-control homicide study of physician Arthur Kellermann and his colleagues, who claimed that because homicide victimization was 2.8 times more likely among persons who kept guns in their homes than among persons in gunless homes, this meant that home gun ownership caused a higher risk of being murdered. The more empirically supported interpretation of their findings is that the same factors that put people at greater risk of violent victimization (e.g., engaging in dangerous activities, frequenting dangerous places, or associating with dangerous people) also motivate people to acquire guns for self-protection.

The credibility of Kellermann's interpretation collapsed when it was found that his own data indicated that no more than 1.67 percent of the homicides committed in the three urban counties he studied were committed with a gun kept in the victim's home. Guns in the victim's household almost never had anything to do with his or her murder, and could not have caused a tripling of the risk of being murdered. People may well be endangered by guns possessed by dangerous people outside their own homes, but their risk of being victimized is not significantly increased by the guns kept in their own homes.

Allowing Private Citizens to Carry Guns Will Not Reduce Crime or Protect Gun Owners

by the *Economist*

About the author: *The* Economist *is a weekly financial magazine.*

The second amendment of the American constitution concerns the "right of the people to keep and bear Arms", and the intent of that language is the subject of a perpetual debate, one that will be sharpened by the [Bush] administration's gun-leaning instincts. Economists are not usually in the business of making value judgments. But some recent research about the effects on crime of gun ownership ought to play a part in informing society's decisions.

From a hypothetical perspective, gun ownership could promote crime by facilitating violence; or it could deter it, by implicitly threatening retribution. Empirically, the question has been hard to resolve. Economists seeking to map the relationship between American gun ownership and crime face a formidable obstacle: data on gun ownership exists only at the national level.

An Academic Debate

It is not for economists, however, to be put off by a paucity of data. Some academics have spent years squirrelling around for proxies for gun ownership in given geographical areas. Until recently, the most notorious of their studies used the passage of legislation that allowed private citizens to carry concealed firearms as a proxy indicator of gun ownership. The findings of John Lott of Yale University and David Mustard of the University of Georgia (both at the time at the University of Chicago) suggested that such laws, and the increases in gun ownership that presumably accompanied them, diminished violent crime.

While the National Rifle Association feasted upon these results, other academics voiced scepticism about their statistical rigour. Just a year later [in 1998], a paper using the same data and more advanced econometric methods showed that concealed-weapon legislation had made only a small contribution to falling murder rates, and may even have boosted robberies. This second paper was feasted upon less than the first.

The search for a more reliable proxy continued, and has now led to a . . . paper by Mark Duggan of the University of Chicago. Mr Duggan obtained state- and county-level sales data from one of America's largest gun magazines, betting that sales would be strongly correlated with gun ownership. This particular magazine concentrates on handguns, the type most commonly used in crime. Although Mr Duggan does not assume that subscribers are likely to be criminals, he does point out that the majority of guns used in crimes

"Increases in gun ownership led to increases in crime . . . but the reverse did not hold."

are obtained through burglaries or second-hand sales. Still, even before considering the link to crime, how do you prove that a correlation exists with magazine sales, when gun ownership is itself such an unknown quantity?

Mr Duggan attacked this problem from several directions. First, he showed that the counties with high gun-magazine sales had similar demographics to those associated with the profile of typical gun-owners in national-level surveys. Next, he found a strong relationship between the level of magazine sales and the number of gun shows in states. To assume that gun shows and gun ownership are highly correlated is no great leap of logic. But then again, the logical link between gun ownership and the sales of gun magazines can hardly be called tenuous. Mr Duggan also used government health statistics to demonstrate that states with higher magazine sales suffered higher rates of gun-related death.

The Relationship Between Crime and Gun Ownership

Armed with a high-powered proxy, Mr Duggan set his sights on crime. With data stretching from 1980 to 1998, he calculated that a 10% increase in an average state's rate of gun ownership, proxied by magazine sales, was associated with a 2% rise in its homicide rate. However, these concurrent changes could support either of two hypotheses: that crime rises when individuals own more guns, or that individuals purchase more guns to defend themselves against rising crime. To sort out this confusion, Mr Duggan checked the direction of the relationship over time; increases in gun ownership led to increases in crime in the following year, but the reverse did not hold. The same pattern was found at the county level.

As a further check, Mr Duggan divided his pool into homicides that involved guns and those that did not. Changes in magazine sales were not associated with changes in non-gun homicides—a reassuring point in favour of the proxy.

Mr Duggan also examined other forms of crime. Perhaps most striking for those who believe in the deterrent effect of gun-ownership, burglary (theft with forcible entry) and larceny (theft without forcible entry or threat of harm) rose significantly following growth in gun ownership, by roughly half as much as homicides. On the other hand, rates of robbery (theft with threat of harm), assault, rape and car theft remained largely unchanged, a finding which, at least for violent crimes, contradicts Messrs Lott's and Mustard's paper.

The author also took on the Lott-Mustard results explicitly. Mr Duggan reasoned that for guns to deter crime, the passage of concealed-weapons laws must either lead to more gun ownership or to more frequent carrying of previously owned weapons. But the passage of such legislation did not lead to significant changes in gun ownership. And those counties where gun ownership was highest (where an increase in gun carrying could occur) did not see any significant changes in crime when their states passed concealed-weapons laws.

Perhaps those in favour of concealed-weapons laws will argue that it is merely the increased fear that your victim might be armed that would be enough to deter criminals; and that concealed-weapons laws might create such fears regardless of whether actual gun ownership, or gun carrying, increased. Still, the central tenet of Mr Duggan's findings stands: on balance, the evidence suggests that guns foster crime, not the other way around.

Gun Ownership Endangers Women

by Josh Sugarmann

About the author: *Josh Sugarmann is the executive director of the Violence Policy Center, an educational foundation that conducts research on gun violence.*

Despite assertions by the gun industry and its allies that the greatest threat to women comes from attack by strangers, in reality the most imminent source of violence to a woman comes from the person with whom she shares her life—in research terms, her "intimate acquaintance." Adding a handgun to this mix can have deadly repercussions. Public health researcher Susan P. Baker has noted that, in cases of assault, people tend to reach for the most lethal weapon readily available. It is no surprise to learn that the very presence of a firearm in households prone to domestic violence creates a lethal situation. Family and intimate homicide is usually preceded by an escalating pattern of violence. A firearm in the home acts as a catalyst, transforming an act of nonfatal spouse abuse into a homicide.

In a seminal study, researcher Arthur L. Kellermann, MD, MPH, looked at U.S. homicides from 1976 to 1987. He found that a firearm, usually a handgun, was the most common weapon used to kill victims of *either* sex. Handguns were involved in 36 percent of all homicides against women. However, the circumstances of firearm homicide differed significantly between men and women. Women were most often shot and killed by their spouses. Men were most likely to be shot and killed by friends or acquaintances. For both men and women, murder by a stranger was rare. During these years, only nine percent of women were killed by strangers, compared to 17 percent of men. Kellermann found that "during the entire 12-year study interval more than twice as many women were shot and killed by their husband or an intimate acquaintance than were murdered by strangers using firearms, knives, or any other means."

A 1992 study by researchers at the Centers for Disease Control and Prevention confirmed the hazard guns in the home pose to women. Firearm-related assaults by family members and intimate acquaintances were 12 times more likely to result in death than were those involving weapons other than a firearm. The authors noted that "studies of male batterers and anecdotal reports suggest that many . . . [domestic-violence assaults] (fatal and nonfatal) are a spontaneous response to conflict or anger and frequently occur without premeditation or planning." The researchers concluded that the greater lethality of firearms increases the chance of homicide in a domestic-violence situation. Conversely, the authors noted, reduced access to firearms would likely result in fewer family and intimate homicides.

> *"Having a firearm in the home may further elevate women's risk of homicide by intimates."*

Research shows that guns are used more often in domestic murders than in other types of homicides. A 1989 study in the *American Journal of Public Health* reported that firearms were used in 71.5 percent of spousal murders, compared to 60.5 percent of non-spousal homicides. The study concluded: "The presence of a firearm in the home may be a key contributor to the escalation of nonfatal spouse abuse to homicide." Another study by Kellermann, "Gun Ownership as a Risk Factor for Homicide in the Home," published in *The New England Journal of Medicine* in October 1993, found that having a firearm in the home may further elevate women's risk of homicide by intimates. Kellermann writes:

> People who keep guns in their homes appear to be at greater risk of homicide in the home than people who do not. Most of this risk is due to a substantially greater risk of homicide at the hands of a family member or intimate acquaintance.

A 1997 study entitled "Risk Factors for Violent Death of Women in the Home" found that prior domestic violence in the household made a woman four times more likely, and having one or more guns in the home made a woman 3.4 times more likely, to be the victim of a homicide. Additionally, when looking at the likelihood of a woman being killed by a spouse, intimate acquaintance, or close relative, the authors found that prior domestic violence in the household made a woman 14.6 times more likely, and having one or more guns in the home made a woman 7.2 times more likely, to be the victim of such a homicide.

Dangerous Accessibility

Finally, a study published in the journal *Homicide Studies* in 1998 found that the ready availability of guns was a key ingredient in many partner homicides. The following two stories, taken from the study and presented in the dry prose of the public health researcher, illustrate the role that an easily accessible handgun can play in turning domestic violence into a domestic homicide:

Earlier in the day he had threatened his wife and gotten angry at other people over an alleged debt. He had been drinking heavily. The wife told her daughter that he was "going to blow her (the wife's) head off." He had held a gun to her head earlier—in one instance the daughter had tried to intervene and was pushed to the floor. He continued to drink and play with the gun. He went into the kitchen where she was cooking and their 13-year-old daughter was doing her homework and told her that she had hurt him so much and that he wanted to hurt her back. She was making plans to leave him, and he said the sooner the better. He was waving a pistol around and kept telling her how bad she hurt him, and she kept telling him he was the one messing up. He was going to shoot her in the heart because of how much pain he felt. The arguing continued and the daughter went upstairs. She told him to get the gun out of her face. He shot the gun into the ceiling, and she asked him why he shot the gun in the house. He shot her in the head about 15 to 20 minutes later. . . .

Dating couple with a long history of domestic violence. He kept coming back after she asked him to move out. Neighbors knew of domestic violence. He had recently threatened her with a small handgun that she managed to wrestle away from him and keep with her for several days. On the afternoon of the murder, a female friend had been visiting her at her home. When the friend left, the boyfriend came into the house. Very shortly thereafter, the neighbors heard loud voices and within minutes he went to the friend's house to say that he shot her. Neighbors saw him with a gun and heard a shot and called police. When police arrived she was dead and he was sitting there with a gun.

Perhaps what is most shocking about these stories is not the sensationalist aspect, nor the inherent tragedy. It is that they are commonplace. Hundreds of times a year the same scenario is played out, until it becomes a dreary, recognizable formula: domestic violence + a gun = homicide. The truth is that the handgun is not the great equalizer for women. It is like pouring gasoline on a fire, turning an already terrible situation of domestic abuse into a horrifying domestic homicide.

The conclusions of these numerous studies are borne out by information regarding female handgun homicide victims for 1997. In 1997, handguns were used to murder 1,169 women. In cases where the victim/offender relationship could be identified, more than half of all female handgun homicide victims were killed by an intimate acquaintance—a husband, ex-husband, common-law husband, boyfriend, or homosexual partner. (An additional 7.2 percent were killed by family members, and 27 percent were killed by others known to the female victim.) Only 13.1 percent were killed by strangers. In comparison, male handgun victims were also most likely to be killed by someone they knew (53.6 percent), but rarely by an intimate acquaintance.

More Victims than Defenders

Women very rarely use handguns to kill in self-defense. According to [Philip Jr.] Cook and [Jens] Ludwig's comprehensive *Guns in America*, 84 percent of women handgun owners say that they own a handgun for protection against crime. Yet how often are handguns used by women in self-defense? And who are they using them against?

In 1997, there were 3,336 female victims of homicide, more than a third (1,169) of whom were killed in handgun homicides. During that same year, there were only *14* justifiable homicides reported to the FBI where a woman used a handgun to kill in self-defense. Of these 14 women who committed justifiable homicides, half (seven) knew their attackers. (These seven attackers were comprised of three boyfriends, one husband, one ex-husband, a father, and a friend.) Six of the attackers were strangers to the women. The relationship in the remaining incident was unknown.

> *"A women is ... 200 times more likely to be murdered by someone using a handgun than to use one to kill a stranger in self-defense."*

Thus in 1997, for every time that a woman used a handgun to kill a stranger in self-defense, 195 women were killed in handgun homicides alone. Considering that a woman is, in an average year, 200 times more likely to be murdered by someone using a handgun than to use one to kill a stranger in self-defense, the gun industry's efforts to exploit women's fears of attack by strangers is revealed in all its cynical glory. . . . And contrary to the gun industry's promises, giving women *even more* handguns isn't going to even the odds.

Fortunately, the overwhelming majority of American women have had the good sense to ignore the industry's blandishments and have rejected handguns from their lives. In 1987, Franklin Zimring and Gordon Hawkins offered an insightful observation on women and guns:

> The American woman of the late 1980s and 1990s . . . [is the] leading indicator of the social status of self-defense handguns in the more distant future. If female ownership of self-defense handguns increases dramatically, the climate of opinion for drastic restriction of handguns will not come about.

Their predictions have held true—and not to the gun industry's advantage. While the gun press abounds with anecdotes of women as fervent proselytes to the shooting sports, overall handgun ownership by women has shown no change over the past 15 years. Although the industry failed to reap benefits from its campaign to win over women's hearts and minds, it remains undaunted.

Keeping a Gun in the Home for Self-Defense Endangers Children

by the Brady Campaign to Prevent Gun Violence united with the Million Mom March

About the authors: *The Brady Campaign to Prevent Gun Violence works to enact sensible gun laws and regulations and increase public awareness of gun violence. The Million Mom March is an organization that supports licensing, registration, and other firearm regulations.*

There are an estimated 193 million guns in America. Some estimates range as high as 250 million. That's almost one gun for every man, woman and child in the United States. Guns are not just in urban and rural homes, they're every-where—cities, towns, suburbs and farms. In fact, there is a gun in 43% of households with children in America. There's a loaded gun in one in every ten households with children, and a gun that's left unlocked and just "hidden away" in one in every eight family homes.

While the Brady Campaign united with the Million Mom March does not seek to prevent law-abiding citizens from owning, using, or purchasing fire-arms, people have the right to know the true risks associated with keeping a gun in the home. The fallacy that a home is safer with a gun in it and that a gun is a necessary means of self-protection is widely promoted by the gun lobby. The gun lobby also downplays or ignores the risks families take when they intro-duce a gun into the home.

Guns Do Not Increase Safety

Despite claims by the National Rifle Association (NRA) that you need a gun in your home to protect yourself and your family, public health research demonstrates that the person most likely to shoot you or a family member with a gun already has the keys to your house. Simply put: guns kept in the home for self-protection are more often used to kill somebody you know than to kill in self-defense; 22 times more likely, according to a 1998 study by the *Journal of Trauma*. More kids, teenagers and adult family members are dying from firearms in their own home than criminal intruders. When someone is home, a gun is used for protection in fewer than two percent of home invasion crimes. You may be surprised to know that, in 1999, according to the FBI's *Uniform Crime Report*, there were only 154 justifiable homicides committed by private citizens with a firearm compared with a total of 8,259 firearm

> *"The risk of homicide in the home is three times greater in households with guns."*

murders in the United States. Once a bullet leaves a gun, who is to say that it will stop only a criminal and not a family member? Yet at every opportunity the NRA uses the fear of crime to promote the need for ordinary citizens to keep guns in their home for self-protection. Furthermore, the NRA continues to oppose life-saving measures that require safe-storage of guns in the home.

Because handguns and other firearms are so easily accessible to many children, adolescents and other family members in their homes, the risk of gun violence in the home increases dramatically. Consider this: The risk of homicide in the home is three times greater in households with guns. The risk of suicide is five times greater in households with guns. What's more, tragic stories of accidental or unintentional shootings from the careless storage of guns at home are all too common. The statistic noted above bears repeating: a gun in the home is 22 times more likely to be used in a criminal, unintentional, or suicide-related shooting than to be used in a self-defense shooting.

A Gun in the Home: Key Facts

From 1990–1998, two-thirds of spouse and ex-spouse murder victims were killed with guns.

Guns are the weapon of choice for troubled individuals who commit suicide. In 1999, firearms were used in 16,599 suicide deaths in America. Among young people under 20, one committed suicide with a gun every eight hours.

A gun in the home also increases the likelihood of an unintentional shooting, particularly among children. Unintentional shootings commonly occur when children find an adult's loaded handgun in a drawer or closet, and while playing with it shoot themselves, a sibling or a friend. The unintentional firearm-related death rate for children 0–14 years old is NINE times higher in the U.S. than in the 25 other countries combined.

Five Tragedies

On March 21, 2002, a 14-year-old South Carolina boy deliberately shot and killed his 12-year-old foster sister. The boy had taken live shotgun shells from his father's house and used them in a shotgun that he had taken from his mother's bedroom. ("Alleged shooter under house arrest," The *Herald* [Rock Hill, SC], March 27, 2002.)

On March 28, 2002, 15-year-old Quinton Bridges was shot and critically injured by his 15-year-old friend, Derek Scott Oaks in Tucson [Arizona]. The youths had been tossing water balloons and wrestling before Oaks loaded his father's rifle and aimed it at his friend's head while the teen sat at a computer playing a game. According to police, the boys were not arguing; Oaks didn't think the firearm worked because he tried to pull the trigger before he went in the room and it didn't fire. Oaks has since been charged with attempted second-degree murder. ("Teen charged with attempted murder," *Tucson Citizen*, March 30, 2002.)

On March 30, 2002, a 9-year-old Seattle boy was wounded when a .22-caliber rifle he and his 13-year-old brother were playing with discharged. The boys were playing with the gun in a bedroom in their uncle's home. ("9-Year-Old Boy Wounded In Apparent Accidental Shooting," KOMO News web site, March 30, 2002.)

On April 6, 2002, 3-year-old Stephon Starks shot and wounded himself with a .22-caliber pistol that he found in a dresser drawer in his mother's bedroom in Nashville [Tennessee]. Police said Stephon had gotten up to get some clean underwear after he wet the bed when he found the gun. He was climbing back into bed when the gun went off. ("Boy, 3, wounds himself after finding gun in mom's room," The *Tennessean*, April 7, 2002.)

> *"Many parents simply do not view guns as a personal threat to their children or their family."*

On April 8, 2002, a 4-year-old Jacksonville [Florida] boy died after unintentionally shooting himself, while playing with his grandfather's gun while the rest of the family was sleeping. ("Boy, 4, accidentally kills self," *Florida Times-Union*, April 9, 2002.)

Parents Have Ignored the Problem

A 1998 study by Peter Hart Research on behalf of the Center to Prevent Handgun Violence (now the Brady Center to Prevent Gun Violence) found that, even though most parents realize that guns in the home endanger their children, many parents still leave guns accessible to kids.

Specifically, in the nationwide survey of 806 parents, 43% of households with children have guns, and 23% of gun households keep a gun loaded. 28% keep a gun hidden and unlocked. 54% of parents said that they would be highly concerned about their child's safety if they knew there was a gun in the home of their child's friend. Despite many parents' concern about the immediate dangers that guns left in the house pose to their children, they are failing to take the necessary steps to help ensure their children's safety. Perhaps most significantly, many parents simply do not view guns as a personal threat to their children or their family whatsoever.

Too often a parent drops off their child at a friend's house for an afternoon play session or a sleep-over party not knowing that the car ride would be the last time they would see their child alive. Why? The study found that most parents don't discuss the issue of guns in the home with the parents of their children's friends. Amazingly, only 30% have asked the parents of their children's friends if there is a gun in the home before allowing a visit. 61% of the parents included in the survey responded that they never even thought about asking other parents about gun accessibility.

Clearly, parents don't think about the tragic possibilities of an innocent visit to another home. While parents are asking each other about supervision, food allergies, adult television access, they are ignoring guns—the one factor that could mean the life or death of their child.

Organizations to Contact

The editors have compiled the following list of organizations concerned with the issues presented in this book. The descriptions are derived from materials provided by the organizations. All have publications or information available for interested readers. The list was compiled on the date of publication of the present volume; the information provided here may change. Be aware that many organizations take several weeks or longer to respond to inquiries, so allow as much time as possible.

American Civil Liberties Union (ACLU)
125 Broad St., Eighteenth Fl., New York, NY 10004-2400
(212) 549-2500
e-mail: aclu@aclu.org • Web site: www.aclu.org

The ACLU champions the rights set forth in the Declaration of Independence and the U.S. Constitution. The ACLU interprets the Second Amendment as a guarantee for states to form militias, not as a guarantee of the individual right to own and bear firearms. Consequently, the organization believes that gun control is constitutional and, since guns are dangerous, it is necessary. The ACLU publishes the semiannual *Civil Liberties* in addition to policy statements and reports.

Americans for Gun Safety (AGS) and the AGS Foundation
(202) 775-0300 • fax: (202) 775-0430
Web site: www.americansforgunsafety.com • Web site: www.agsfoundation.com

AGS is a nonpartisan, not-for-profit advocacy organization that supports the rights of law-abiding gun owners and promotes sensible and effective proposals for fighting gun crimes and preventing criminals and children from having access to guns. The organization's priorities include promoting gun safety and improving the background check system on gun purchases. The AGS Foundation provides background, research, and reference materials to the public and to policy makers on gun-related issues, including the reports *Broken Records: How America's Faulty Background Check System Allows Criminals to Get Guns, Stolen Guns: Arming the Enemy,* and *Selling Crime: High Crime Gun Stores Fuel Criminals.*

Brady Campaign to Prevent Gun Violence and Brady Center to Prevent Gun Violence
1225 Eye St. NW, Suite 1100, Washington, DC 20005
(202) 898-0792 (Brady Campaign) • (202) 289-7319 (Brady Center)
fax: (202) 371-9615 (Brady Campaign) • fax: (202) 408-1851 (Brady Center)
Web site: www.bradycampaign.org • Web site: www.bradycenter.com

The Brady Campaign to Prevent Gun Violence was formerly known as Handgun Control, Inc. The goals of the campaign are to enact and enforce sensible gun laws, regulations, and public policies through grassroots activism, increase public awareness of gun violence, and elect public officials who support gun control. The Brady Center works to reform the gun industry and educate the public about gun violence through litigation and grassroots mobilization and to develop sensible regulations to reduce gun violence.

The Web site offers dozens of issue briefs, fact sheets, legislative updates, and links to news stories on gun control, as well as links to the affiliated organizations Million Mom March and Legal Action Project. Reports available on the Web site include *Domestic Violence and Guns* and *CONCEALED TRUTH: Concealed Weapons Laws and Trends in Violent Crime in the United States.*

Cato Institute
1000 Massachusetts Ave. NW, Washington, DC 20001
(202) 842-0200 • fax: (202) 842-3490
e-mail: librarian@cato.org • Web site: www.cato.org

The Cato Institute is a libertarian public-policy research foundation. It evaluates government policies and offers reform proposals and commentary on its Web site. Its publications include the Cato Policy Analysis series of reports, which have covered topics such as "Fighting Back: Crime, Self-Defense, and the Right to Carry a Handgun" and "Trust the People: The Case Against Gun Control." It also publishes the magazine *Regulation*, the *Cato Policy Report*, and books such *The Samurai, the Mountie, and the Cowboy: Should America Adopt the Gun Controls of Other Democracies?*

Citizens Committee for the Right to Keep and Bear Arms
12500 NE Tenth Pl., Bellevue, WA 98005
(425) 454-4911 • (800) 486-6963 • fax: (425) 451-3959
e-mail: www@ccrkba.org • Web site: www.ccrkba.org

The committee believes that the U.S. Constitution's Second Amendment guarantees and protects the right of individual Americans to own guns. It works to educate the public concerning this right and to lobby legislators to prevent the passage of gun-control laws. The committee is affiliated with the Second Amendment Foundation and has more than six hundred thousand members. It publishes several magazines, including *Gun Week, Gottlieb-Tartaro Report, Women & Guns*, and *Gun News Digest.*

Coalition for Gun Control
PO Box 90062, 1488 Queen St. W., Toronto, ON M6K 3K3 Canada
e-mail: 71417.763@compuserve.com • Web site: www.guncontrol.ca

The coalition is a Canadian organization that was formed to reduce gun death, injury, and crime. It supports strict safe storage requirements, possession permits, a complete ban on assault weapons, and tougher restrictions on handguns. Its Web site provides information on firearms death and injury, illegal gun trafficking, Canada's gun control law, and kids and guns. The coalition publishes press releases and backgrounders.

Coalition to Stop Gun Violence (CSGV)
1000 Sixteenth St. NW, Suite 603, Washington, DC 20002
(202) 530-0340 • fax: (202) 530-0331
e-mail: webmaster@csgv.org • Web site: www.csgv.org

The CSGV lobbies at the local, state, and federal levels to ban the sale of handguns to individuals and to institute licensing and registration of all firearms. It also litigates cases against firearms makers. Its publications include various informational sheets on gun violence and the *Annual Citizens' Conference to Stop Gun Violence Briefing Book*, a compendium of gun-control fact sheets, arguments, and resources.

Independence Institute
13952 Denver West Pkwy., Suite 400, Golden, CO 80401
(303) 279-6536 • fax: (303) 279-4176
e-mail: anne@i2i.org • Web site: www.i2i.org

The institute is a pro–free market think tank that supports gun ownership as both a civil liberty and a constitutional right. Its publications include issue papers opposing gun control, such as "Children and Guns: Sensible Solutions," "'Shall Issue': The New Wave of Concealed Handgun Permit Laws," and "Some Frequently Overlooked Facts in Gun Policy Discussions," as well as the book *Guns: Who Should Have Them?* Its Web site also contains articles, fact sheets, and commentary from a variety of sources.

Jews for the Preservation of Firearms Ownership (JPFO)
PO Box 270143, Hartford, WI 53027
(262) 673-9745 • fax: (262) 673-9746
e-mail: webmaster@jpfo.org • Web site: www.jpfo.org

JPFO is an educational organization that believes Jewish law mandates self-defense. Its primary goal is the elimination of the idea that gun control is a socially useful public policy in any country. JPFO publishes the quarterly *Bill of Rights Sentinel*, the booklet *Will "Gun Control" Make You Safer*, and regular news alerts. The Web site also features a special section on doctors and guns.

Johns Hopkins Center for Gun Policy and Research
Johns Hopkins Bloomberg School of Public Health
624 N. Broadway, Baltimore, MD 21205
(410) 614-3243 • fax: (410) 614-9055
e-mail: jhcgpr@jhsph.edu • Web site: www.jhsph.edu/gunpolicy/index.html

The Johns Hopkins Center for Gun Policy and Research, which is operated by the Johns Hopkins Bloomberg School of Public Health, aims to provide public health expertise to the issue of gun violence prevention. The center conducts original research and policy analysis into topics such as guns as consumer products, reducing illegal firearms trafficking, and technology for safer guns. The center also publishes fact sheets on topics such as assault weapons and firearm injury and death, policy analyses, and reports, including *Myths About Defensive Gun Use and Permissive Gun Carry Laws.*

Join Together
1 Appleton St., Fourth Fl., Boston, MA 02116-5223
(617) 437-1500 • fax: (617) 437-9394
e-mail: info@jointogether.org • Web site: www.jointogether.org

Join Together, a project of the Boston University School of Public Health, is an organization that serves as a national resource for communities working to reduce substance abuse and gun violence. Its publications include research briefs and reports, such as *Gun Violence: Making Connections with Suicide, Domestic Violence, and Substance Abuse.*

National Crime Prevention Council (NCPC)
1000 Connecticut Ave. NW, Thirteenth Fl., Washington, DC 20036
(202) 466-6272 • fax: (202) 296-1356
e-mail: webmaster@ncpc.org • Web site: www.ncpc.org

The NCPC is a branch of the U.S. Department of Justice. Through its programs and educational materials, the council works to teach Americans how to reduce crime and to address its causes. It provides readers with information on gun control and gun violence. The NCPC's publications include the newsletter *Catalyst*, which is published ten times a year, the book *Reducing Gun Violence: What Communities Can Do*, and brochures on crime prevention.

National Rifle Association of America (NRA)
11250 Waples Mill Rd., Fairfax, VA 22030
(703) 267-1400
Web site: www.nra.org

With nearly 3 million members, the NRA is America's largest organization of gun owners. It is also the primary lobbying group for those who oppose gun-control laws. The NRA believes that such laws violate the U.S. Constitution and do nothing to reduce crime. In addition to its monthly magazines *America's 1st Freedom, American Rifleman, American Hunter, InSights*, and *Shooting Sports USA*, the NRA publishes numerous books, bibliographies, reports, and pamphlets on gun ownership, gun safety, and gun control.

Second Amendment Foundation
12500 NE Tenth Pl., Bellevue, WA 98005
(425) 454-7012 • (800) 426-4302 • fax: (425) 451-3959
e-mail: www@saf.org • Web site: www.saf.org

The foundation, which is affiliated with the Citizens Committee for the Right to Keep and Bear Arms, is dedicated to informing Americans about their Second Amendment right to keep and bear firearms. It believes that gun-control laws violate this right. The foundation publishes numerous books, including *The Amazing Vanishing Second Amendment, The Best Defense: True Stories of Intended Victims Who Defended Themselves with a Firearm*, and *CCW: Carrying Concealed Weapons*. The complete text of the book *How to Defend Your Gun Rights* is available on its Web site, along with articles from *Journal on Firearms and Public Policy* and *Gun Week*.

U.S. Department of Justice (Bureau of Justice Statistics)
810 Seventh St. NW, Washington, DC 20531
(202) 307-0765
e-mail: askbjs@ojp.usdoj.gov • Web site: www.ojp.usdoj.gov/bjs/welcome.html

The Department of Justice strives to protect citizens by maintaining effective law enforcement, crime prevention, crime detection, and prosecution and rehabilitation of offenders. Through its Office of Justice Programs, the department operates the National Institute of Justice, the Office of Juvenile Justice and Delinquency Prevention, and the Bureau of Justice Statistics. The Bureau of Justice Statistics provides research on crime and criminal justice. It publishes a variety of crime-related documents, including *Background Checks for Firearm Transfers, 2002* and *Firearm Use by Offenders*.

Violence Policy Center
1140 Nineteenth St. NW, Suite 600, Washington, DC 20036
e-mail: info@vpc.org • Web site: www.vpc.org

The center is an educational foundation that conducts research on firearms violence. It works to educate the public concerning the dangers of guns and supports gun-control measures. The center's publications include the reports *Handgun Licensing and Registration: What It Can and Cannot Do; License to Kill IV: More Guns, More Crime;* and *Really Big Guns, Even Bigger Lies*.

Bibliography

Books

Elliot Aronson	*Nobody Left to Hate: Teaching Compassion After Columbine.* New York: Worth, 2000.
Michael Bellesiles	*Arming America: The Origins of a National Gun Culture.* New York: Alfred A. Knopf, 2000.
Carl T. Bogus, ed.	*The Second Amendment in Law and History: Historians and Constitutional Scholars on the Right to Bear Arms.* New York: New Press, 2000.
Peter Harry Brown and Daniel G. Abel	*Outgunned: Up Against the NRA—the First Complete Insider Account of the Battle over Gun Control.* New York: Free Press, 2002.
Philip J. Cook and Jens Ludwig	*Gun Violence: The Real Costs.* New York: Oxford University Press, 2000.
Jennifer Croft	*Everything You Need to Know About Guns in the Home.* New York: Rosen, 2000.
Constance Emerson Crooker	*Gun Control and Gun Rights.* Westport, CT: Greenwood, 2003.
Alexander DeConde	*Gun Violence in America: The Struggle for Control.* Boston: Northeastern University Press, 2001.
Donna Dees-Thomases and Alison Hendrie	*Looking for a Few Good Moms: How One Mother Rallied a Million Others Against the Gun Lobby.* Emmaus, PA: Rodale Press, 2004.
Tom Diaz	*Making a Killing: The Business of Guns in America.* New York: New Press, 1999.
Jan E. Dizard, Robert Merril Muth, and Stephen P. Andrews Jr., eds.	*Guns in America: A Reader.* New York: New York University Press, 1999.
Kathleen M. Heide	*Young Killers: The Challenge of Juvenile Homicide.* Thousand Oaks, CA: Sage, 1999.
Harry Henderson	*Gun Control.* New York: Facts On File, 2000.

William G. Hinkle and Stuart Henry, eds.	*School Violence.* Thousand Oaks, CA: Sage, 2000.
Deborah Homsher	*Women & Guns: Politics and the Culture of Firearms in America.* Armonk, NY: M.E. Sharpe, 2001.
James B. Jacobs	*Can Gun Control Work?* New York: Oxford University Press, 2002.
Gary Kleck and Don B. Kates	*Armed: New Perspectives on Gun Control.* Amherst, NY: Prometheus, 2001.
Wayne Lapierre, James Jay Baker, and Charlton Heston	*Shooting Straight: Telling the Truth About Guns in America.* Washington, DC: Regnery Press, 2002.
John R. Lott Jr.	*More Guns, Less Crime: Understanding Crime and Gun-Control Laws.* New York: New York University Press, 2002.
Joyce Lee Malcolm	*Guns and Violence: The English Experience.* Cambridge, MA: Harvard University Press, 2002.
Mike Males	*Kids and Guns: How Politicians, Experts, and the Press Fabricate Fear of Youth.* Monroe, ME: Common Courage Press, rev. 2004.
Andrew McClurg, Dave Kopel, and Brandon Denning	*Gun Control and Gun Rights: A Reader and Guide.* New York: New York University Press, 2002.
Richard Poe	*The Seven Myths of Gun Control: Reclaiming the Truth About Guns, Crime, and the Second Amendment.* Roseville, CA: Prima Lifestyles, 2001.
Ted Schwarz	*Kids and Guns: The History, the Present, the Dangers, and the Remedies.* New York: Franklin Watts, 1999.
Michael A. Sommers	*The Right to Bear Arms.* New York: Rosen, 2001.
Robert J. Spitzer	*The Right to Bear Arms: Rights and Liberties Under the Law.* Santa Barbara, CA: ABC-CLIO, 2001.
Peter Squires	*Gun Culture or Gun Control: Firearms, Violence, and Society.* New York: Routledge, 2000.
Mary Zeiss Stange and Carol K. Oyster	*Gun Women: Firearms and Feminism in Contemporary America.* New York: New York University Press, 2000.
Josh Sugarmann	*Every Handgun Is Aimed at You: The Case for Banning Handguns.* New York: New Press, 2001.
Glenn Utter	*Encyclopedia of Gun Control.* New York: Oryx Press, 1999.

Periodicals

Akhil Reed Amar	"Second Thoughts," *New Republic*, July 12, 1999.
Anil Ananthaswamy	"The Way of the Gun," *New Scientist*, July 12, 2003.
Paul Begala	"A Hunter for Gun Control," *George*, June 2000.

Bibliography

Alfred Blumstein	"Youth, Guns, and Violent Crime," *The Future of Children*, Summer/Fall 2002.
H. Sterling Burnett	"Suing Gun Manufacturers: The Protection of Lawful Commerce in Arms," *Vital Speeches of the Day*, June 15, 2002.
Christian Science Monitor	"Unfit to Bear Arms," May 10, 2002.
Congressional Digest	"Firearms in America: The Link Between Guns and Violence," November 1999.
Dick Dahl	"Whatever Happened to Gun Control?" *In These Times*, October 1, 2001.
Julian Epstein	"Doublespeak on Guns," *Nation*, August 5–12, 2002.
Miguel A. Faria Jr.	"The Tainted Public-Health Model of Gun Control," *Ideas on Liberty*, April 2001.
Elisabeth Frater	"Checking Up on the Brady Law," *National Journal*, July 22, 2000.
Charlton Heston	"Our First Freedom," *Saturday Evening Post*, January 2000.
Issues and Controversies on File	"Gun Control," July 14, 2000.
Issues and Controversies on File	"Gun Industry Lawsuits," October 15, 1999.
Bronwyn Jones	"Arming Myself with a Gun Is Not the Answer," *Newsweek*, May 22, 2000.
Rachel Jurado	"Gun Control Victims," *American Enterprise*, January/February 2004.
Benjamin Kepple	"Gun Crazy," *Heterodoxy*, April/May 2000.
David B. Kopel	"America's Fascination with Firearms," *World & I*, October 2003.
Daniel Lazare	"Your Constitution Is Killing You," *Harper's*, October 1999.
John Lott	"Half Cocked," *American Enterprise*, July/August 2003.
Frank J. Murray	"Despite Risks, Americans Use Guns in Self-Defense," *Insight on the News*, June 14, 1999.
Clarence Page	"Good Gun Policy—Good Politics," *Liberal Opinion*, November 4, 2002.
Richard North Patterson	"Slaughterhouse of Civilization," *Los Angeles Times*, October 20, 2003.
Gary Rosen	"Yes and No to Gun Control," *Commentary*, September 2000.
Roger Rosenblatt	"Get Rid of the Damn Things," *Time*, August 9, 1999.
Dave Shiflett	"In Defense of Brother Heat," *National Review*, April 17, 2000.

Jeff Snyder
"The Supreme Court Will Never Safeguard Your Gun Rights," *American Handgunner*, September 2000.

Richard W. Stevens
"Just Dial 911? The Myth of Police Protection," *Ideas on Liberty*, April 2000.

Eugene Volokh
"Guns and the Constitution," *Wall Street Journal*, April 12, 1999.

Michael W. Warfel
"Why Gun Control?" *America*, April 15, 2000.

Leslie Wayne
"'Smart' Guns Prove to Be No Quick Fix in Firearm Violence," *New York Times*, June 15, 1999.

Douglas S. Weil
"Closing Gun Control Loopholes," *National Forum*, Fall 2000.

Index

197

Index